CONTEMPORARY CATHOLICISM

Edited by John Littleton and Eamon Maher

Contemporary
Catholicism in Ireland

A CRITICAL APPRAISAL

the columba press

First published in 2008 by
the columba press
55A Spruce Avenue, Stillorgan Industrial Park,
Blackrock, Co Dublin

Cover by Bill Bolger
Origination by The Columba Press
Printed in Ireland by ColourBooks Ltd, Dublin

ISBN 978 1 85607 616 6

Table of Contents

Preface

Readers might wonder what, if anything, there is to add to the edited volume *Irish and Catholic? Towards an Understanding of Identity,* published in 2006.[1] Many aspects of Irish Catholicism remain largely unchanged. The same downward spiral in relation to attendance at religious ceremonies has continued – although the arrival of a large immigrant Catholic population from countries like Poland has meant bigger congregations in particular parts of the country. The dearth of vocations to the priesthood has led to difficulties in running certain parishes due to an ageing clerical population, or to a simple lack of manpower. One of the most noticeable developments in recent times is the spread of an aggressive form of secularism that is intolerant of opinions that do not coincide with the widely embraced 'liberal agenda'. In this regard, globalisation continues to exert a massive influence on what we perceive to be important in life. More often than not, material prosperity takes precedence over religious observance. As Tom Inglis observes:

> [...] The Irish [...] have become the same as their Western counterparts in their immersion in the material world, their pursuit of pleasure, quest for excitement, fulfilment of desire, obsession with consuming and obsession with self. They have moved from being quiet, poor Catholic Church mice embodying a discourse and practice of piety and humility, to becoming busy, productive, self-indulgent rats searching for the next stimulation.[2]

---

1. Fuller, Louise, John Littleton and Eamon Maher (eds), *Irish and Catholic? Towards an Understanding of Identity* (Dublin: The Columba Press, 2006).
2. Tom Inglis, *Global Ireland: Same Difference* (London: Routledge, 2008), pp 189-190.

The Irish have definitely changed, and not only in the area of their attitude to religion. We are more self-confident (some might say brash), prosperous, cosmopolitan, liberal than we were a few decades ago. We are certainly no longer quiet 'Catholic Church mice'. One of the ways we used to acquire social capital was by being perceived to be 'good Catholics'; it is now more likely to be determined by the type of property (or properties) we own, or by the car we drive, or our holiday destinations. There can be no denying that in the past the Catholic Church in Ireland exerted an undue influence on the affairs of state. It was also intrusive in its attempts to control the sexual lives and practices of its members. Similarly, a tiny minority of priests and religious abused their power and indulged in what were heinous crimes against innocent and vulnerable children. Nevertheless, the great work the Church did in the realms of education, health and culture is often conveniently forgotten. The strong social justice agenda of the Church has the potential to run contrary to the tide of consumerist values that have come centre stage since the advent of the Celtic Tiger. The very idea that anything other than market-force capitalism is good for the country is deemed blasphemous in the same way as sex outside of marriage was roundly denounced from the pulpit during the 1960s and 70s. Our embrace of modernity has brought in its wake a new form of intolerance towards those voices that are raised in dissent at the path on which we are embarked. Joe Cleary offers the following assessment:

> It must be acknowledged that the economic modernisation programme, and the attendant neo-liberalisation, European-isation and Americanisation (sometimes mistakenly termed 'globalisation') of Irish society have enjoyed considerable intellectual and popular support. The most audible opposition to this social agenda was a conservative Catholic backlash, which mobilised considerable opposition to various forms of social liberalisation – especially on divorce, sexuality and abortion – for a period in the eighties, only then to dramatically collapse in the nineties when the economic boom arrived to vindicate the modernisation programme, and a litany of highly publicised clerical sex and physical abuse scandals

discredited the authority of the Catholic hierarchy that had earlier given a lead to such campaigns.[3]

The problems encountered by the Church were mirrored by those experienced by certain politicians who were found guilty of making unlawful gain from their insider knowledge and potential to influence the planning process. In the words of Eugene O'Brien: 'The transcendentality of the Church and State could no longer be taken as a given. Instead, they, too, became part of a system of differences, and hence capable of interrogation.'[4] O'Brien cites Ben Dunne's antics in a Florida hotel room as the beginning of a series of revelations concerning a number of our most senior politicians, including the Taoiseach of the day, Charles J. Haughey. A Tribunal was set up to investigate payments to politicians and revelations emanating from this source shook the very foundations of the State. Public outcry was directed against what had heretofore been the untouchables of Irish life: the Church hierarchy and politicians. The reaction to the Church was the more virulent, however, as the chance to 'get even' with a once all-powerful institution was too tempting to resist for those who had in the past suffered at the hands of priests and religious. The anger persisted for a long time, and still persists today. But there comes a stage when it is important to reappraise our relationship with Catholicism. Because, for all its faults, the majority religion has always held a particular fascination for Irish men and women. As Tom Inglis observes: 'However, although Catholics may have become detached from the teachings and regulations of the Church as a guide as to how to live a moral life, being Catholic is still an endemic part of most people's lives.'[5] The ways of 'being Catholic' may have changed enormously, but the relationship is still an important one for many people.

---

3. 'Introduction: Ireland and Modernity', in Joe Cleary and Claire Connolly (eds), *The Cambridge Companion to Modern Irish Culture* (Cambridge University Press, 2005), pp 14-15.
4. Eugene O'Brien, 'Ireland in Theory: The Influence of French Theory on Irish Cultural and Societal Development', in Eamon Maher and Grace Neville (eds), *France-Ireland: Anatomy of a Relationship* (Frankfurt: Peter Lang, 2004), p 35.
5. Tom Inglis, *Global Ireland*, p 148.

This collection of essays is an attempt therefore to tease out in a critical and detached manner the state of contemporary Catholicism in Ireland. Two thirds of the contributors are different from those who appeared in the *Irish and Catholic?* collection. Four are the same, although hopefully they explore new angles. The contributors include social scientists, educationalists, media experts, a priest, a poet, historians, cultural theorists and literary critics. Some relate personal histories in a moving manner and others the conclusions emanating from years of research. We hope that readers will find some food for thought, as well as some provocation, in the various chapters.

We are grateful to the contributors for agreeing to be involved in the project and for being so professional in their dealings with the editors. We would also like to express our sincere appreciation of the support given by The Priory Institute and ITT Dublin, adjoining institutions in Tallaght, who enjoy a relationship based on mutual respect, synergy and collaboration.

John Littleton and Eamon Maher

PART ONE

What is the Current State of Irish Catholicism?

Being a Catholic in Ireland today

John Littleton

All the Christian churches have in recent years being making a big push to spread the gospel. Certainly in the Catholic Church there has been a lot of talk about evangelisation. Dioceses and parishes have drawn up ambitious plans to let people know about our faith. Usually these have had little effect. We talk about love, freedom, happiness, and so on, but unless our churches are seen really to be places in which people are free and courageous, then why should anyone believe us?[1]

The passage of time inevitably brings change, sometimes good and periodically bad, which could never have been anticipated. Such a transformation has occurred particularly in the Roman Catholic Church in Ireland during the past 50-60 years. In contrast, during the preceding centuries there was little significant variation in its status and conventions. Today the Catholic Church no longer benefits automatically from the privileged and powerful position it once occupied; and the dramatic and far-reaching changes experienced have serious implications for what it means to be a Catholic in Ireland during the opening decade of the twenty-first century.

The context

It is not an exaggeration to say that we now live in a global village. In many instances communication happens instantly. Travel is easier and more appealing (apart from the inconvenience of traffic gridlock in cities and stringent security at airports). Border restrictions between many countries are effectively disappearing, while pluralism and multi-culturalism characterise much of western society.

---

1. Timothy Radcliffe, *What is the point of being a Christian?* (London: Continuum, 2005), p 3.

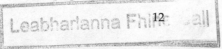

However, there is also a negative aspect to this seemingly unstoppable progress. People's attitudes are now more individualistic, materialistic and consumerist. For example, most urban dwellers neither know nor care about their next-door neighbours; instead, they are preoccupied with their own plans and activities. Likewise, people are more often than not less interested in joining voluntary and charitable organisations because there is no perceived material advantage in doing so. This attitude is quite different from the old Irish custom of *Meitheall*.[2]

The fast-moving pace of change is most epitomised by the information technology sector. Almost as quickly as new products are launched on the market, they are classified as being already out-of-date – such is the speed of the technological advances in an increasingly sophisticated world. It is no wonder, then, that many people believe that this is the 'age of disposables' where almost nothing has any enduring value. Transience is the order of the day and people wait impatiently for the next passing craze.

This entire cultural shift has major implications for the Catholic Church where the pace of change has traditionally been measured in terms of decades if not centuries. The implications are well summarised by the question: What is the point of being a Catholic? This question is a modification of the title of Timothy Radcliffe's recent book, *What is the point of being a Christian?* In the opening quotation of this chapter, above, Radcliffe comments rather startlingly on the growing irrelevance of the Christian churches, including the Catholic Church, to the lives of countless people. This surely has implications for being a Catholic in Ireland today.

The Catholic Church in Ireland today
The reality in twenty-first-century Ireland is that although the Roman Catholic Church is still the majority church, at least nominally, it does not exercise the unquestioned power and signifi-

---

2. *Meitheall* was the Irish rural tradition of local farmers gathering to help one another with specific tasks, for example, threshing the corn, saving the hay and digging the potatoes. It was based on the principles of neighbourliness and companionship, which many people believe to be fast disappearing in these more individualistic and materialistic times.

cant influence it had during the previous few centuries. Observers agree that, in the past, the terms 'Irish' and 'Catholic' were so compatible that they were almost synonymous in the sense that being Irish – with very few exceptions – also meant being Catholic.[3] The two terms were used interchangeably. But that cannot be presumed anymore.

The hierarchical Church has lost much of its power and credibility. Consequently, its moral authority has diminished greatly. There are several reasons for this, not least of which is the totally unprofessional and profoundly unChristian manner in which its leaders dealt with the dreadful revelations of child sexual abuse perpetrated by a few priests and religious who, having exploited the trust of parents, teachers and care-workers – but especially the trust of the victims themselves – destroyed the lives of so many innocent and vulnerable children. No one knows when, if ever, that trust will again be forthcoming. The revelations of sexual abuse by Church officials have horrified some Catholics so much that they have ceased practising their faith; and their outrage is understandable. However, in the interests of accuracy, it must be acknowledged that other people, who stopped going to church for no particular reason, sometimes use the child abuse scandals as a convenient excuse to justify decisions made independently of the scandals. This is unfair.

But it would be a mistake to think that the decline in the influence of the Catholic Church is due entirely to the child sexual abuse scandals. In addition, Ireland, like so many Western countries, is becoming increasingly secular. Large numbers of people are not interested in organised religion because they can manage themselves and their activities without it. Therefore, they argue that religion – in any of its expressions – should not be given any recognition.[4] Numerous people do not perceive a need for God, more than ever in the booming Celtic Tiger economy

3. See, for example, John Littleton, 'Catholic identity in the Irish context', in Louise Fuller, John Littleton and Eamon Maher (eds), *Irish and Catholic? Towards an understanding of identity* (Dublin: The Columba Press, 2006), pp 26, 29-30.
4. A relevant instance is the recurrent campaign, especially in letters to the national newspapers, to have RTÉ (Ireland's National Television and Radio Broadcaster) cease broadcasting the Angelus bells at 12.00 noon and at 6.00 pm.

that has made such a vast difference to the Irish nation's prosperity. For many people, religious practice has become redundant; it is merely a memory from the past. Yet it is amazing to observe how many 'non-practising Catholics' visit churches to have their throats blessed on the Feast of Saint Blaise (3 February) and to receive the blessed ashes on their foreheads on Ash Wednesday at the beginning of Lent.[5] Likewise, popular novenas to various saints (especially Our Lady of Perpetual Help, Saint Francis Xavier, Saint Martin de Porres and Saint Gerard Majella), Christmas Midnight Mass and the Good Friday ceremonies still attract relatively large congregations. It would be inaccurate to describe these anomalies as pure superstition; nevertheless, it is difficult to offer a coherent rationale for them.

There is undoubtedly no shortage of negative images of the Catholic Church. According to many people, the hierarchical Church is out-of-touch with the reality of contemporary life, especially in the areas of sexual morality, the role of women, the rights of minority groups, and the lack of accountability and democratic structures at all levels. This has resulted in what are stereotypically described as 'lapsed Catholics' (those who have abandoned the practice of the Catholic faith) and the so-called 'à-la-carte Catholics' (those who choose whichever doctrines and moral guidelines suit themselves, while ignoring the remainder).[6] Again, it would be erroneous to assume that it is only teenagers and those in their twenties and thirties who forsake the practice of their faith; middle-aged and older people are doing it too (this is quite significant because it did not happen so much in the past). Then there are sizeable numbers of immigrants arriving in Ireland, not all of whom are Catholics and some of whom form significant ethnic minorities with their own particular social, religious and pastoral needs.

---

5. For example, the current Taoiseach (Irish Prime Minister), Bertie Aherne TD, often features on television news reports from Dáil Éireann (the Lower House of the Irish Parliament) wearing the distinctive mark of the blessed ashes on his forehead. Some commentators suggest that this typifies an era that is no more.
6. This is not to suggest, however, that thinking Catholics should not engage critically with their Church's beliefs and teachings. Human experience necessarily informs belief.

When considering what it means to be a Catholic in Ireland today, there are several factors that merit particular deliberation. Among the most important are: (1) the disappearance of Catholic culture; (2) the demise of sacramental confession; (3) the crisis in vocations to the priesthood and religious life; and (4) the lack of effective Church leadership. Obviously, these factors do not have a critical impact on non-Catholics; but they are crucial for Catholics in terms of understanding and articulating what they believe about their faith and its ramifications for daily life.

(1) The disappearance of Catholic culture

The disappearance of Catholic culture is widely evidenced by a lack of awareness, among many Catholics, of what it means to profess Catholicism by participating in the Church's sacramental life and other rituals, and by living in accordance with its ethical teachings. It relates to their inability to explain the central truths of their faith and their ignorance of basic Catholic customs and devotional practices.

Examples of the absence of Catholic culture on the level of knowledge of the faith include doubts about the Church's core teachings such as the Real Presence of Jesus in the Eucharist, the resurrection of the dead (including the resurrection of Jesus) and the existence of the afterlife. In similar vein, some Catholics, if asked, would not be convinced about the existence of God; also, they would argue that one religion is as good as another or that all religions are basically the same. Similarly, many Catholics under 30 years of age would not be able to say how many sacraments there are, much less name them.[7] While this may seem incredible to older, more traditional Catholics, various surveys indicate that increasing numbers of Catholics, especially those who are younger, are uninformed about the essentials of their faith.[8]

7. According to a 2007 poll conducted by Lansdowne Market Research on behalf of The Iona Institute and the Evangelical Alliance, 63% of those over 65 years old, 38% of those aged 15-24 years and 50% of the total population knew that, according to Catholic belief, there are seven sacraments. See the website of the Iona Institute (http://www.ionainstitute.ie/).

8. See, for example, the 2002 Irish Social/Lifestyle Research Results prepared by Millward Browne IMS for the Power to Change campaign.

This, in turn, has serious consequences for the handing on of the faith. Even seminary training is introducing a propaedeutic year – an introductory year before formal studies begin – because of the rather impoverished levels of faith development in candidates presenting for priesthood.

The primary responsibility for handing on the faith lies with parents; it is explicitly stated in the Catholic baptismal liturgy. But nowadays, younger parents frequently do not practise the faith or, if they do, have not been well-grounded in its fundamental teachings. Thus they are unwilling or unable to share confidently their faith experience with their children. Ironically, often it is grandparents who pass on the faith because it is they – mainly the grandmothers – who pray with their grandchildren and take them to visit 'Holy God's house' where they regularly 'light a candle'. Regrettably, these activities are often the only elements of faith formation received by children before they commence formal schooling when the responsibility for faith formation is then unjustly transferred exclusively to teachers. This is wrong because, as catechists consistently argue, 'the faith is caught, not taught'.[9] In other words, it needs to be experienced by children with their parents in the home. Other educators in the faith, including schoolteachers and clergy, have a role that is rightly secondary to that of parents.

Examples of the disappearance of Catholic culture on the level of customs and devotional practices include the lack of familiarity among many Catholics of what to say when they go to confession, and how to be reverent in church during liturgical celebrations. This is especially evident at funerals and weddings when it becomes immediately obvious that many people in the congregation are simply 'out of practice' regarding the language and routine gestures used. Similarly, many couples preparing for marriage engage the hotel, photographer and florist ever before contacting the priest to reserve the church and discuss the religious aspects of their wedding. Also, parishioners generally do not inform the local priest that a member of their family is ill

---

9. This does not imply that teaching is an unimportant dimension of passing on the faith; simply that it is not the only dimension. The faith needs to be taught in a systematic way, but in the wider context of lifestyle and good example.

in hospital, and it is the undertaker who contacts the priest when someone has died. This is so different from the past, when the priest was contacted first – even before the doctor.

What is urgently needed to restore a sense of Catholic culture is basic evangelisation (which is a logically prior step to a more thorough catechesis). The proof that evangelisation and catechesis were achieving their aims would be that people would not be embarrassed to mention the name of Jesus and that they would readily admit to having a personal relationship with him in their daily lives which is nurtured through prayer and the frequent celebration of the sacraments. Furthermore, their commitment to the teaching of Jesus and his Church would be evident in their Catholic lifestyles. Thus there would be an obvious link between liturgy and life; or, in the words of older people, people would be 'living the Mass'.

(2) The demise of sacramental confession

The demise of sacramental confession has become one of the most noticeable traits of contemporary Catholicism. Whereas previously people 'went to confession' regularly, for example, once every month or, in some cases, once every week, nowadays almost nobody goes to confession. A glance inside the confessionals in most Catholic churches reveals that they are increasingly used for storage purposes. Yet it could easily be argued convincingly that confession was never needed more than it is now.

Undoubtedly confession, in the sense of sacramental confession, is no longer relevant for many people because there has been such a loss of the sense of sin, which in turn in due to a loss of the sense of the sacred.[10] But confession – understood in terms of the psychological need to experience the fundamental truth that 'a trouble shared is a trouble halved' – happens all the time. Observe, for instance, the vast numbers of people who attend counsellors and psychotherapists; that did not happen in the past. Nowadays, however, people almost boast about being 'in therapy'. Notice too how, particularly in Ireland, talk-radio has

---

10. Sin is a theological terms; it makes no sense in the absence of belief in a personal God.

become the norm; this did not happen by chance. There are non-stop live phone-in radio programmes and, remarkably, people reveal the most intimate details of their personal lives on national radio, often encouraged by the skilful interviewing techniques of the presenters whose main aim is to create sensational radio so that listenership figures will remain high and compete favourably with rival broadcasters.[11]

We all need people to listen to us (the Samaritans report that many people telephoning them say 'You are the first person who listened to me for so long') and offer us affirmation, encouragement, clarification or an objective alternative opinion. In the past, quite apart from the sacramental absolution that was given by the priest to the penitent in confession, the advice and counselling were also helpful. Now, instead of going to confession in the safety and confidentiality of the confessional, people are confessing their innermost thoughts, fears and fantasies publicly in a context that is frequently voyeuristic and unsympathetic. This cannot be wholesome.

Finally, when the Sacrament of Reconciliation (another name for Confession or Penance) is celebrated using penitential services in churches several times every year (usually during Advent and Lent, or during a parish mission) many people think that they have not been to confession – despite having individually confessed their sins to a priest and received absolution – simply because they have not entered the confessional. Thus significant catechesis is required – both to encourage people to avail of the sacrament again and to help them understand that penitential services (where individual sacramental confession and absolution are included) constitute the Sacrament of Reconciliation just as much as going to confession in the confessional.

(3) The crisis in vocations to the priesthood and religious life
The general perception is that there is a crisis in vocations to the priesthood and religious life. However, the reality is not as it is often presented. For example, there are plenty of vocations to

11. Currently, two of the most successful and popular live radio programmes are *Liveline*, presented by Joe Duffy on RTÉ's Radio One, and the *Gerry Ryan Show*, presented by Gerry Ryan on RTÉ's 2FM.

the priesthood and religious life in countries around the Catholic world where the Church is being persecuted or where the Church is new. Here in Ireland (and in other western European countries, Australia and America), there is undeniably a great shortage of vocations when comparisons are made with the early decades of the twentieth century. Here, too, the dramatic fall-off in vocations to the priesthood has resulted in all of the seminaries in Ireland, except the National Seminary in Maynooth, closing. Even in Maynooth, the total number of seminarians is now less than the number in each of the six or seven years of training in the past.

Nonetheless, it could be argued that the current decline in vocations is not really a crisis. Perhaps the 'good old days' were atypical – they certainly were when compared with the statistics over the Church's long history. For much of the twentieth century, Ireland experienced an economic recession. Families had more children to rear then too. So having a son or daughter enter the priesthood or religious life solved some of the problems about the future of individual family members. Most of the clergy came predominantly from a middle-class, farming background when family status was measured, as is often said, in terms of 'having a (water) pump in the yard, a bull in the field and a son in the priesthood'.

How times have changed! Parishes are now being clustered – and some are being closed – due to the lack of available priests to service them. Likewise, the number of Masses is being reduced. But this can only be good. Hopefully, it will increase the quality of participation in liturgical celebrations and will also give lay people the opportunity to exercise their own legitimate ministry by virtue of being baptised. It must be remembered, too, that much of priests' working time has traditionally been occupied by duties and tasks that are not essential to the nature of priesthood – for example, being involved in fundraising for parish properties and being chairpersons of schools' boards of management.

Giving lay people greater responsibilities in the Church's mission and ministry will release priests to focus on their priestly work. Then the shortage of clergy may not be experienced in quite the same way. It must be remembered that vocations to the priesthood and religious life emerge from lay people; paradoxically, then, encouraging the laity to become more involved in the Church's structures and ministry will invariably result in clerical and religious vocations. The real crisis is arguably a crisis of ideas rather than a crisis in vocations. Thus the situation regarding the crisis in vocations to the priesthood and religious life might well be expressed: 'What crisis? There is no crisis!' That opinion is indeed provocative but, if given serious consideration, it might challenge all Catholics to reassess their attitudes towards the much-talked-about crisis in vocations.

(4) The lack of effective Church leadership
Most commentators today agree that a major flaw in the Roman Catholic Church in Ireland during recent decades has been its lack of effective leadership. Unfortunately, the bishops – both individually and collectively – have generally assumed that they alone must bear the burden of leadership, without sharing it with their priests and engaging meaningfully with the laity about how to deal properly with the various crises and pastoral needs.

This was strikingly noticeable in how the bishops dealt with the victims and perpetrators of clerical sex abuse. There were serious systemic failures at all levels. This has resulted in a period of unprecedented crisis in the Church. The lack of transparency was inexcusable. The decisions to instigate formal legal processes in preference to suitable pastoral strategies, when dealing with abuse allegations, were unwise. Similarly, the unwillingness to communicate openly with the news media was counterproductive. In fact, the bishops would have been much better advised to learn from the incomparable expertise of parents (especially mothers) when devising appropriate procedures to ensure the safety of children.

Furthermore, the relationship between priest and bishop (that, apart from his relationship with God, is meant to be the most important relationship in a priest's life), which should be based on mutual respect, trust and obedience, has been seriously undermined by the manner in which some bishops have dealt with complaints and allegations against priests. Significantly, most parishioners now identify their local parish clergy as being linked with themselves rather than with the hierarchy. This is certainly a major change among Irish Catholics because it means that their frustration and anger over the revelations of child sexual abuse are clearly directed towards the bishops, not priests (other than priests who are abusers).

But just as sexual abuse is symptomatic of the wider malaise of the abuse of power, the hierarchy's inadequate responses to child protection issues are symptomatic of how it deals with many broader issues and concerns. More generally, there is no satisfactory means of dialogue between the bishops and other groups in the Irish Church that is mutually enhancing and life-giving. Journalists are mostly treated with suspicion and mistrust. A proactive approach to communications, media and public relations is not evident. It is often forgotten that the teaching Church is also the learning Church.

While the Catholic Church is not a democracy, theologically speaking, nevertheless some elements of democracy could operate at all levels. The absence of democratic structures is particularly noticeable in the appointment of bishops, which is surrounded with secrecy. Bishops are the leaders of the local church; yet they are appointed centrally from Rome, often with very little meaningful communication at diocesan level.

For example, it is somewhat ironic that priests who are appointed bishops are referred to as 'bishop elect' between the public announcement of their appointments and their ordination/installation as bishop. Surely it would be more accurate and honest to refer to them as 'bishop designate'. Also, in the sophisticated and complex world in which we live today, it is asking too much of any fallible human being to possess all the skills that are required for effective leadership. All the more reason, then, why much greater consultation is needed about the appointment of bishops. That is why more participation by greater numbers of people needs to be encouraged at all levels in the Church. Such involvement, if properly facilitated, would naturally lead to a synod-type approach to debate and discussion in the Church – and maybe towards a national assembly of the Catholic Church in Ireland which has been advocated by several groups (especially the National Conference of Priests of Ireland) for some time.

The need for prophetic leadership in the Church
Contrary to much popular opinion, prophets – at least in the biblical understanding of the term – do not foretell the future but speak out in the present context. Neither do they speak on their own authority. Throughout Judeo-Christian history, prophets have been first and foremost God's spokespersons, literally people who speak for God; but prophets have also interceded with God on behalf of their people, thereby exercising a dual role in divine-human relationships. Thus the role of prophets has been, and continues to be, tremendously important and necessary in the lives of God's people. Without prophets, and more particularly without people heeding their teaching, believers in God cannot be knowledgeable about the authentic meaning of God's revelation (self-communication).

In the Book of Deuteronomy, there are crucial lessons about prophecy in the words spoken by Moses. He said to the people: 'Your God will raise up for you a prophet like myself, from among yourselves, from your own brothers [and sisters]' (Deut 18: 15). There Moses explained that prophets emerge from the ordinary people; they do not drop from the sky and, in general, they are not extra-special people. Indeed, they are reluctant people, doing what is necessary. This is significant because we tend to dismiss the possibility that we ourselves, family members, friends or colleagues could be called by God to be prophets in our Church and in the world.

The call to be prophetic is part of our baptismal commitment whereby we decide to bear witness to the teaching of Christ and his Church. The fact is that, through the commitment we make in baptism and confirmation, we are obliged to speak the truth, especially when confronted with evil and sinful situations. The challenge is to accept God's invitation to speak the truth with conviction and compassion.

Moses also explained that prophets would be people who would be like him. This, too, is significant. Moses shared a deeply personal relationship with God. He met God face-to-face and talked to God with ease and familiarity. He taught God's commandments and challenged people to abandon their sinful practices. In doing so, he often made the people uncomfortable and he was unpopular with them sometimes. Nevertheless, Moses regularly mediated with God on behalf of the people.

Such are the characteristics that are necessary in any true prophet. Essentially, prophets bring words of consolation or judgement – occasionally both – depending on what the situation requires. Sometimes the prophetic word of God is calling people back to judgement; at other times it offering consolation to people who are experiencing trauma and other kinds of difficulty.

Prophets are holy people. They are uncompromising in their faithfulness to the word of God. They always speak the truth, regardless of the consequences. They offer encouragement and hope to people who have no sense of meaning or purpose in life. They challenge people to repent for their sins and to seek God's mercy. There is still a need for prophets in our society, men and women who come from among the ordinary Church members and who are faithful to their baptismal commitment. The future of the Catholic Church in Ireland lies in realising this potential in the lives of people.

'Thinking Catholic'

This chapter has focused on the question: What is the point of being a Catholic in Ireland today? Most Roman Catholics were born into Catholicism and reared as Catholics. To that extent at least, they initially made no formal choice to embrace the Catholic way of life – although such a choice was made for them by their parents and godparents when they were baptised. But that does not mean that they do not subsequently have to choose the Catholic lifestyle. That choice needs to be made everyday and, regardless of how one thinks and feels as a member of the Catholic Church, it is better to work for reform from within rather than to leave. Being a Catholic in Ireland today is about 'thinking Catholic'. Thinking Catholic is more than knowing the teaching of Christ and his Church. It is really a distinctive mindset which guides the practice of Catholicism in one's life; it involves doing whatever is necessary in terms of faith development to think critically about what Catholicism means and about what its implications are for daily living.

CHAPTER TWO

The Catholic Church in post-Celtic Tiger Ireland

Peadar Kirby

Madam, Last weekend, in the absence of the parish priest, I was the priest-celebrant at all three Masses in the parish of Our Lady of Lourdes in Limerick. I saw nobody in church between the ages of 10 and 40 years.

There was a certain sadness in the fact that the 'Mass intention' for the 10:30 am Eucharist was: 'For all our young people who were sitting their Leaving and Junior Certificate exams'.

– Letter to the editor of The Irish Times *from Fr Patrick Seaver CC, published on 16 June 2007.*

The issue of the abuse of children by priests and religious over the past 60 years or so, and particularly the cases of sexual abuse that have come to light, weigh heavily on today's Irish Catholic Church, among both the clergy and lay people. Yet, Father Seaver's letter to the editor of *The Irish Times* raises issues of even more fundamental significance to which far less attention appears to be paid, even if the absence of young people from our churches is lamented by many. For a Church top-heavy with older people not only lacks a future but it shows a failure to find a role for itself in the vastly changed society that has emerged over recent decades. In other words, it points to a fundamental failure to evangelise a new generation, to relate the message of the Gospel in a liberating and penetrating way to the values, lifestyles, concerns and life horizons that predominate among them.

Far more than clerical sex abuse scandals, this failure of evangelisation is the great drama of contemporary Irish Catholicism. While scandals may have alienated some who would have continued a marginal involvement in the Church in their absence, even if no Irish priest or religious had ever sexually abused any-one, the Irish Catholic Church would still be in the midst of arguably its most serious crisis for many centuries. What the abuse scandals help to do is to highlight why the Church is in the crisis it is in. For experts tell us that abusers use their position of power to satisfy unfulfilled sexual needs. The reality of rela-tively widespread abuse therefore points to the pervasive cul-ture of clericalism that grew up in the nineteenth century Irish Church which saw the emergence of what can only be called a clerical caste or elite that dominated the Church and kept lay people in a submissive and largely ignorant situation. What the cases of abuse do is to highlight and make visible the perverse legacies of the past to which the situation described by Fr Seaver in his letter is directly attributable.

This chapter analyses the situation of the Irish Church in the vastly changed society that has emerged over recent decades, what we can call 'post-Celtic Tiger Ireland' since it is largely the creation of the processes of modernisation and capitalist expan-sion that came to full fruition in the economic boom of the late 1990s. It begins by identifying some of the key legacies of the past that help account for the situation in which the Irish Catholic Church now finds itself. The chapter then turns to ex-amine the contours of today's Ireland and the challenges for spirituality and ecclesial life that these throw up. The third sec-tion offers some suggestions about what might be done to ad-dress these challenges and focuses in particular on one concrete proposal. The analysis in this chapter is made in the knowledge that the author is no expert in pastoral action but it derives from a certain expertise in socio-political analysis of contemporary Ireland and is offered in a spirit of ecclesial concern and commit-ment. The chapter will end with some closing reflections on the need for prophetic leadership and courageous action at this time in our history.

Legacies of past options
The letter with which this chapter opens raises the most funda-mental questions for pastoral agents in today's Irish Catholic Church yet there is little evidence that these questions are being addressed with the thoroughness they require. In essence, the

key question is as follows: Why is it that a generation, most of whom were educated in schools dominated by Catholic Church personnel and who grew to adulthood in a culture still deeply impregnated by ecclesial language and concerns, has seemingly severed a meaningful relationship with the Church? Does this not indicate a most serious failure of pastoral action? If so, what are the causes of this failure and how should the Church begin remedying them? In the absence of a sustained conversation in Irish life and the Irish Church addressing these questions, this section offers some reflections on them in the hope that it might stimulate such a conversation.

It is important to begin by avoiding personalising the question being addressed. It would be difficult to sustain an argument that the failure reflects the personal failings of pastoral agents since there is no evidence to suggest that the quality and commitment of these agents was any worse in the second half of the twentieth century than it was in earlier periods. As many can vouch from personal experience, the Irish Church was blessed with dedicated, inspiring, loving and hard-working personnel (clergy, religious and lay people) who helped form the generation that now seem little interested in ecclesial life and involvement. Inevitably, among these personnel were some whose influence was not as positive (and indeed some who should never have been given pastoral responsibility by the Church) but this was presumably equally true in earlier periods when the Irish Church had much greater pastoral success. Instead of any search for failings of personnel, the question needs to be addressed at the level of the role the Church took on in Irish life and the strategies adapted to give effect to that role. This offers a much more fruitful terrain of inquiry as it draws attention to the highly successful role that the Church found for itself in Irish life in the early nineteenth century, a role that effectively institutionalised Irish Catholicism in a very new way. The subsequent successes of this newly emergent Church, not only at home but throughout the English-speaking world, made it an extremely powerful institution. It is the crisis of this model of Church, of this particular form that Irish Catholicism took and that lasted for about 200 years, that lies at the heart of the difficulties and challenges now facing the Irish Church.

The Irish Catholic Church emerged from the eighteenth century as a very strongly believing body of faithful but in a very weakened institutional state and with a big shortage of clergy and religious to service a fast growing population. The story of the nineteenth century was one of institution-building on a massive scale as an extensive infrastructure of churches, schools and hospitals was built throughout the island and, particularly in the post-Famine period, the numbers of clergy and religious grew as the population began its long decline. As this fast expanding institution grew in confidence, it came to see its role as being the creation of a Catholic nation to counter the dominance of Irish economic and political life by Protestants. While not totally wedded to the nationalist project (many bishops were only too happy to do business with the British government and a portion of the emerging Catholic business class was unionist in political outlook), extensive sectors of the Church were increasingly key actors in this project, not least through the Catholic education system. In this regard, the role of the Christian Brothers and other religious congregations in mapping out a new 'imagined community' of Irish Catholic nationalism was essential to the long-term success of that project. While the impact on concepts of the Irish nation of its increasing identification with Catholicism has received much critical attention, particularly in the period since the 50th anniversary of the 1916 Rising and in the context of the Northern Troubles, what has received less attention is the impact of this identification on the Church.

Arguably this identification was central to the remarkable success of Catholicism in nineteenth and twentieth century Ireland. As the Irish language and Gaelic culture fast declined as a distinguishing badge of separate identity, Catholicism filled the void so that being Irish and being Catholic began to appear synonymous. In other words, Catholicism replaced Gaelic culture as the central element of what it was to be Irish and this has continued down to our own day. Of course, this identification on its own was not sufficient to maintain the active allegiance to the Church of the majority of the Irish faithful. After all, Catholicism was also a core part of French, Spanish and Italian identity and this did not prevent the steady decline of Catholicism in these countries. Part of the difference in the Irish case is that Catholicism was an active part of an emerging project of anti-colonial cultural nationalism that was deeply popular and democratic, so that the Church was not wedded to the power structures of the past but was a core element of the challenge to these power structures. Also, however, the Church was very successful in offering a new diet of devotional practices to replace the native and deeply rooted spirituality that was a central part of the Gaelic worldview.[1] For it has not been realised enough how the language shift of the nineteenth century impacted on people's spirituality, severely eroding the rich inheritance of a faith practice that was deeply integrated into people's everyday lives, not least their interaction with the natural world. The devotional revolution of the second half of the nineteenth century therefore filled a vacuum opened up by swift anglicisation. But this devotionalism was very different to the spirituality it replaced. Imported from Victorian Britain and from France and Italy, it created a world of devotional practices parallel to people's everyday lives rather than being a central part of their lives. Secondly, it was largely centred in church buildings and therefore under the control of clergy. The identity that deeply shaped the emerging Irish nation, therefore, was nurtured on a sentimental piety that had the effect of divorcing faith practice from the everyday lives and struggles of people.

An essential element of this devotional revolution was its anti-intellectualism. For Church leaders set their face against the theological education of people in this new emerging Catholicism. Bishops struggled throughout the nineteenth century for a separate Catholic educational system but this was not to be used to educate people to think critically about their faith but rather to immerse them in a highly devotional Catholicism. It was bizarre in the extreme that once an essentially Catholic university system was achieved in the guise of the National University of Ireland (NUI), theology was excluded from the curriculum. Ireland must be the only country in the world where lay Catholics were effectively excluded for a century from the option of achieving theological literacy. Even the religious education that lay people got at school was devoid of a robust theolog-

---

1. For an indepth analysis of this issue, see John J. Ó Riordáin, *Irish Catholic Spirituality* (Dublin: The Columba Press, 1998).

ical content – it was largely devotional and polemical in earlier decades and has degenerated into a mild form of social studies in more recent times. Only as we enter the twenty-first century has religious studies finally become a subject on the curriculum of secondary education. The predictable result of this neglect was that the Church effectively excluded itself from the intellectual debates of Irish society, largely losing the intelligentsia, something that became ever more obvious amid the ferment of the modernisation and liberalisation of Irish life since the 1960s (though there is little sign that this worries most Church leaders).

The devotional revolution did not have to go hand in hand with an anti-intellectualism. The latter was caused rather by what emerged as undoubtedly the most distinguishing characteristic of the new Irish Catholicism, namely clericalism. The swift growth in the numbers of clergy and religious from the middle of the nineteenth century until the last quarter of the twentieth century, coupled with the centring of Catholic practice in the institutions they controlled, led to the emergence of what can only be called a clerical caste, wielding immense social and cultural power. Offering opportunities for the theological education of lay Catholics, and the climate of debate and contestation this would have undoubtedly fostered, would have helped counter this excessive power and one can only speculate that this was the reason, whether conscious or subconscious, why Irish Catholics were kept largely intellectually childish in their faith for over a century. Instead, clerical power inculcated an excessive and often uncritical regard for clergy and religious among lay people which, at least for some, would be more accurately described as a fear. While many of these clergy and religious were very dedicated and good people, they lived within this caste system and inevitably were shaped by some of its features, not least in terms of how they were regarded by lay people. To use a term taken from the writings of the Brazilian theologian, Leonardo Boff, this has been perhaps the greatest pathology of Irish Catholicism and it is deeply implicated in the sexual scandals now rocking the Irish Church.[2] Indeed, it has

---

2. See Leonardo Boff, *Church: Charism and Power* (London: SCM Press, 1985).

taken these scandals to begin to break open this caste system and allow the human lives and frailties of priests and religious to find more widespread airing and acknowledgement. That this is going hand in hand with a vigorous tide of anti-clericalism is only to be expected and indeed is something healthy when it does not degenerate into a blanket hostility to clergy and religious which, unfortunately, it often seems to do in today's Ireland.

There are therefore two interlinked inheritances that today's Irish Catholic Church carries as a very heavy legacy. The first is the shaping of Catholicism as a largely devotional set of practices, parallel to people's everyday lives and devoid of robust intellectual content, and the central link shaped between this and the form of Irish identity that emerged triumphant, both culturally and politically, in the early twentieth century. This devotionalism speaks little to the well-educated, highly literate and internationalised Ireland of today but the Church struggles to offer intellectual and spiritual resources that resonate with the needs of the generations of Irish people below the age of 50 or so. It is little surprise that, after keeping lay people in a passive and obedient state for generations, the Irish Church now finds such a vacuum of lay leadership, lay movements, lay spirituality and lay theological debate. Indeed, most of the Catholic lay activism visible over recent decades seemed motivated by a desperate attempt to reinforce the clericalised and devotional Church of the past rather than to sow the seeds of new forms of ecclesial life. Furthermore, as the identification of faith and nation is being critically interrogated for its narrowness, its intolerance, its inability to open to the opportunities of what we now call a more globalised world, by extension Catholicism is being seen as an element that has also to be jettisoned. What is extremely worrying is just how deeply this view of Catholicism has taken hold among a younger generation, as those of us who teach this generation can only too readily vouch for.

The second inheritance is clericalism. This has been the central reason for the lack of a reforming current in the Irish Church as the caste which ran it and wielded such immense power saw the mildest form of critical thinking or any autonomous mobilisation among the faithful (or even among clergy and religious) as a threat to be opposed and stamped out. For this reason, the promise of Vatican II was never realised in the Irish Church as its reforms were introduced in form but its spirit was largely absent. As Archbishop John Charles McQuaid famously said on his return from the Council, nothing was to upset the tranquil lives of the Irish faithful. Yet, perhaps there is more hope that this inheritance is fast becoming an historical relic. One reason is simply the lack of vocations as young people are not attracted any more to joining this clerical caste. The second, of course, as stated already, comes as a result of the scandals that have opened some of the most unsavoury features of this clericalism to public scrutiny so that Church leaders are being forced to address these. More and more, a Church that for a century and a half kept lay people in a passive and obedient state is now being forced to turn to them as pastoral partners. It is little surprise that, as Fr Seaver's letter states, it finds so few below the age of 40.

Post-Celtic Tiger Ireland
If the form of Irish Church now dying was successful because it addressed the needs of its society, so a new and vibrant form will emerge only through addressing the needs of the very different society that is taking shape in today's Ireland. A renewal of Irish Catholicism requires therefore an intense scrutiny of the contours of that society through the lens of Gospel values, in other words a 'reading of the signs of the times'. For Ireland today is indeed a different country but one desperately in need of the refinement that comes from a thorough evangelisation. Yet, the forms of pastoral ministry, ecclesial leadership and spiritual life that dominate and define today's Irish Church seem largely inadequate to this daunting task.

What then are the contours of this new Ireland? The task of discernment is guided here by the reading given by the Irish Catholic Bishops in their pastoral letter *Prosperity with a Purpose*, published in 1999.[3] In the opening of this document, the Bishops

---

3. Irish Catholic Bishops' Conference, *Prosperity with a Purpose: Christian Faith and Values in a Time of Rapid Economic Growth* (Dublin: Veritas, 1999). All subsequent references will be to the relevant paragraphs in this edition.

speak of the need for a 'careful appraisal' of today's Ireland to 'ensure there is moral purpose to Ireland's new prosperity' (pars 2 and 3). They then structure their appraisal into four sections: Looking Back, Looking Around, Looking Within and Looking Forward. The Bishops rightly devote extensive attention to the many social problems and deficits of today's Ireland. The section on 'Looking Around' is the longest section of the document and covers a list of what are many of the glaring injustices of today's Irish society – housing and homelessness, the environment, income adequacy and poverty, long-term unemployment, early school leavers, urban disadvantage, people with disabilities, the prison population, former low-skilled emigrants, the Travelling People, refugees and asylum-seekers. They pose the principal challenge now facing Ireland as being to redress 'fundamental problems that have beset its society for a very long time'. They continue:

> The performance of the Irish economy during the last decade of the twentieth century has been described as 'peerless'. Irish people should now be determined that future commentators will have cause to speak of equally impressive social achievements on the island during the first decade of the new century. These years will, in all probability, present unprecedented opportunities: to reduce poverty and educational disadvantage from among the highest to among the lowest levels in the EU; to ensure no child is reared in poverty; to end extreme social segregation in the Irish pattern of housing; to adopt best practice in every area of care for the island's environment; to become an increasingly credible and effective advocate of the cause of the poorest nations (par 4).

From the vantage point of almost a decade later, it would be difficult for even the most sympathetic observer to claim that these unprecedented opportunities for impressive social achievements have been grasped. How they might be, is addressed in the next section below. Here, what is important is to highlight the huge imbalances in Irish society to which the Bishops draw attention and which constitute perhaps the greatest contradiction of contemporary Ireland. As they state, income inequalities in Irish society are continuing or even accelerating; this is widely known by any informed observer. What the Bishops go on to emphasise, however, is that worsening relative income poverty (of which Ireland has among the highest levels in the EU in the mid 2000s) 'should not be lightly dismissed, nor assumed to be largely a temporary phenomenon. Living on an income far below what most others enjoy can bite painfully; a person may feel, and be perceived by others to be, a failure' (par 56).

Amid all the hype that we have never had it so good, the Bishops are right to focus on the fact that 'the fractures beginning to widen in Irish society are capable of souring life for everyone, and materialism is capable of undermining people's ability to find contentment in what they already own' (par 126). Here they get to the heart of what makes contemporary Ireland such a morally distasteful place to live: for what we see daily is a culture of obsessive and gross consumerism (shopping as recreation, consumption as a 'lifestyle choice') side by side with the real harsh material deprivation in which at least one fifth of our population live, among them very many children and elderly people. If, as the Economic and Social Research Institute (ESRI) claims, this is the 'best of times' for Irish people, then clearly this 20 per cent is simply being forgotten about in such a judgement.[4] As the Bishops so incisively comment: 'It is, arguably, becoming more difficult for those benefiting the most from economic growth to see what the same process is entailing for others' (par 116) and yet 'policies expressing solidarity … will only be formulated and find political support when more of the better-off in society *do* see, and when they accept that an economy that is moving faster is more demanding of people who are poor also, not more benign' (par 115; emphasis in original).

In this comment, the Bishops join the socio-economic with the moral and cultural; indeed, they draw attention to the fact that any advance towards the sort of society they aspire to as outlined in paragraph 4 quoted above depends on fostering 'an ethic of civic responsibility' (title of Section 5.7) to counter the 'growing individualism and competitiveness in Irish society' (par 167). Nor is this some vague feeling of goodwill towards

4. Fahey, Tony, Helen Russell and Christopher T. Whelan (eds), *Best of Times? The Social Impact of the Celtic Tiger* (Dublin: Institute of Public Administration, 2007).

those less well off; the Bishops are very realistic (and run completely against the prevailing ideology accepted without question by all our mainstream political leaders of left and right as well as by our media) in making the point that better public services depend on raising more income for the State through taxation. The section is worth quoting at some length since it makes well the obvious point that the leaders of our society (and most of our fellow citizens if option surveys are to be believed) seem to have great difficulty in grasping:

> Equity and efficiency questions about how the current level of tax revenue is being raised ... should not be allowed to hide the fact that, by the standards of other small, prosperous European societies, Ireland has low overall taxation and correspondingly low public social expenditures. It is quite consistent to argue at the same time for lower tax rates on modest personal incomes and better public services, if the tax base is appropriately widened. The key moral issue for the individual is whether there is any type of extra taxation (for example, on property or energy use) or foregone tax reduction he or she will accept in order to support the state in raising the levels of healthcare, educational attainment, income protection and housing provision associated with Irish citizenship *per se* (par 168).

The Bishops are right to pose reform of the taxation system not as a technical issue for the State but as a moral issue for citizens. And, as if to make clear that the State is not morally blameless in this situation, the Bishops go on immediately to argue for an indexing of all social welfare payments to the growth of average earnings, something successive governments have opposed. As the Bishops state: 'Christians find it morally indefensible to maintain a financial incentive to work, which is appropriate and important in many instances, at the expense of a higher poverty risk being run by recipients of, for example, unemployment assistance and supplementary welfare allowances. It is, also, a minimalist form of solidarity when only minor real increases are granted to social welfare beneficiaries at a time when the average earnings in society are rising steadily' (par 169). In these paragraphs, the bishops accurately identify the causal connections between the moral choices of citizens, the political choices of the governments they elect and the social outcomes that these same citizens so regularly decry. It is a rare piece of clear moral and social scientific thinking in a society so widely confused and befuddled by incessant media clatter.

Another theme so hidden in the discourse of contemporary Irish society that this pastoral letter highlights is the role of the market. For, if the Celtic Tiger has any essential meaning, it is as the period when the Irish State became largely subservient to the power of private market actors in the guise especially of global corporations but also of Irish speculators, at great cost to Irish society (even if a small elite enriched itself immensely). The costs are well documented in this pastoral letter. But this essential shift of power from the public authorities of the State to the private authorities of market players is subjected to frighteningly little critical scrutiny.

The Bishops acknowledge that there are causes for concern:

The common good is not automatically served by market forces. Without at all denying the positive role of markets, including the social advances they make possible, it is important that more people in Ireland expect and support the public authorities to intervene resolutely wherever it is necessary to protect the common good. The extent to which the country's rapid economic growth is due to opening the economy to more intense competition in wider markets underlines the need for constant vigilance. There is disconcerting evidence from other countries of how rapid growth through deeper integration into today's global economy creates winners and losers inside the same national society (par 41).

Again the Bishops advocate what can only be called citizens' activism, this time in regard to the influence of market forces on our polity and our society. This call for constant vigilance of the market is most important, not least for academics and journalists.

A Christian reflection on post-Celtic Tiger Ireland, therefore, highlights and exposes the contours of a very different society. It is a society of deep injustice in which the class structure has been shaken up, creating a new wealthy elite of global market actors who exercise immense influence over public authorities, but also creating a entrenched and deepening marginalisation of around one-fifth of the population. Amid a booming economy, the contradictions are glaring: pervasive consumerism side by side with growing poverty, deprivation and social breakdown; a yawning gap between the reality of stressed and worried lives and the euphoric rhetoric from political and cultural leaders and from the mass media that we have never had it so good; the erosion of moral discourse and the celebration of an intense and amoral individualism; the construction and careful policing of a culture of consensus and the failure to generate contestatory analyses and readings which reflects not just the neoliberalisation of the Irish media but also the takeover of our universities by market actors and interests. While some may seek to persuade us that we have never had it so good, this is a completely pointless exercise more calculated to deflect critical reflection on contemporary Ireland than to make any valid social scientific point about comparing the present with the past.

As the Bishops so rightly point out, it is a challenging society in which to live as a Christian. It invites us not just to retain the spiritual values that have characterised Irish society in the past but to deepen them (par 16). And, in making very clear that the huge social challenges we face depend, at heart, on moral values, the pastoral letter highlights the central role for Christian faith in addressing these social challenges, in building a society of greater justice, equality and solidarity. Yet, as pointed out above, there is little evidence that such a society is being built in today's Ireland, raising in a stark way the issue of how the Church could be a more effective actor for change. The next section addresses this issue.

Challenges and a proposal

The Irish Catholic Bishops have offered a very rich and challenging reading of post-Celtic Tiger Ireland in their pastoral letter. Yet, it would be hard to argue that it has had much impact on thinking in Ireland over the intervening period and I suspect that it is largely unknown not just by most Irish citizens but, indeed, by most Irish Catholics. Obviously, the Bishops are not to be faulted for this but it does draw attention to the context in which the pastoral letter is published, a context marked by the legacies outlined earlier in this chapter. For most Irish Catholics do not expect from their bishops insightful and challenging commentary on the socio-economic circumstances of their lives and on the challenges we face as a society. The largely anodyne treatment the pastoral letter received from the media reflects this expectation. Instead of it becoming a major discussion point in the media, with bishops and other Catholics forcefully advancing their critiques of contemporary Ireland and generating something of a moral consensus around the sort of society we might want for Ireland, it received cursory coverage and was quickly forgotten about. Bishops might lament that it was not taken more seriously, and they have every reason to, but it is hard to expect otherwise until the legacies of the past are put well and truly behind us.

This raises a second point about the dissemination of the pastoral letter for which the Bishops can be blamed. For there was, as far as I know, no strategy to ensure that it became widely read and discussed. One might have expected that parishes up and down the country would devote major attention to it, that study groups would be established, that lay movements would take up its message and act on it, contesting the many injustices of Irish society. Again this relates to the legacies of the past, as the dominance of a clerical caste effectively marginalised the laity and left the Irish Church with very few of the sort of active and vibrant lay movements that one finds, for example, throughout Latin America. In the absence of such a world of lay Catholic activism, it is hard to imagine how the pastoral letter is going to have much of an impact. This is not meant to deny the great work that lay groups like the St Vincent de Paul Society are doing, and they are to the forefront of critiquing government social policies as well as offering practical support to the marginalised in our society. They certainly play a major role in trying to develop values of social solidarity. But much more needs to be done, particularly in the ministry of consciousness raising and social activism that in Latin America is called 'conscientisation'. We need contestatory movements in the Irish Catholic Church that find innovative ways to embarrass our political, economic and social elites, that highlight the grave injustices from which they benefit, that mobilise the marginalised to find an effective voice, and that do all this in the name of the Gospel. Issuing a pastoral letter at a time of major social change offered the Bishops a golden opportunity to try to foster the development of such a world of lay Catholic activism but they failed to take this opportunity. This may reflect a reality that, while they speak about the need for a fundamental change of values among citizens, about the grave damage that inequality is doing to our society and about the need for vigilance of the market, they would be very uncomfortable indeed if groups took this on as a serious task of Christian living. Perhaps this is being unfair, but I remain to be convinced that it is untrue.

Yet, if we take the message of this pastoral letter seriously, then it imposes a serious responsibility on us to find effective ways of reversing the drift in our society towards the deterioration in the quality of life and the two-tier system of social services that the Bishops say in paragraph 166 concern many people. Are the Irish Catholic Church and its active members going to be identified by a serious commitment to this task? For, if as our leaders tell us, this is the challenge of the Gospel in today's Ireland, then our following of Christ imposes nothing less upon us. But how do we do this? How do we grasp the unprecedented opportunities for impressive social achievements that the Bishops say we now have? How do we develop moral values and a culture of solidarity? How do we develop the sort of social activism that the Bishops seem to expect from their fellow Catholics? Answering these questions offers the potential to fashion a new form of Irish Catholicism, with new institutions and new forms of devotion and spiritual practice, adequate to the challenges of our times. But this cannot be done without first dealing with the heavy legacies of the past so that we can be free to move on.

This will involve two intertwined tasks. The first is an honest and searching facing of the past, acknowledging as fully as possible the sort of Church that we have inherited, its strengths but also its limitations and pathologies. Such a facing of the past will require a very special quality of authentic leadership and time to allow a real healing among so many who were hurt and abused. And the abuse referred to here is something far wider than physical or sexual abuse but refers to the narrowing of the

Gospel message, its identification with rigid and inflexible moral precepts and intellectual dogmatism, the terrible poverty of liturgical life that still unfortunately is the fare offered to some Irish Catholics, the failure to open the riches of scripture to lay people, and the lack of intellectual sustenance or debate within the Church. For example, it is most worrying that some Irish people seem to have had bad experiences of the priests, brothers and nuns who educated them and the institutions they live in. We need an open identification of what went wrong, before a healing can take place. Only then can the Church fully disentangle itself from the shackles of the past and turn its face to the challenges of today and tomorrow in the freedom of spirit that Christ asked of his followers.

The second task requires that this be done, not as an elite exercise of Church leaders seeking forgiveness for the sins of others, but as an open process among all the faithful. Generous gestures by Church leaders may be important in individual cases of hurt but the task being referred to here is an exercise for all Catholics. This is not to deny, however, that careful planning and visionary leadership are required if such a mobilisation of healing energies can take place. Many will resist, feeling that something they treasure is being taken from them, and their feelings and experiences must be fully respected and heard by others. But, in the light of Fr Seaver's letter with which this chapter opens, it is equally important to initiate a process that could attract many young people, those who have been hurt by the Church and those who have been indifferent to it, never having being touched by the call of the Gospel. Such a process cannot therefore just be confined to parishes – or at least not to parish institutions. Like the priests in Tipperary who recently organised meetings in pubs to allow people freely air their views, ways must be found to gather those who aspire to something better for our society, those who are seeking spiritual ways far from Catholicism or Christianity, those whose lifestyles and interests might at first glance seem far from the Church. In other words, what is required is a process of re-evangelisation, reaching out beyond the comfort zones and the predictable, to spark an awakening to the liberating and transforming presence of Christ in our midst. This is a very urgent task.

My modest proposal for one way of beginning to address the great task of evangelisation is to begin a process for a national pastoral congress of the Irish Church, with preparatory assemblies at parish and diocesan level. Such a process, if well planned, honestly undertaken, and given time to take root among the faithful and the alienated, could be the beginning of the renewal so urgently needed. The focus of such a process would have to be on the future, not on the past, though the healing of past hurts would be one of its many challenges. But its central concern would be with the Ireland of today and tomorrow, not in any narrow confessional sense, but in the conviction that the Christian Gospel has the potential to profoundly transform that society, to challenge it to its core, to humanise and complete it. Irish society today cries out for the energies such a process could release.

Prophetic leadership, courageous action
Though rarely acknowledged by the media, there is much that is hopeful taking place in today's Irish Church. Celebration of the liturgy has improved enormously in many parishes, the quality of preaching is much better, a new relationship of warmth and equality has grown up among priests and lay people, there are many seeds of new forms of pastoral ministry and presence being sown particularly by religious, there is a rich flowering of more authentic forms of spiritual practice and, being less embedded in the power structures of Irish society, the Church is being freed to stand more with those on the margins of that society. The Irish Catholic Church is therefore beginning to show the face of Christ more clearly. But this is only a beginning and the malaise of our society demands a more forceful response from the Church. Not only do the statistics on alcohol abuse, drug consumption and suicide among young males indicate a profound spiritual vacuum that stands as an urgent challenge to the Church, but the growing violence and rifts in our society point towards an ever more ominous future.

It was indeed heartening to hear Archbishop Diarmuid Martin in July 2007 describe the increase in violent crime as being close to a national emergency and to call on the government to devise a new strategy to deal with the problem, including the calling of a summit of community leaders. He is a rare senior figure to acknowledge in this way the seriousness of these issues. But, useful and all as government action might be, the problem is a far more profound one than simply the actions of some criminals. It touches on the value systems of our society and is one manifestation of the erosion of values of solidarity and the common good, the essential underpinnings for any humane and decent society. Addressing these issues is beyond any government (though what government does has a huge effect on them, and it is by no means without blame for what is happening). The common good is the responsibility of us all and some way of mobilising and channeling the energies of society to reinforce it is very, very badly needed. The Catholic Church has in the past profoundly moulded this society, not always for the better. The challenges of the present call it to find with urgency new ways of bringing the Gospel of Christ to bear on the life and concerns of today's generation of Irish people.

Embracing Change:
The remodelling of Irish Catholic primary schools in the 21st century

Patricia Kiernan

The task is huge. We are to bring the Gospel into a new century to face challenges we have not begun to imagine, to respond to opportunities we have not anticipated, with the great variety of gifts (1 Cor 12: 4-11) which we do not fully realise we have.[1]

The Catholic Church exercises a vast influence on the Irish educational system through its patronage, management and ownership of primary and post-primary schools. However, many dispute whether this involvement is beneficial to Irish society, to schools or to the Church. Catholic schools exhibit variation in type (primary, special, secondary, community, comprehensive, fee paying) and contain radical (often associated with religious orders) as well as conservative elements. Consequently Irish Catholic schools are heterogeneous institutions 'characterised by internal differentiation and by internal ideological struggles'.[2] This chapter investigates some recent ideological struggles concerning the legitimacy, efficacy and future of Catholic schools in Ireland. It focuses on the key debate of whether Catholic schools, which inherited a nineteenth century structure and management system, can educate diverse religious and cultural groups in twenty-first century Ireland while still maintaining their Catholic identity and mission. It concentrates mainly on Irish Catholic primary schools since the most intense recent debates have focused on them.[3]

---

1. Bishop Donal Murray, Lenten Pastoral, 2001.
2. Gerald Grace, *Catholic Schools: Mission Markets and Morality* (London: Routledge Falmer, 2002), p108.
3. For a recent account of Catholic schools in Ireland see Grace, Gerald R, and O'Keefe, Joseph (eds), *International Handbook of Catholic Education*

The influential and long established tradition of Catholic involvement in Irish education can be interpreted in radically different ways. A positive reading suggests that the high percentage of Catholic schools in Ireland, their considerable academic achievements and emphasis on social justice, provide a valuable service to the learning community and to society at large. As a rule, Irish Catholic schools are in a healthy financial position as they benefit from State funding while the Church maintains control over school ethos, the provision of religious education as well as ownership of many school buildings. Of late, there is a discernible energy around Catholic schooling in Ireland manifest in a collaborative trustee body and innovative projects focusing on the role, mission and ethos of Catholic schools.[4] Moreover, the Irish hierarchy consistently supports Catholic schools with initiatives such as a National Catechetical Office, Catechetical Sunday, the commissioning of new Catholic syllabi and guidelines for RE in primary and post-primary schools, the commissioning of a National Directory, the establishment of a national Congress on RE as well as producing statements and documents on Catholic education.

On the other hand, it is possible to engage in a less positive reading of Catholic involvement in Irish schools. The latter have been seriously harmed by the withdrawal of religious teaching orders, allied to public repugnance at the Catholic Church's role in recent child abuse scandals. Increasingly dissident voices suggest that the Catholic Church has unfairly monopolised the Irish educational system to its own advantage and cite as evidence Catholic enrolment procedures that disadvantage non-Catholics.[5]

Challenges for School Systems in the 21st Century, Vol 2 (New York: Springer, 2007).
4. For example a collaborative trustee body CEIST (Catholic Education - an Irish Schools Trust) came into operation in 2007. The Catholic School – Imagining the Future (2002) project gave rise to a national conference and a renewed role for Catholic schools and the Wellsprings (2007) project concerns the ethos of Catholic schools.
5. Gráinne Faller, 'Is your child Catholic enough to get a place at school?', in *The Irish Times*, 1 May, 2007. Fionnuala Kilfeather, outgoing chief executive of the (National Parent's) Council, says: 'The assumption has to be made that a school, denominational or not, is a community school. If it is giving clear preference to children of one denomination over other children in the community, I think questions have to be asked.'

Additionally some see Catholic schools as redundant in a culturally diverse society. As the Irish Catholic population declines and parents simultaneously look for greater choice in educational provision, the prevalence of Catholic schools in every part of Ireland appears as a kind of inflexible systemic educational anachronism which serviced the educational needs of a bygone age yet fails to meet the needs of a changing society. If many send their children to Catholic schools, some argue, it is not because they desire a Catholic ethos: rather, it is because they have no choice. Those less positively inclined towards Catholic education sometimes speak of Catholic schools as something they have endured, survived and recovered from. For others, Catholic schools are Catholic in name only as they are 'market-driven, smart-targeted and commodified' secular organisations that are confused and embarrassed in equal measure by their Catholic heritage and mission.[6]

New wine in old wineskins:
Can history shed light on the Irish school system?
The question arises as to why faith-based schools are so prevalent in the Irish educational system and why the Catholic Church operates such an influential role within that system. Indeed it is impossible to understand the contemporary denominational Irish primary school system, which classifies schools according to religion, without understanding something of the historical context out of which it emerged. One of the ironies of the current Irish educational system is that it is at odds with the vision of its founder, E. G. Stanley (1799-1869), who opposed religious separatism in education. The national school system was not founded by an Act of Parliament but instead by a letter written by Stanley, the Chief Secretary of Ireland, to the Duke of Leinster, in 1831. In this letter, Stanley outlined his vision for a mixed or inter-denominational, national system of education. Mixed national schools meant that children from different religious traditions including Anglican, Catholic, Presbyterian and Methodist, would be educated together. It must be noted that the principle of mixed education was more politically than religiously moti-

6. See Ned Prendergast and Luke Monahan (eds), *Reimagining the Catholic School* (Dublin: Veritas, 2003), p 11.

vated as it was envisaged that, after the Irish Rebellion of 1798, a non-sectarian system of education could help neutralise radical political leanings. Indeed a written general moral and religious lesson exhorting tolerance and understanding was displayed prominently in every mixed classroom. A sample form of this General Lesson stated:

Christians should endeavour, as the Apostle Paul commands them, to 'live peaceably with all men' (Rom. Ch. Xii. V. 17); even with those of a different religious persuasion.[7]

Despite this laudable emphasis on mutual respect, Stanley's vision of mixed education never came to fruition. The story of the development of the Irish national school system is one where different denominations favoured segregated rather than mixed education. In one sense this is unsurprising since in 1826, prior to the founding of the national school system, the Catholic Bishops made it abundantly clear that no Catholic teacher should be trained by those professing a different faith.[8]

Subsequently Archbishop Paul Cullen (1803-1878) spearheaded Catholic resistance to the system of interdenominational national schools because he saw it as a proselytising and anglicising mechanism that was inherently dangerous for the faith of Catholic children. The Synod of Thurles (1850) condemned the state system of mixed education and warned that 'the separate education of Catholic youth is, in every way, to be preferred to it.'[9] It would be unwise to suggest that Catholics were the only ones who had difficulty with the mixed system of education.[10] Protestants, who were just coming to terms with the implications of Catholic Emancipation in 1829, feared that a religiously

---

7. Thomas Joseph Durcan, *History of Irish Education from 1800* (North Wales: Dragon Books, 1972), pp 15-16.
8. Áine Hyland and Kenneth Milne (eds), *Irish Educational Documents, Vol 1*, (Dublin: CICE, 1987), p 91. There were members of the Catholic hierarchy such as the liberal Dr James Doyle, Bishop of Kildare and Leighlin, who supported mixed education.
9. John Coolahan, *Irish Education History and Structure* (Dubln: Institute of Public Administration, 1981), p 18.
10. J. D. King, *Religious Education in Ireland: A Survey of Catechetics in the Primary and Secondary Schools, and in the Training Colleges and Catechetical Centres of Ireland* (Dublin: Fallons, 1970), p 6.

mixed educational environment would be exploited by Catholics as a mechanism for proselytising Protestant children. Some Presbyterians objected to Catholics being given a seat on the Board of Education which administered funding for schools and they refused to submit joint applications for funding with Catholics. As a consequence of these concerns, by 1838 denominational education was allowed in national schools and the relevant clergy members came in to provide segregated religious instruction for pupils. In such a manner the clergy gained increasing control of the educational system and by 1840 a local bishop or clergyman from each denomination could apply to become a patron of a mixed school. The patron appointed a manager and the manager appointed, or dismissed, the teacher in the relevant school. This marks the development of a patronage structure that still exists as well as the powerful placement of religious authorities at the heart of the national system of education. The vast majority of schools were subsequently built on grounds owned by religious denominations so that the denominationalisation and clericalisation of the educational system gained momentum. When the national school system was established in 1831 it was intended *de jure* to be fully mixed or inter-denominational. However, the system that developed *de facto* was denominational and differed radically from Stanley's foundational principles. In the 1850s and 1860s the Catholic Church gained increasing power within the national system of education and it called for state-funded education for Catholics. Likewise, Methodist, Presbyterian and Anglican children were sent to their own denominational schools. Subsequently it was argued that the system of schooling provided by religious patrons was adequate to the educational needs of the people of Ireland and therefore there was no need for any alternative.

In Ireland provision was never made for a separate system of primary schools controlled by the local authority, largely because it had been found by the Powis Commission in 1870 that voluntary effort had adequately met the demand for elementary education in this country.[11] The gradual denominationalisation

---

11. Áine Hyland, 'The Multi-denominational Experience', in *Irish Educational Studies*, 8(1), p 1.

of Irish schools is evident in statistics which show that by the early 1880s just over half (55%) of national schools were attended by both Catholic and Protestant children whereas this figure was reduced to over one quarter (28%) by 1912. The pattern of denominational and clergy-controlled national school continued in the twentieth century.

> Practically all of the national schools are managed by boards which are chaired *ex officio* by clergymen and whose other membership is determined partly by Church decision; in addition the legal trustees of the school property also come from the ranks of senior diocesan clergymen and church parochial officers.[12]

Some have argued that since independence the State has benefited financially from the involvement of the Churches in education. Religious or parish owned schools contribute financially to the building cost and maintenance of the school thereby reducing the State's financial obligation. For their part the Churches have benefited significantly from their involvement in education and they have been granted a huge degree of autonomy in the management of schools, in the formation and appointment of teachers, and in the design, delivery and assessment of syllabi for religious education.[13]

Catholic Schools Today

A brief historical overview shows that the Irish national school system evolved on denominational lines as a result of ecclesiastical objections to inter-denominational schooling. Catholic suspicion of inter-denominationalism was fuelled by the memory of religious discrimination in the Penal Laws. It is worth remembering that the Catholic Church stood to gain increased power through involvement in a denominational national system of education. In the Irish context, religion was neither separated from education nor deemed peripheral to it. The idea of omitting religion in the name of equality of opportunity was uncon-

---

12. S. O'Buachalla, *Educational Policy in Twentieth Century Ireland* (Dublin: Wolfhound Press), p 205.
13. S. Drudy and K. Lynch, *Schools and Society in Ireland* (Dublin: Gill and Macmillan, 1993), pp 75-6.

scionable for the hugely influential religious bodies in the nineteenth century. According to the thinking of the time, a corrective to religious discrimination was not the exclusion of religion from education but rather its placement at the centre of the educational enterprise in order to uphold the denominational rights of children and parents. In the twentieth century the *de facto* denominational structure of national schools was given support by the government. For example, in 1965 the revised *Rules for National Schools* emphasised that 'the state provides for free primary education for children and gives explicit recognition to the denominational character of these schools'.[14]

When the Rules (for National Schools) were eventually revised by the Minister for Education in 1965, no cognisance was taken of the fact that not all national schools were attended exclusively by children of the same denomination. Neither was there any provision made for parents who might not wish their children to attend denominational schools.[15] This denominational system may have suited the majority religious tradition but school provision gave relatively little choice to those from minority religious traditions and those with no desire for faith schools. Even the term 'denominational', meaning a subgroup within a religion, is a problematic descriptor of the current Irish system of primary education. In twenty-first century Ireland there are eight types of primary school including Muslim, Jewish and Educate Together schools. None of these are subgroups within a religion so the application of the term is inaccurate.

Structural and ideological issues
concerning Catholic involvement in education in Ireland
The question of whether the Irish denominational national school system, which evolved over the last one hundred and seventy plus years, is capable of adapting and responding to the educational needs of a culturally and religiously diverse postmodern society, must be taken seriously. This question focuses on structural and ideological concerns. From a structural per-

---

14. *Rules for National Schools*, 1965. The phrase 'provide for free primary education' echoes article 42.4 of the 1937 Constitution.
15. Áine Hyland, 'The Multi-denominational Experience', p 1.

spective it explores whether a school patronage structure and management system which evolved in the wake of the Penal Laws, just after the emancipation of Catholics in the nineteenth century, is adequate to the complex task of educating children in a radically different twenty-first century context. From an ideological perspective challenging questions are raised about the desirability and legitimacy of religious involvement in the Irish educational system. These two concerns are inter-related and focus most acutely on the Irish primary school system where 93% of schools are managed by the Catholic Church. Consequently Catholic primary schools are particularly vulnerable to the suggestion that their patronage and recruitment of staff is over-representative of one denomination and under-representative of other religious and secular groups.[16] This in turn highlights the lack of an alternative state system of primary schools and the consequent lack of parental choice.[17]

A number of landmark events have focused national and international attention on these interlinked structural and ideological concerns. In the mid 1980s it was argued that a religious monopoly of state schooling in Ireland was unconstitutional.[18] The Irish Humanist Association stated that a religious-based, State funded, denominational primary school system was discriminatory. Central to its argument was the fact that such a system unjustly excluded those of a different religious affiliation or those who were non-religious.

This is a major bone of contention for non-religious, tax-paying parents who feel strongly the injustice of a national school system which discriminates against their children. Allied with this is the issue of discrimination against teachers who may be

---

16. The present Irish Primary School System consists of: 2,911 Catholic schools; 183 Church of Ireland schools; 44 Multi-denominational or Educate Together Schools; 14 Presbyterian; 4 Inter-denominational; 1 Jewish school; 2 Muslim schools; 1 Methodist school. Source: DES Statistics Section (2005-6).

17. Dympna Glendenning, *Education and the Law* (Dublin: Butterworths, 1999), 1:02.

18. Desmond Clarke, *Church and State: Essays in Political Philosophy* (Cork: Cork University Press, 1984). See also Dympna Glendenning, *Education and the Law*, p 99.

barred from employment because of their religious or non-religious position.[19]

This perception of faith-based state-funded education as inherently discriminatory has been a recurring *leitmotif* in recent discussions about Catholic education in Ireland. Commentators such as Fintan O'Toole see Ireland's primary education system as 'a system funded by a secular state and run to an overwhelming extent by lay people [...] according to the ethos of one church.'[20] Others focus on the by-product of Catholic education and blame it for turning the population into 'a crass, money-grubbing *(sic)*, vulgar, possession-worshipping population without finer philosophical values.'[21]

These concerns about Catholic education have been given considerable national and on occasion international coverage. In 2005, in the wake of the publication of the *Ferns Report*, Liz O'Donnell of the Progressive Democrat Party made a speech in the Dáil calling for a radical examination of the 'Church's almost universal control of education' and an end to the 'special' relationship which the Catholic Church enjoyed with the State. What was extraordinary about her speech was the explicit and irresponsible link that she made between the religious management of Catholic schools and child sex abuse. She stressed that there were child protection concerns in relation to the Church's management of schools and argued that in the light of its 'systemic maladministration and dereliction of duty to protect children' the Catholic Church could not be entrusted with the management of schools.[22] O'Donnell conflated and confused two separate issues and in so doing rashly undermined the Catholic system of school management.

19. Dick Spicer and Ellen Sides, *The Humanist Philosophy* (Bray: Humanist Publishers, 1996), p 58.
20. Fintain O'Toole, *The Irish Times*, 12 October 2004.
21. Emer O'Kelly, 'The church is responsible for today's moral mess', in *Sunday Independent*, 11 November 2007, p 23.
22. Liz O'Donnell stated 'the Church is neither democratic nor accountable. In many ways it is a secret organisation – with its own diplomatic service, civil service, laws and self-regulatory codes, which have failed the public ...' She also emphasised the Church's 'systematic maladministration and dereliction of duty to protect children.' Liz O Donnell Dáil statement on *Ferns Report*, Wednesday 9 November 2005. 24 October 2007.

It must be noted that serious objections to the State's support of the system of primary education in Ireland, where 98% of schools are denominational, have come from other sectors. In 2005 a United Nations Committee (On the Convention on the Elimination of all Forms of Racial Discrimination) received a submission which argued that the Irish Government failed to fund and provide an adequate choice of non-denominational or multi-denominational schools for Irish parents, teachers and children. In 2006 a Council of Europe's Advisory Committee urged the Irish authorities 'to pursue their commitment to widen schooling options, including in terms of non-denominational and multi-denominational schools, in a manner that ensures that the school system reflects the growing cultural and religious diversity of the country'.[23]

Race, Religion and a Shortage of Places
– a recent debate in Primary Schooling

The Catholic Church has been aware of this backdrop of critique and dissatisfaction with the current school system but, despite this, it has generally focused its energy on supporting and managing its schools. However, the failure of parents to find primary school places for over 90 non-Catholic children in Balbriggan, north County Dublin, in September 2007, has acted as a barometer indicating the desire to change the current system.[24] The lens of public scrutiny focused on the Catholic Church as the majority and, according to some, the monopoly stakeholder in Irish primary education. Under current equality legislation denominational schools have the right to maintain school ethos by giving priority of place to children of the school's faith.[25] In the North

---

23. 'The Committee encourages the State party to take fully into consideration the recommendations made by the Committee on the Elimination of Racial Discrimination (CERD/C/IRL/CO/2, par. 18) which encourages the promotion of the establishment of non-denominational or multi-denominational schools and to amend the existing legislative framework to eliminate discrimination in school admissions.' http://www.educatetogether.ie/2_campaigns/humanrights-andirished.html

24. Alison Healy, '106 children left without school places in Dublin', in *The Irish Times*, 14 September 2007.

25. 'An educational establishment shall not discriminate in relation to

Dublin district of Balbriggan, one unforeseen consequence of this policy, allied to a paucity of primary schools, was the exclusion of over 90 mainly black children from existing local schools. When headlines such as 'Black Children Left Out of Irish Schools' circulated in media reports, Ireland's school system came under considerable criticism. As the largest stakeholder in Irish primary education, the Catholic Church was vulnerable to the suggestion that it was excluding religious and ethnic minority groups.[26] The children without school places were almost all black and while the majority of them were Irish born, some were of Muslim, evangelical Protestant denominations or of no religious faith. Media reports suggested that children without baptismal certificates were excluded from Catholic schools. It was alleged that what was operative in this instance was a school system that discriminated on racial and religious grounds. The Balbriggan crisis seemed to indicate that Ireland had difficulty integrating its increasingly diverse population and that its school system, including its Catholic schools, was deficient in responding to the task.[27] This prompted the Equality Authority to express concern at 'the emergence in effect of segregated primary school provi-

---

the admission [...] of a person [...] where the establishment is a school providing primary or post-primary education to students and the objective of the school is to provide education in an environment which promotes certain religious values, it admits persons of a particular denomination in preference to others or it refuses to admit as a student a person who is not of that denomination and, in the case of a refusal, it is proven that the refusal is essential to maintain the ethos of the school.' Equal Status Act, 2000. 7 (1) c.

26. See CBS News 5 September 2007 for an article titled 'Black Children Left Out of Irish Schools', with a subheading 'Black Immigrants to Ireland Struggling to Find School Places: 1st All-Black School to Open.' Paul Rowe, CEO of Educate Together, opened Bracken Educate Together National School, on 24 September 2007. He stated 'We have been disappointed by the media description of this school as being "a school for blacks" and wish to state categorically that this is not the case. Bracken Educate Together National School operates the same "first come first served" enrolment policy of other Educate Together schools and will not permit any discrimination in access on religious, racial, cultural or social grounds.' *The Electronic Newsletter from Educate Together* (*ETEN*) 7 (8), 2007.

27. CBS News, 5 September 2007.

sion for black and minority ethnic students' and it suggested that 'management groups could no longer use an exemption allowed under the Equal Status Act if this had the effect of excluding persons of other religions or other races.'[28]

All those involved in primary schooling in Ireland contributed to the ensuing debate. The Minister for Education (Mary Hanafin) strongly defended existing legislation and the exemptions afforded to schools under the Equal Status Act while announcing the imminent piloting of a new model of community primary schools under Vocational Education Committee (VEC) patronage.[29] This led to speculation that a new sector of state-financed and controlled primary schools was being introduced.[30] The Irish National Teachers' Organisation (INTO) called for a National Forum on Education to discuss all issues pertaining to education in a non-confrontational manner. Educate Together expressed the view that there was no evidence of institutional racism in Irish patronal bodies yet it stated: 'There is profound, embedded and institutionalised religious discrimination throughout the system particularly at primary level. This discrimination is the responsibility of the state, not of schools or religious bodies.'[31]

For its part, the Catholic Church was not silent on the issue of the structural deficits of the Irish educational system. Archbishop Martin emphasised that the Catholic Church could not be held responsible for the State's lack of planning in the area of education and stressed that he 'would be very happy to see a plurality of patronage and providers of education. I have no ambition to run the entire education system in Dublin [...] And it is not my job to provide teachers and classrooms [...] that is the State's job.'[32] The Church robustly countered the notion that it was in-

28. Seán Flynn, 'School admission Policies open to equality challenge', in *The Irish Times*, 13 September 2007, p 1.

29. Marie O'Halloran, 'Hanafin defends policy on schools', in *The Irish Times*, 6 September 2007.

30. Diarmuid Martin, the Catholic Archbishop of Dublin, warned that an exclusively State run system of schooling would not necessarily improve upon the denominational system and he cited the example of England as a system which had become overly politicised.

31. *ETEN* 7 (8), 2007.

32. *The Irish Times*, 6 September 2007, p 1.

terested in monopolising the Irish educational system or that it discriminated against religious minorities.[33] It emphasised that its primary duty was to provide Catholic schools for Catholic parents while taking seriously its mission to serve the educational needs of the wider society. Furthermore Church authorities stressed that it was inappropriate to blame it for a shortage of school places since its duty was to provide schools primarily for Catholic parents and children while the State's duty was to plan for the entire population's schooling. Archbishop Martin succinctly affirmed: 'The Catholic education system has been far-seeing and has provided Catholic schools for Catholic parents. We have done our job, if there are others who are left without schools they should not blame us.'[34]

That said, the Irish Catholic Church has recently illustrated its consciousness of the need for change. Its document *Catholic Primary Schools: A Policy for Provision into the Future* (2007) maintains that a publicly-funded denominational school system is a basic human right for parents who wish to send their children to such schools. However, the document is characterised by a recognition of the need for a plurality of models of provision and educational providers in Ireland. Furthermore the Catholic Church has placed an increased emphasis on working collaboratively with other patronage bodies. The basis of this pluralism, which the Church welcomes, is the recognition that the educational system of a country must adapt in order to address its population's changing educational needs. Not only is the Church using the rhetoric of change, it is simultaneously imagining what that structural change might look like. Diarmuid Martin, perhaps the most outspoken member of the hierarchy on the issue of Catholic schooling, has spoken of 'divesting current Catholic schools', thereby, in certain circumstances, relinquishing Catholic patronage and management. He envisaged this type of reconfiguration in situations where there is a surplus of Catholic schools and a need for alternative types of schooling.

---

33. Diarmuid Martin cited St Teresa's School (in Balbriggan) and Scoil Choilm (Diswellstown) as examples of schools 'almost exclusively made up of children with an international background'. Séan Flynn, 'Archbishop says State to blame for schools crisis', in *The Irish Times*, 6 September 2007, p 1.
34. *The Irish Times*, 6 September 2007, p 1.

Take an area where there are five schools [...] over a period of time, and in consultation with parents and teachers, you could rationalise that and ensure you have sufficient number of schools for Catholics and other patrons.[35]

The piloting of new enrolment policies for two Catholic schools in the Dublin diocese, with a quota of places (one third) assigned to non-Catholic pupils, is a clear indication of the Church's willingness to rethink its Catholic-first policy and to respond to religious and cultural diversity. Moreover the Catholic Church is involved in a consultative process with those for whom it is providing a service. Bishop O'Reilly, Chair of the Bishops' Commission for Education, has signalled that qualitative research into parental choice and satisfaction with the Irish Catholic school system is being undertaken by the Bishops' Council for Research and Development.[36] In general one can say that the Bishops' attitude to schooling in Ireland is marked by a recognition of the need for change and the importance of collaboration with the main stakeholders in Catholic education, other patronage bodies and the Government. Commentators unsympathetic to the Catholic position may note that it is only when the existing school system shows significant signs of fracture that the Church has begun to adopt the rhetoric of change, knowing perhaps that the *status quo* is untenable. On the other hand, the fact that the Church has begun to embrace the notion

---

35. *The Irish Times*, 6 September 2007.
36. At the Press Conference to launch *Catholic Primary Schools: A Policy for Provision into the Future*, Bishop Leo O'Reilly, Chairman of the Bishops' Commission for Education stated: 'In order to ascertain the desires of parents in this regard the Bishops' Council for Research and Development is carrying out quantitative research among parents who send their children to Catholic schools in Ireland. A preliminary report from this research will be available to the Conference in December and a full report will be complete for the March Conference. This will give us valuable information not only in relation to the wishes of parents for the education of their children but also the role they see for the Catholic school. As a result of this research we hope to be in a better position to plan for the time ahead.' http://www.catholiccommunications.ie/pressrel/02-october-2007.html accessed 13 November 2007. See also Patsy Mc Garry, 'Pluralism in education best, says bishop', in *The Irish Times*, 3 October, 2007 p 11.

of change is positive, although whether or not the idea of divesting Catholic schools moves beyond rhetoric remains to be seen.

Can Irish Catholic primary schools
address the educational and religious needs of 21st century Ireland?
At the heart of this debate on Catholic education is the question of whether the Catholic school system is capable of addressing the needs of the Catholic community which it serves as well as the needs of an increasingly diverse Irish society. Even if an alternative system of schools develops under non-denominational or state patronage, the question remains whether Catholic schools are capable of addressing the needs of a religiously pluralist society. In recent years Ireland has become religiously and culturally diverse at a pace more accelerated than its closest neighbour, the United Kingdom.[37] Up to the early 1990s Ireland was home to a comparatively small percentage of minority religious groups. Nevertheless it is well documented that Ireland has been religiously and culturally diverse for millennia. The ancient religious practices of the Celts are visually embodied in numerous sculptural monuments dotted around the country. Christianity came to Ireland in the fifth and sixth centuries and flourished with the aid of monastic communities that functioned as centres of evangelism and learning. There is evidence that Jews arrived in Ireland in the year 1079, and while the number of Jewish immigrants in the twelfth and thirteenth centuries was small, more substantial communities of Jews settled in Ireland during the sixteenth and seventeenth centuries.[38] The Jewish community has exercised considerable influence on Irish life. In Joyce's *Ulysses*, Leopold Bloom, arguably one of the most iconic characters in the whole of Irish literature, is both Jewish and Irish. In the post-Reformation era the plantation of Protestant English and Scottish settlers in Ulster by 1610 had huge implications for a religiously plural society. The arrival of French-speaking Huguenots who fled to Ireland in the seventeenth century left a distinctive legacy in paces such as Portarlington (St Paul's

---

37. In contrast England has a long history of ethnic diversity where minority ethnic groups compose 9% of its population.
38. Maurice Ryan, *Another Ireland* (Stranmillis College: The Learning Resources Unit, 1996), p 1.

Church), Dublin (Huguenot Cemetery off St Stephen's Green) and Lisburn (Christ Church Cathedral). Sizeable numbers of Hindus settled in the North of Ireland in the early twentieth century and members of the Sikh community came to Ireland in the 1920s and 1930s.[39] Furthermore, documentary evidence suggests that a small active Muslim community was established in Ireland from the 1950s onwards.[40]

Since the early 1990s Ireland has witnessed extraordinary change in its population's composition and religious affiliation. The population has become ethnically and religiously diverse at an accelerated rate relative to many of its European counterparts.[41] For instance between the 2002 and 2006 censuses, the number of non-Irish nationals who were resident in the State increased by 87%.[42] The 2006 Census revealed that over 10% of the usually resident population in Ireland were composed of non-Irish nationals. These recent population changes have been propelled by a variety of factors including a rapidly growing

---

39. At present the majority Sikhs are located in the Dublin region. There is a *Gurdwara* in Ballsbridge and the Irish Sikh Council is based in Dublin and actively provides support for the Sikh community.

40. The Dublin Islamic Society was founded in 1959.

41. Nearly 420,000 (10%) persons who were usual residents of the State in April 2006 indicated that they had a nationality other than Irish. The corresponding figure in 2002 was 224,000 (5.8%). 'Comparing Ireland to other EU countries underlines its rapid changes. During 1990-1994, Ireland was the only country among the member states of the EU-15 with a negative net migration rate. In contrast, between 1995 and 1999, Ireland's average annual net migration rate was the second highest in the EU-15, surpassed only by that of Luxembourg. And according to recently released Organization for Economic Cooperation and Development (OECD) data, by 2002, the estimated share of non-nationals in Ireland's population had surpassed those of the UK and France, countries with much longer immigration histories.' Martin Rhus, in *Ireland: A Crash Course in Immigration Policy*, Centre on Migration, Policy and Society (*COMPAS*), Oxford University http://www.migrationinformation. org/Profiles/display.cfm?ID=260

42. 'Non-Irish nationals who were resident in the State increased from 224,000 to 420,000 (+87%) over the same period. The fastest growing categories were EU nationals, apart from Irish or UK nationals, along with Africans and Asians. Polish nationals numbered 63,300 while the number of Lithuanian nationals was 24,600.' *2006 Census Summary* (Dublin: Central Statistics Office), p 25.

economy and immigration.[43] Under more favorable economic circumstances the majority of immigrants in the late 1990s were returning Irish nationals who had emigrated in previous decades.[44] This changed significantly in the twenty-first century when the number of non-Irish immigrants outnumbered returning Irish nationals. The growing number of individuals seeking asylum in Ireland has risen dramatically from the mid twentieth century when successive groups of Hungarian (1950s), Chilean/Vietnamese (1970s), and Iranian (1980s) refugees came to Ireland. Numbers of people seeking asylum rose from just 39 applications in 1992 to a peak of over 11,000 in 2002. Apart from those seeking asylum in Ireland, the robust economy continues to attract many international companies and immigrant workers.

This new wave of immigration has had a dramatic effect on Ireland's religious and educational landscape. The Muslim community in Ireland has increased from a relatively small population of around one thousand in 1992 to an official census figure of 32,500 in 2006. The Christian communities have also experienced major change as a consequence of immigration and migration. A significant example is that the Orthodox community which doubled in number between 2002 and 2006. The 2002 census marked the end of a long period of decline for the Church of Ireland, Presbyterian and Methodist Churches and the 2006 census reveals that this growth has continued. Since 1 May 2004, the inflow of migrant workers from ten new EU member States means that large numbers of Polish, Lithuanian, Latvian, Slovakian, Estonian, Hungarian and Czech workers are now living in Ireland. Indeed the numerous Catholic economic migrants who have come to Ireland from countries such as Poland have contributed both numerically and pastorally to the Irish Church. Their presence has fostered an increased variety of Catholic ritual and spiritual life. The *Irish Catholic* newspaper has a weekly page written in Polish which caters for its changing readership

---

43. Between 2002-2006 there were 46,000 more immigrants than emigrants annually. *Census 2006 Preliminary Report*, Central Statistics Office.
44. 55% of inward migrants in 1999 were returning Irish nationals. See the Immigrant Council of Ireland, *Labour Migration into Ireland* (Dublin: ICI, 2003).

and the translation of a recent pastoral letter into Polish indicates that the Catholic Church is beginning to address its faith community in diverse ways.[45]

When it comes to Irish schools, however, there is relatively little research on the impact which new religious groups and immigrant communities are having on the Catholic primary and post-primary sector. This is not to suggest that those working in Irish schools are not acutely aware of the need for 'ongoing inservice, upskilling and training' to cater for Ireland's diverse population.[46] It is simply to place Irish Catholic schools in the context of a larger international trend where there is a lack of research into religious diversity and Catholic schools. J. Kent Donleavy comments that while reviewing the literature on non-Catholic students in Catholic schools:

> [...] there was a paucity of information dealing with the topic. In fact, after a search which included contacting individuals in the United Kingdom, Australia, the United States of America, and Canada, all that was revealed was a small 25-page, opinion-based pamphlet [...] a short comment in a recent book ... a series of qualitative studies primarily from one researcher ... and a tangentially relevant number of doctoral and masters degree theses [...]. In all other respects, the academic literature was silent. Ostensibly, the topic seemed by this lack of attention to be of little significance to the Catholic community.[47]

The situation, while needing improvement, is not as drastic as Donleavy presents it. For instance, in the UK there have been a number of recent reports into teaching world faiths in Catholic

---

45. Bishops' Conference Pastoral Letter, *Blogoslawiony jest owoc Twojego Iona* (2007).
46. *Intouch* No.= 81, 2006, p 27. Every decade the INTO carries out a survey of members' attitudes and approaches to the primary curriculum. The results for its 2005 survey show that teachers specified the teaching of non-nationals as an area in need of attention.
47. J. Kent Donleavy 'Ten Dimensions of Inclusion: Non-Catholic Students in Catholic Schools', in *Catholic Education*, 10: 3, (2007), pp 293-4.

schools[48] and in Ireland some small-scale research has been carried out on diversity and inclusivity in Catholic schools.[49] One study argues that Ireland's denominational and confessional primary school system 'does not allow for equal recognition or respect for difference.'[50] The researcher, Anne Lodge, conducted interviews with people of minority belief and people of personal belief,[51] about their experience of denominational primary education. While Lodge's research sample is small, her research concluded that children sometimes feel alienated because of their different religious or personal beliefs; sacramental preparation heightens this sense of exclusion and alienation; bullying and teasing can be based on the perception of the child as religiously different;[52] and that both participation in and withdrawal from

48. Ann Casson 'The Teaching of Other Faiths in Catholic Schools in the North East' (Farmington Fellowship, 2003) and Catharine Speroni 'Teaching Other Faiths in the Catholic Primary School' (Farmington Fellowship, 2005). Astley J., Francis L J., Wilcox C., Burton L., 'How different is religious education in Catholic schools?', in *International Journal of Education and Religion*, 1 (2), 2000. Deirdre Mc Govern, *Hospitality to the Other in Faith-based School*, PhD research, University of Glasgow.

49. Micheál Kilcrann, 'Welcoming the New Irish', in R. Topley and G. Byrne (eds), *Nurturing Children's Religious Imagination*, (Dublin: Veritas, 2004), p 86ff; Patricia Kieran, 'Promoting Truth? Inter-faith education in Irish Catholic Primary Schools', in *Teaching Religion in the Primary School Issues and Challenges*, (Dublin: INTO, 2003), pp 119-130. P. J. Boyle, 'Engaging with Ethnic Minorities', in Ned Prendergast and Luke Monahan (eds), *Reimagining the Catholic School* (Dublin:Veritas, 2003), pp 141-153; Cooke Michael, 'Interfaith Perspectives: More questions than answers', in M. Hayes and Liam Gearon, (eds), *Contemporary Catholic Education* (Leominster, Gracewing, 2002). Masters Theses in St Patrick's College, DCU: Micheál Kilcrann, *The Challenge to Primary Religious Education posed by a Multicultural Society* (2003); Helen Bhreathnach, *Living with Difference and Discovering a Common Heritage: Bringing Nostra Aetate into the Primary School Religious Education Programme in the light of the Writings of James Dunn* (2004).

50. Jim Deegan, Dympna Devine and Anne Lodge (eds), *Primary Voices: Equality, Diversity and Childhood in Irish Primary Schools* (Dublin: Institute of Public Administration, 2004), p 32.

51. Lodge, in Deegan (ed), *Primary Voices*, p 22.

52. See Chapter 6 on Religious Belief, especially section 6.4 on 'Harassment', in Lodge, A. and Lynch, K., *Diversity at School* (Dublin: Institute of Public Administration, 2004).

Religious Education can be problematic. This research is worrying as it contends that 'differences in belief are denied in the denominational primary system and those whose beliefs are different are rendered invisible and subordinate.'[53] This study is given some support by preliminary findings from a five-year research project into education systems in 13 EU member states. The preliminary report entitled *Include-ED* suggests that, with regard to initiatives dealing with equal opportunities and intercultural education, Irish schools are ahead of their European counterparts in preventing social exclusion. When it comes to the issue of initiatives in the area of religion Irish schools are less noteworthy. *Include-ED*'s preliminary findings for Irish schools states:

> [...] in terms of the recognition of cultural and religious diversity within schools, major reforms need to be undertaken in particular at primary level. The report also stresses the importance of creating schools in which all religions can freely and equally find their expression.[54]

These are serious charges and Irish Catholic schools must ensure that in addressing the religious and educational needs of the Catholic community they do not marginalise or ignore those who are religiously different. However, while taking such studies seriously, the Catholic Church must also implement and promote its own positive teaching on Catholic schools as inclusive schools. The Catholic Church teaches that Catholic schools should promote 'civil progress and human development without discrimination of any kind'.[55] The very word Catholic origi-

53. Lodge, *Primary Voices*, p 32.
54. Georgina O'Halloran, 'Irish Schools top of EU class in tackling social exclusion', in *The Irish Times*, 14 September 2007. Bishop O'Reilly quotes from the *Include-ED* preliminary report to substantiate the view that Catholic schools are inclusive schools. 'We are very happy to see that the preliminary results of a five-year research project on education systems in 13 member states of the EU by staff at Dublin City University (the title of the study is *Include-ED*) found that Irish schools are far ahead of their European counterparts in preventing social exclusion. Catholic primary schools are acknowledged to be among the most inclusive in the country.'
55. *The Catholic School on the Threshold of the Third Millennium*, (Congregation for Catholic Education, 1997), par 16.

nates from the Greek *kath'holou* which means 'according to the whole' or 'universal'. To be Catholic is to be called to live a life focused on inclusivity. This inclusivity does not involve an abandonment or dilution of the Catholicity of a school. Catholics are called to live the Gospel of Jesus Christ, to build communities of service for others, in a just and loving manner. Catholic instit-utions, including schools, should not be immune or unrespon-sive to the religiously different, but are called to witness to their faith in Jesus Christ in the vibrant context of religious difference without diluting that faith.

The Church's own teaching and tradition should function as a major source of guidance for those involved in Catholic educ-ation. The Church recognises the unity and dignity of all human life since 'humankind form but one community [...] all stem from one stock which God created.'[56] Successive recent docu-ments testify to the fact that inter-religious dialogue is a crucial imperative for Catholics.[57] Addressing the Foundation for Interreligious and Intercultural Research and Dialogue in 2007, Pope Benedict XVI insisted 'research and interreligious and in-tercultural dialogue are not an option but a vital necessity for our time.'[58] In a sense the controversy surrounding his address at Regensburg in September 2006 has served to augment and reinforce the Pontiff's emphasis on the need for inter-religious dialogue.[59]

---

56. *Nostra Aetate (The Declaration on the Church's Relations with non-Christian Religions)*, (Vatican II, 1965), par 1.
57. *Nostra Aetate; Evangelii Nuntiandi (On Evangelisation in the Modern world)* (Paul VI, 1975); *The Attitude of the Church toward the Followers of Other Religions. Reflections and Orientations on Dialogue and Mission*, (Pontifical Council for Interreligious Dialogue, 1984). *Redemptoris Missio*, (John Paul II, 1990).
58. *Zenith*, 1 February 2007.
59. Cardinal Tauran, newly appointed President of the Pontifical Council for Interreligious Dialogue, told Vatican Radio: 'I think it (his appointment) is a sign of the importance that the Pope gives to dialogue among religions, in particular with Islam...' Speaking about the link be-tween his appointment and the Regensburg address in September 2006, he added: 'I think it had a decisive influence, because thanks to the reac-tions, the Pope was able to clarify his words,' the cardinal said. 'By reading the Pope's speeches to the ambassadors of Arab countries, and also to those who have come from Asia to present their credentials, you

When it comes to schooling it appears that Catholic teaching on inclusivity is sometimes unknown or invisible in the very centres where it is most relevant. The Church rejects the notion of a values or a religiously 'neutral' school.[60] Catholic education 'focuses on the human person in his or her integral, transcendent, historical identity' and this includes religious identity.[61] Vatican II teaches that governments 'must acknowledge the right of parents to make a genuinely free choice of schools'.[62] Where Catholic schools exist the Church readily acknowledges that not all members of the Catholic school community are Catholic and it offers general principles on how Catholic schools might include and celebrate religious diversity while being true to its own mission and teaching.[63] The Church upholds its mission to proclaim the Gospel of Jesus Christ and to evangelise but it does so in a manner which explicitly recognises human freedom and the rights of all to follow their conscience.[64] Vatican II's *Declaration on Christian Education, Gravissimum Educationis,* makes it clear that the church cherishes non-Catholics who attend Catholic schools.[65] So the Church teaches that Catholic schools are not restricted to Catholics and are open to those who share its educational project.[66]

The Catholic Church does not wish to render invisible the 'religious other' in the Catholic school or to coerce the religious or non-religious other into conformism to Catholic belief and practice. Rather, it teaches that the 'Catholic school offers itself to all, non-Christians included, with all its distinctive aims and

---

can see a common thread in the thought of the Pope, who thinks that interreligious dialogue is important for peace, and that religions are at the service of peace.' As quoted in *Zenith,* 27 June 2007.

60. *The Catholic School on the Threshold of the Third Millennium,* par 10.
61. *The Catholic School on the Threshold of the Third Millennium,* par 10.
62. *Dignitatis Humanae (The Declaration on Religious Liberty)* (Vatican II, 1965), par 5.
63. *Lay Catholics in Schools: Witnesses to Faith,* (Congregation for Catholic Education, 1982), par 3; *The Religious Dimension of Education in a Catholic School,* (1988), par 6; *The Catholic School on the Threshold of the Third Millennium,* par 16.
64. *Dignitatis Humanae* (1965), par 3.
65. *Gravissimum Educationis* (1965), par 9.
66. *The Catholic School on the Threshold of the Third Millennium,* par 6.

means, acknowledging, preserving and promoting the spiritual and moral qualities, the social and cultural values, which characterise different civilisations.'[67]

This does not mean that Catholic schools relinquish their mission for evangelisation and proclamation of the Gospel of Jesus Christ in deference to the students of other world faiths which they serve. *Redemptoris Missio* (1990) asserts that while elements of truth can be found in other world religions, this does not cancel the call to faith and baptism in the Catholic Church.

> [...] a Catholic school cannot relinquish its own freedom to proclaim the Gospel and to offer a formation based on the values to be found in a Christian education; this is its right and its duty. To proclaim or to offer is not to impose, however; the latter suggests a moral violence which is strictly forbidden, both by the Gospel and by Church law.[68]

So the manner in which a Catholic school includes and educates members of different faiths is crucial. It prohibits any form of discrimination and coercion. The Church presents the Catholic school as a lively centre of proclamation, apprenticeship and dialogue between people of different social and religious backgrounds.[69] Still, one might question whether or not people involved in Catholic schools are familiar with this positive body of Church teaching on inclusivity. Furthermore one might wonder if this teaching is recognisable in the Irish system of Catholic schools where there is sometimes little freedom of choice for religious or non-religious minorities and where inter-religious learning is in its infancy.

---

67. This mirrors *Nostra Aetate*, par 2 ,which exhorts 'Sons and daughters to enter with prudence and charity into discussion and collaboration with members of other religions. Let Christians, while witnessing to their own faith and way of life, acknowledge, preserve and encourage the spiritual and moral truths found among non-Christians, also their social life and culture.'
68. *The Religious Dimension of Education in a Catholic School*, par 6.
69. Apostolic Exhortation *Ecclesia in Africa* (John Paul II, 1995), par 2, see also *The Catholic School on the Threshold of the Third Millennium*, par 11.

Conclusion

This chapter began with positive and negative appraisals of the Catholic system of education. It focused on structural and ideological concerns surrounding Catholic primary schools in Ireland. The Catholic Church's current management of schools was placed in the larger historical context of the emergence of a *de facto* denominational system of schooling in the nineteenth and twentieth centuries. However, the limitations of that denominational system, where the Catholic Church currently manages the majority of primary schools, without any viable alternative for a significant number of parents and children, is undeniable.

As a country on the cusp of change, Ireland is attempting to forge a *via media* between its traditional system of informal denominational education and the excesses of rigid formality. While striving to accommodate the needs of all creeds and none, it desires to protect its existing denominational system on behalf of the majority of parents.[70]

The call for reform and the establishment of an alternative primary school structure has originated from a variety of sources, including the Catholic Church. The Church teaches that it is wrong for any sector to monopolise the educational system of a country.[71] Further, it prohibits coercion in the matter of education and delineates the Government's duty to 'acknowledge the right of parents to make a genuinely free choice of schools and of other means of education.'[72] Catholic teaching on education supports change and choice so that no child is coerced into attending a school where their family's faith or conscience is compromised. The Catholic Church has pledged to work collaboratively with other patronage bodies and the Government to respond to Ireland's changing educational and religious needs. The Church in Ireland has rightly supported the call for a pluralism of patronage bodies and the need for greater choice. In supporting choice, the Catholic Church is remaining true to its own teaching which acknowledges parents' rights 'to determine, in accordance with their own religious beliefs, the kind of religious

---

70. Dympna Glendenning, *Education and the Law*, 1.13.
71. *Gravissimum Educationis*, par 6.
72. *Dignitatis Humanae*, par. 5

education that their children are to receive' or not to receive as may be the case.[73]

As Ireland becomes more religiously diverse, Catholic schools are called to serve the needs of a religiously plural society. The teachings of Vatican II encourage Catholics to 'acknowledge, preserve and promote' the spiritual and moral goods found among the followers of other religions and the values in their society and culture.[74] Catholic schools must celebrate and make visible their commitment to the Catholic faith, which is rooted in the Gospel of Jesus Christ, which is focused on social justice and love of neighbour. They cannot be indifferent to the plight of children who are excluded in a school system where the Catholic Church is the majority shareholder. They have a duty to work for structural reform so that there is greater equality of provision.

Today Catholic schools need to be less apologetic and more self-conscious and self-confident about their Catholic identity and mission. Ironically in an educational system which offers greater choice, Catholics will begin to reflect more profoundly on the religious foundation and ethos of their Catholic schools and to select them for religious as well as educational reasons. There are already new projects, a new trustee body, and new signs of life in Irish Catholic schools. In response to the question as to whether these schools can respond to the needs of a religiously plural society it must be stated that many Catholic primary schools are already providing high quality education and support for religiously diverse groups. One suspects, however, that they are motivated more by guidelines from the Department of Education and Science and the Irish National Teachers Organisation (INTO) rather than the teachings of the Catholic Church. The Catholic Church needs to continue to publicise and implement its teaching on inclusivity and freedom of educational choice. The challenge facing Catholic schools is to remain faithful to the specific, unique and particular message and mission of the Catholic tradition while simultaneously being welcoming, open and respectful to the truths and wisdom, the vision and values found in other faith traditions.

73. *Dignitatis Humanae*, par 5.
74. *Nostra Aetate*, par 2.

Catholic schools are challenged to live out this tension in their patronage systems, school management structures, enrolment policies, mission statements, and in their day-to-day life. The fact that the Catholic Church has begun to embrace change is a great sign of hope.

CHAPTER FOUR

From Modernity to Ultramodernity:
The Changing Influence of Catholic Practice
on Political Practice in Ireland

Jean-Christophe Penet

In his well-known book entitled *The Disenchantment of the World* (*Le désenchantement du monde*, 1985), Marcel Gauchet provides us with a most enlightening insight into the primordial and onto-logical link between politics and Catholicism. The latter, in Gauchet's view, was the religion which gave men the paradoxi-cal possibility of freeing themselves from their religiously-struc-tured view of the world and of society. Gauchet argues that Christianity is fundamental to the political organisation of con-temporary societies, as it paved the way – however unexpectedly – for technological advancements and the rise of democracy. Indeed, whereas primeval societies were characterised by the law of immanence (which was marked by a strong temporal divide in which the past set the rules, thereby creating constant immobility), the development of the idea of the State was con-temporary with the rise of monotheistic religions which were founded on the new notion of transcendence during what was called the 'axial era'.[1] It was in this context that Catholicism, a religion bringing together both transcendence and incarnation, emerged. In Catholicism, God is both absent and distant as he belongs to other spheres and is simultaneously present at the heart of human history, since he became flesh through his son. And because God sent Jesus to save men, they, according to Catholic dogma, must devote themselves exclusively to works of salvation, not by ignoring this world, but by inhabiting it fully (*DM*, p 96). Thus, in Marcel Gauchet's interpretation of Catholicism as a religion which presupposes the separation and the autonomy

---

1. Marcel Gauchet, *Le Désenchantement du monde, une histoire politique de la religion* (Paris: Gallimard, 1985), p xv. My translation. All subsequent references will be to this edition and will be denoted in brackets by *DM*, followed by the page number.

of this world from the other, Catholic practice is intrinsically linked to political practice, as politics becomes a fundamental way to achieve salvation.

History itself, in the person of Constantine, confirmed this primordial link between Catholic practice and political practice. The converted Emperor's Edict of Milan in 314, which turned Christianity into the official religion of the Roman Empire, gave the Christian Church a unique opportunity to infiltrate thoroughly and permanently the Empire's political life. Later on, by the end of the eleventh century, the Gregorian Reformation, which resulted in a definitive schism between what was to become Eastern Orthodoxy and Western Catholicism, took the marriage of political and Catholic practice to its zenith, since it made the Pope Supreme Head of a Europe united by a common Catholic faith, to whom the princes and monarchs of Europe owed obedience.

It was only in the eighteenth century, in the wake of the various European manifestations of the Enlightenment – which found its inspiration in humanist and, therefore, Christian precepts – and its political corollary, the 1789 French Revolution, that Europe entered modernity, that is to say the process whereby European societies, which had remained heteronomous, religiously-structured societies up to that time, slowly started turning into autonomous, self-governing entities. In opposition to the traditional, past-oriented form of political practice that had prevailed until then, modernity was thus characterised by the emergence of a new form of political practice, which was definitely future-oriented and in which the notions of national sovereignty and progress were strongly emphasised. From 1789 onwards, in a country like France, for instance, the new national, republican ideology was therefore constructed in constant opposition to the monarchy and, above all, to the Catholic Church. There ensued from this hostility the 1905 Act on the Separation of Church and State (*Loi sur la laïcité*), which officially severed all links between Catholic practice and political practice. Thus in France, as in many other European countries, modernity was characterised by a will to assert the superiority and, more importantly, the complete independence of political practice (that of the Republic) over Catholic practice.

As for Ireland, its attitude to modernity and to the link between political and Catholic practice appears somewhat trickier. Throughout most of the nineteenth century, Ireland seemed to be succumbing to the lure of a sometimes constitutional, at other times revolutionary, form of nationalism which, though Protestant in origin, gradually became synonymous with Catholicism. One could therefore believe that, due to the withdrawal of Irish society into an inclusive form of nationalism progressively associated with Catholicism throughout the nineteenth century, Ireland did not experience modernity, since its political practice as defined by nationalism was definitely past-oriented, glorifying a Golden Age in which everyone in Ireland was supposedly Catholic and Irish-speaking and condemning progress such as that found in the United Kingdom during the Industrial Revolution. However, this interpretation ignores the fact that one of the main characteristics of modernity was, as shown by Eric Hobsbawm, the invention of tradition. Indeed, in its efforts to 'restore' the Irish nation to the way it used to be under the banner of religion, nationalism in Ireland was much more a political practice than a religious one. Nationalists in Ireland wanted to stop the concept of 'Nation' from being associated with the stream of modernist ideas where the French Revolution had taken it, so as to lodge in it, instead, their plan to restore a past Irish nation. By so doing, Irish nationalists were in fact unconsciously changing the divine order by imposing their own nationalist – and therefore human – will on this order. And they were thereby making modern history, and history modern.

From such nationalist aims a new link between Catholic and political practice was created, which, from the 1801 Act of Union to the 1961 application for EEC membership, shaped most of modern Irish history. In such a nationalist history, the Catholic Church in Ireland enjoyed the full support of the country's popular forces, achieved by having cemented links with them during the time of Daniel O'Connell and his Catholic Association's political fight for Catholic Emancipation in the 1820s and thereafter.[2] Throughout the nineteenth century, the – at first fragile – alliance between the Catholic Church on the one hand, and

---

2. Brian Girvin, *From Union to Union. Nationalism, Democracy and Religion in Ireland – Act of Union to EU* (Dublin: Gill & Macmillan, 2002),

nationalism and popular forces on the other hand, grew ever stronger and it eventually gave birth to a triangular structure of power – Church, State and Nation – which was to dominate most of the twentieth century. To Fintan O'Toole, with its symbolic occurrence at Easter and its imagery of sacrifice and redemption, the founding act of the modern Irish State, the 1916 Rising was therefore '[...] a religious as much as a political act, and conceived by its leader, Patrick Pearse, as such.'[3]

Thus, as soon as Ireland became a Free State, whose two national objectives were the reunification of the island and the restoration of the Irish language, it took Catholicism as its main ideology. As Máire Nic Ghiolla Phádraig argued in her article, 'The Power of the Catholic Church in the Republic of Ireland', even though Church and State were formally separate, the State's lack of civic ceremonial soon created a reliance on Catholic rituals with, for example, a special Mass being said for the opening of the Oireachtas each autumn. She concludes that 'The [State's] willingness to concede further influence [to the Church] can be attributed to [...] a requirement for legitimation and cohesion. The Church offered the State continuity and stability and in return sought its support for continuity and stability in its own work.'[4] This alliance between Catholic and political practice in Ireland, whereby the Church gave the state the necessary legitimacy and vice versa, was even enshrined in the letter of the law, since the 1937 Constitution recognised the special position of the Catholic Church on the basis that, as de Valera himself stated in the Dáil, '93% of the people on this part of Ireland [...] belong to the Catholic Church' and 'their whole philosophy of

---

p 10. All subsequent references will be to this edition and will be denoted in brackets by *FUU*, followed by the page number.

3. Quotation taken from Mary Kenny, *Goodbye to Catholic Ireland. A Social, Personal and Cultural History from the Fall of Parnell to the Realm of Mary Robinson* (London : Sinclair-Stevenson, 1997), p 60. All subsequent references will be to this edition and will be denoted in brackets by *GCI*, followed by the page number.

4. Máire Nic Ghiolla Phádraig, 'The Power of the Catholic Church in the Republic of Ireland', in P. Clancy, S. Drudy, K. Lynch and L. O'Dowd (eds), *Irish Society: Sociological Perspectives* (Dublin: Institute of Public Administration, 1995), pp 593-619, p 609.

life is the philosophy that comes from its teachings'.[5] As a result, the new Irish Constitution, which linked Catholicism and nationalism, enabled the Irish to present themselves as special, as God's chosen people, and thereby justified the State's efforts at constituting on a political level the Catholic practice of missions by establishing 'Ireland's spiritual empire', which was thought of as a parallel of – if not a competitor to – the British Empire (*GCI*, p 117). This anti-liberal constitution, which did not clearly distinguish between the secular and the religious spheres, but which had the support of the popular forces, therefore achieved '[…] a synthesis between Catholic, nationalist and democratic values in a way that provided a stable basis for constitutional continuity for the next forty years' (*FUU*, p 82).

Therefore, in modern Irish society, unlike most liberal societies, there was no clear-cut boundary between the sacred and the secular and, as a result, between political and Catholic practice. Actually, such a correlation between both practices allowed for the development of what Tom Inglis called, following Pierre Bourdieu's sociological theory, a Catholic 'habitus' in Ireland.[6] Indeed, in his study, *Moral Monopoly*, Tom Inglis showed how important it was, in the Catholic habitus created by modern Ireland, to be perceived as a good practising Catholic, as this gave one greater religious capital which, in turn, led to greater

5. Quotation of Dáil Debates, 67, col 1890 (4 June 1937) taken from Louise Fuller, 'New Ireland and the Undoing of the Catholic Legacy: Looking back to the Future', in Louise Fuller, John Littleton and Eamon Maher (eds), *Irish and Catholic? Towards an Understanding of Identity* (Dublin: The Columba Press, 2006), pp 68-87, p 71. All subsequent references will be to this edition and will be denoted in brackets by *I&C?*, followed by the page number.

6. 'To help make these connections, I rely on the work of Pierre Bourdieu. Society and everyday social life can be divided into a number of different fields. Each of these fields is characterised by a *habitus* which revolves around being spiritual or moral. It is this habitus which generated the habit of what it means for believers to be religious. (…) In Catholic Ireland, religious capital was not only important in attaining high positions in the religious field, but it could be used to attain other forms of capital and, thereby, high positions in other social fields.' Tom Inglis, 'Catholic Church, Religious Capital and Symbolic Domination', in Michael Böss and Eamon Maher (eds), *Engaging Modernity* (Dublin: Veritas, 2003), pp 43-65, p 44.

social prestige: 'In other words, being a good Catholic helped get contracts and jobs, be elected, be educated, be well-known and liked.'[7] Such a process gave Catholic practice a moral mono- poly in Ireland which justified the Catholic Church's constant interference in Irish political life. This was exemplified by the Mother and Child scheme, which was interpreted by the Church as an encroachment on one of its private domains, the health sector. In 1950, when the then Minister for Health, Noël Browne, decided to introduce a scheme which would give all mothers free maternity care and all teenagers free healthcare, regardless of income, he met with vehement resistance from the Church au- thorities and from conservative members of the medical profes- sion. The case was rapidly blown out of proportion, so much so that 'the Taoiseach cancel[ed] all his appointments *instanter* and rushe[d] to Drogheda to attempt to negotiate with the Cardinal at a time of crisis.'[8] The Taoiseach's reaction is the perfect illus- tration of the power of the Catholic Church at that time, and of its influence on political practice. Because Irish Catholic authori- ties considered the scheme to be against Catholic teachings (they feared it might have paved the way for birth-control and abor- tion), it was withdrawn without further ado and Noël Browne, who had to apologise, resigned shortly afterwards. As John Whyte noted, up to the 1970s the reluctance of politicians to be seen as opposing the Catholic hierarchy is a clear sign that '[...] there was no electoral dividend to be gained from appearing to stand up to the bishops.'[9]

If the Catholic Church had institutional power stemming from the 1937 Constitution and, therefore, the power to influ- ence Irish political life, its influence largely rested on its moral power in a religious society. There was little or no anticlerical-

7. Tom Inglis, *Moral Monopoly: The Rise and Fall of the Catholic Church in Modern Ireland* (Dublin: UCD Press, 1998), p 11. All subsequent refer- ences will be to this edition and will be denoted in brackets by *MM*, fol- lowed by the page number.

8. Tony McNamara, 'Church and State in the Twenty-First Century' in *Doctrine and Life*, 54 (1), 2004, pp 31-36, p. 33.

9. James H. Whyte, 'Recent Developments in Church State Relations', in *Journal of the Department of the Public Services*, 6 (3), 1985, pp 4-10, p 4. All subsequent references will be to this edition and will be denoted in brackets by *RDCS*, followed by the page number.

ism in a modern Ireland where lay opinion appeared to be more orthodox than that of the Pope himself, and religion apparently gave meaning to everyday life. That is why, according to Brian Girvin, 'Catholic-nationalist Ireland became democratic but it did not become liberal. Its anti-liberalism was a consequence of the Catholic Church's opposition to modernism and Irish nationalism's hostility to Britain. As a consequence, the nation's religious and political leadership could share in the rejection of the liberal version of modernity, especially in its individualism and secularism' (*FUU*, p 18). In such a context, Fianna Fáil became increasingly more conservative from the 1960s well into the 1980s, protecting the Church's moral monopoly by refusing to change the Constitution and following its teachings by opposing more liberal views on moral issues. By doing so, it probably tried to fulfil the expectations of a population that Michael Fogarty, in his 1984 report of the *European Values System, Irish Values and Attitudes*, depicted as being still overwhelmingly Catholic, with people trusting the Church more than their political institutions, and consequently being more conservative – or more 'right-wing' – than most European nations.[10] However, further evidence seems to suggest that the apparently unconditional adherence to Catholic precepts in those days rested on a rather legalistic conception of religion. We can therefore question the sincerity of the faith of the Irish as early as in the 1970s. Indeed, unlike most European countries, the rate of believers in Ireland was lower than the rate of churchgoers; in 1973-1974 there were only 59% of respondents who completely agreed with the Catholic *credo*, whereas 91% of them were regular churchgoers. In 1984, at the time when Michael Fogarty was writing his report, there were respectively 46% and 87% of them, which means a 14% drop in the number of people who genuinely believed in Catholic dogma but only a 4% drop in church attendance.[11] Such figures confirm the idea that the Irish had a particularly legalistic conception of religion, since they abided

---

10. Michael Fogarty, Liam Ryan and John Lee, *Irish Values and Attitudes* (Dublin: Dominican Publications, 1984), pp 10, 68 and 96. All subsequent references will be to this edition and will be denoted in brackets by *IVA*, followed by the page number.

11. Figures taken from Marguerite Corish-Arnal, 'Pratiques et croyances

by the Catholic ethos without necessarily sharing it, and the continuing high level of church attendance well into the 1980s can be seen as the sign that Catholic practice in Ireland remained closely linked to social capital. Yet, however small it might appear to be, the 4% drop in church attendance over a decade can be seen as the sign of the gradually waning influence of the Church on political, and as a result on social attitudes from the 1970s onwards.[12]

In an article about religious and political beliefs entitled 'Croyances religieuses, croyances politiques', Marcel Gauchet noticed the same downward trend in terms of the influence of the Church on French social and political life from the 1960s. He concluded that believers themselves had so fully assimilated the notions of pluralism and liberalism that are the essence of French democracy that their religious beliefs were transformed in the process, and, eventually, so was their faith. Faith was now conceived as a personal matter that should no longer dictate a country's social and political organisation. Indeed, even the staunchest of believers would no longer dream of declaring him or herself a simple member of a community designed by the hand of God. They would be more likely to affirm that men, and men only, have the political power to build a community that

religieuses, valeurs morales' in Paul Brennan (dir), *La sécularisation en Irlande*, pp 131-154, p 140. My translation.

12. 'Fogarty (1984) had already detected signs of questioning and criticism of the church among Catholics in the Republic in 1981, so that declining confidence in the church may not have been new even in the 1980s – compare, for example, the reverential respect for the church revealed by Biever's survey of Dublin Catholics in 1962 (Biever, 1976) with the more critical attitudes pointed by Fogarty (1984). It is plausible that, as has been suggested earlier, the sex scandals in the Catholic church in the 1990s did not so much engender a radical new loss of confidence in the church as carry forwards a downward momentum that had begun up to two decades earlier.' T. Fahey, B. Hayes and R. Sinnott, *Conflict and Consensus, a Study of Values and Attitudes in the Republic of Ireland and Northern Ireland* (Dublin: Institute of Public Administration, 2005), p 49. All subsequent references will be to this edition and will be denoted in brackets by *C&C*, followed by the page number.

brings everyone together.[13] Such conceptions illustrate how secularised our societies have become, since secular ideas – according to which social and political organisations should be completely independent from religious organisations, as they are primarily political and not religious – have now made their way into Catholic minds and attitudes. In Ireland, even though some traces of such secular ideas can be found as early as the 1960s and a secular influence definitely grew more perceptible in Irish political and social organisations throughout the 1970s, it only became crystal clear that those organisations were being secularised when they underwent a series of institutional reforms in the 1980s.

If the first signs of a secular influence were felt in Ireland in the 1960s, this was probably due to the redefinition of Catholic practice and of the role of the Church in society brought into the island by the Second Vatican Council. Indeed, in its efforts to adapt the Catholic Church to the modern world, Vatican II seems to have encouraged – albeit unconsciously – some sort of secularisation of both political and Catholic practices, since according to its pastoral constitution, *Gaudium et spes*, the Church accepted the notion of religious freedom in the name of human rights. With Vatican II, the Catholic Church could no longer champion values such as truth and justice in isolation from men and women. In 1971, the Church's new conception was reasserted with the publication of the apostolic letter, *Octogesima Adveniens*, in which the Pope clearly stressed the legitimacy of the notion of pluralism – a notion the Church had always fought until then – and justified it in the political field, a field where Christians should exert their freedom of conscience.[14] By so doing, the Catholic Church acknowledged the world as it was, one that was ruled by cultural pluralism. Of course, this did not mean that the Church started adhering to a liberal conception of the world – and more specifically to a *princeps* distinction between private and public spheres – but this undoubtedly meant that pluralism, the most distinctive mark of a secularisation which

13. Marcel Gauchet, 'Croyance religieuse et croyance politique', in *Le débat*, n°115, May-August 2001, pp 3-13, p 8. My translation.
14. Jan Grootaers, *De Vatican II à Jean-Paul II: le grand tournant de l'Eglise catholique* (Paris : Editions du Centurion, 1981), p 106.

was leading to an ever-growing distinction between the temporal and the spiritual, the secular and the sacred, the political and the religious, was being recognised and accepted.[15] Thus, because it accepted the notion of pluralism and now insisted on the concept of private conscience, Vatican II undoubtedly represented a watershed in Catholic practice in Ireland and elsewhere. In the wake of this 'religious liberation', a new type of Catholic emerged who was characterised by 'an informed appreciation of the value of the supernatural and sacramental life of the church, but [...] an independence of mind mainly on moral matters' (*IVA*, p 104).

It seems that such drastic changes in terms of the redefinition of Catholic practice were bound to entail a redefinition of political practice in the Emerald Isle. Indeed, it is interesting to note that the Catholic liberalisation of the Second Vatican Council coincided with what Liam Ryan calls the 'creation of the second Ireland' – the one that came after de Valera's. This second Ireland '[...] emerged from a lively duet on the horn by Sean Lemass and Ken Whitaker' and brought economic as well as psychological transformation to the country by providing a solid economic base (*IVA*, p 101). It also coincided with the advent of television and more outward-looking national policies – such as the first EEC membership application and the country's involvement in the United Nations peace-keeping process, both signs of its opening up to foreign influences. To John Whyte, a specialist in Church-State relations in contemporary Ireland, the wide-ranging transformations in Irish society from the 1960s to the 1980s which gradually turned Ireland into an affluent, urbanised country, created the conditions which permitted a more flexible and innovative leadership.[16]

Indeed, considering the case of the rising majority of 'new Catholics' in the 1970s, he concludes: 'Even if a minority of Irish Catholics have drifted away from old attitudes, it is not surpris-

---

15. Jean-Marie Donegani, *La liberté de choisir. Pluralisme religieux et pluralisme politique dans le catholicisme français contemportain* (Paris : Presses de la Fondation Nationale des Sciences Politiques, 1993), p 372. My translation.
16. James H. Whyte, *Church and State in Modern Ireland* (Dublin: Gill & Macmillan, 1971), p 335.

ing that admonitions from the hierarchy no longer have their former influence' (*RDCS*, p 7). And, as a matter of fact, in 1972 the Lynch Government held a referendum asking the Irish to consent to the deletion of the clause in Article 44 of the 1937 Constitution which recognised the 'special position' of the Catholic Church. If such an amendment was justified by the necessity to appease Protestants in the North at a time when steps were being taken towards reconciliation, the huge support in favour of the deletion of the clause (85%) can also be seen as the obedience – however reluctant it might have been – of the Irish hierarchy to the new precepts of Vatican II that promoted a more ecumenical view of religion. Such a view would explain why Cardinal Conway, the then Catholic primate, said that he would not shed a tear if the clause disappeared. The lack of opposition to the referendum can henceforth be paradoxically interpreted as Irish Catholics continuing to have a legalistic interpretation of their religion, by following the instructions of their hierarchy. One year later, however, the same Irish hierarchy distanced itself from its until then usual dogmatic stand during the debate over Mary Robinson's highly polemical Abortion Bill, since, in a joint statement, they declared: 'There are many things which the Catholic Church holds to be morally wrong and no one has ever suggested, least of all the Church herself, that they should be prohibited by the state'.[17] Even though the bill never became law, the reaction of the hierarchy to the matter was of paramount importance, as it made clear that the State was not expected 'to defend by legislation the moral teachings of the Catholic Church' (*RDCS*, p 7) and that this was a matter of private conscience for voters and politicians alike.

Encouraged by this new attitude of the Catholic hierarchy towards politics, the Fine Gael/Labour coalition government led by Garret FitzGerald that was elected in 1981 did not hide its ambition to further enhance the liberalisation of Irish political and social life from Catholic teachings. Soon after the election, it launched a 'constitutional crusade' that aimed to reform Ireland's institutions by making them more secular. Even though, as Louise Fuller has noted, developments in Irish soci-

---

17. *The Irish Independent*, 26 November 1973.

ety back then made FitzGerald's reform programme difficult, as voters remained divided between liberal and conservative camps, each wanting to define Irish identity in what Fogarty calls the 'tension management years',[18] the new Taoiseach's crusade nevertheless set the tone for the whole of the 1980s (*I&C?*, p 82). The 1980s and 1990s were consequently decades of intense reform characterised by politicians proposing a series of laws to the Dáil and referenda to the people to make Catholic prohibitions legal in Ireland. In February 1985, for instance, despite strong opposition from the hierarchy, FitzGerald's Minister for Health, Barry Desmond, passed the Family Planning (Amendment) Act in the Dáil, which amended the 1979 Family Planning Act by making non-medical contraceptives available to adults without a medical prescription. According to John Whyte, this legislation represented nothing less than the Church's greatest defeat since the State was established (*RDCS*, p 4). However, if this was the worst, it was certainly not the last, as a cascade of referenda on abortion (1983, 1992 with the infamous 'X' Case and 2002) and on divorce (1986 and 1995 with the victory of the 'Yes' vote) were to follow – each of them further undermining the legitimacy of the Church's influence on social and political matters. To that effect, Louise Fuller showed how the latest referendum on abortion (2002), which ended in a victory of the 'No' by a narrow margin, can be seen as evidence of the collapsing support of popular forces for the Catholic hierarchy in Ireland, and therefore marks 'the final stage in the dismantling of legislative and constitutional support for the Catholic ethos in Ireland' (*I&C?*, p 87).

So, even though the Church remained more powerful in Ireland than in most other European countries, it nevertheless

---

18. 'The years between 1960 to 1980 in Ireland can best be described in sociological language as years of "tension management", tension between the old and the new: between old ideologies and recent, between Catholicism and nationalism on the one hand and liberalism and materialism on the other; between an older male-dominated society and new emancipated females; between frugal comfort preached by de Valera and the affluence made possible by Lemass; between ethics preached by the church and the ecstasy promised by the media; [...]; between the ways of God and the ways of the world' (*IVA*, p 101).

lost a lot of influence in the areas of education, health and social welfare through the 1980s and 1990s. Nowadays, due to this progressive loss of moral monopoly – a phenomenon which was not provoked but undoubtedly accelerated by the notorious child sex abuse scandals of the 1990s – it is no longer necessary to be seen as a good practising Catholic to have social prestige, as confirmed by the general drop in church attendance since the 1990s. Moreover, despite the long standing association between Irishness and Catholicism, less than 30% of today's population regard being Catholic as very important for being fully Irish (*C&C*, p 69). This redefinition of Irish identity outside the traditional bond between Irishness/nationalism and Catholicism that had made Ireland enter modernity is a clear sign that it has now abandoned it to enter a new era commonly referred to as postmodernity. As a result, it is no longer necessary for politicians to be seen as devout Catholics to be elected. They therefore feel much freer to oppose the hierarchy openly and to propose laws that they know will certainly please the electorate and displease the bishops. In fact, it would hardly be conceivable, nowadays, for the Taoiseach to rush *instanter* to negotiate with the Catholic hierarchy, were they to oppose the proposed legislation, as was the case with the Mother and Child Scheme.[19]

These are clear signs that secularisation intensified in Ireland during the 1990s and that, as a consequence, 'the easy and intimate relationship between the Church and State elites' during the decades after independence has now turned 'edgy and mistrustful'.[20] Ireland's further integration into the European Union during the 1990s also intensified the secularisation of its political practices, as successive governments became more aware of the criticism by the European Court of the sometimes too Catholic nature of their country's legislation on social and moral issues.

19. 'Contrast this with the report in *The Irish Times* on 29 October 2006 – 'Cardinal to meet Ahern on "life issues".' It reported on the delegation from the hierarchy which was officially meeting the Taoiseach to put forward its views on life issues such as cloning, euthanasia and assisted human reproduction – a very brief account of a delegation being received by the Taoiseach in the normal way' (*CS21*, p 33).

20. Joseph Ruane, 'Secularisation and Ideology in the Republic of Ireland', in Paul Brennan (ed), *La sécularisation en Irlande*, pp 239-254, p 251.

In the case of homosexuality, EU membership even forced Ireland to change its legislation. Consequently, the Irish have become much more liberal in terms of marriage, abortion and homosexuality, thus clearly distancing themselves from the Catholic stronghold of bygone days.[21] In postmodern Ireland, where rampant secularisation has introduced the notions of pluralism and liberalism, Catholic practice no longer officially dictates political practice. Unlike modern Irish history, in which Catholic values helped the Irish shape their ideal political and societal organisation as a nation, the Irish are now moving away from their religiously-structured view of society and their Catholic definition of the Republican ideal inspired by their Catholic *habitus*, according to which they conformed automatically to Church teaching. On the contrary, they are now working on the construction of a political organisation free(r) of Catholic influence, as shown by the progressive secularisation of two traditional strongholds of the Catholic Church in Ireland – education and the health system. However, this assessment does not go without qualification. Even though secularism in Ireland means that Catholic practice has become privatised, having lost most of what Tom Inglis called its 'symbolic domination' (*MM*, p 208) this does not mean that it has been completely wiped out of the public arena. Recently enough, for example, a perfect illustration of the persisting influence of Catholic practice on political practice in Ireland was the Taoiseach's interview with *The Irish Times*, in which he stated that 'religious belief and practice is not purely a private matter, with no place in public discourse [...] on the contrary, a truly democratic and inclusive society values its faith community and respects the voice of those who offer spiritual insight and leadership' and that his

---

21. 'EVS data from 1981, 1990 and 1999-2000 indicate that, in the Republic, opposition to homosexuality and abortion has declined since 1981, though with abortion eliciting consistently higher levels of opposition than homosexuality. In 1999-2000, 38% in the Republic expressed strongly negative attitudes to homosexuality, compared to 62% in 1981. Sixty% in 1999-2000 had similarly negative attitudes towards abortion, as compared to 83% in 1981' (*C&C*, p 122).

faith '[…] is both a personal matter for [him] as well as being an important part of […] [his] perspective on public affairs.'[22]

Such a statement by Ireland's current Taoiseach in one of the country's leading newspapers can be understood as evidence that, in spite of secularism the link between Catholic and religious practice in Ireland has not been completely severed. It is true that, on a more universal level, the Roman Catholic Church since Vatican II admitted defeat in the battle for political power when it recognised the legitimacy of pluralism, even in the political field. However, it has never – as yet – completely surrendered its claim to dictate in certain areas in relation to morality. Consequently, in order to maintain some influence in the political sphere, the Church never fails to remind politicians who also happen to be practising Catholics that their duties as politicians do not free them from their moral obligations as members of the Church. In his 1983 programme for a new evangelisation, for instance, Pope John Paul II vividly condemned the permissive mentalities of the day and implored his prelates to recover some of their lost authority over the faithful on the public scene.[23] Thus, the Catholic Church, as far as Rome is concerned, does not only want to make its views heard, it would also like to impose them on society as a whole. And it seems to be more or less successful, as some sociological studies show that the presence, or even the absence, of Catholic practice among the repositories of democratic power, for example, voters, still influences their political practice.

Indeed, in his article on political values and religious identity in Europe (*Valeurs de gauche, valeurs de droite et identité religieuse en Europe*) based on the 1999 European Value Survey, French sociologist Pierre Bréchon shows how, as far as politics is concerned, it is possible to consider that rightwing and leftwing values transcend national boundaries and that all have a similar content in every country. He then goes on to show that conservative people generally hold more traditional views than their

22. *The Irish Times*, 23 February 2006. Quotation taken from Gerry O'Hanlon, 'Religion and Society', *Studies*, 95 (378), pp 141-152, p 141.
23. Jean-Louis Ormières, *L'Europe désenchantée. La fin de l'Europe chrétienne? France, Belgique, Italie, Espagne, Portugal* (Paris: Fayard, 2005), p 257.

more liberal counterparts on matters relating to morality, family and sexuality and that, as far as religious identity is concerned, it must be understood as a continuum of attitudes ranging from antireligious views to people showing a very constructed and integrated system of religious belief and practice.[24] He then notes that, in Europe, people with a weak religious identity are more likely than not to be left-wingers and vice versa, even though numerous nuances persist. Such an analysis can help us understand better why Ireland does not have any traditionally important leftwing party, since its two big parties, Fianna Fáil and Fine Gael, are both at the centre of the political spectrum.[25] Even though Fianna Fáil, the most popular party of the last decade, has liberalised its traditional values in recent times, it still remains fairly conservative and tilts noticeably to the right on the political spectrum. This could suggest that the political practice of Irish voters, who still attend Mass much more frequently than their European counterparts, remains significantly influenced by their Catholic practice. Or, as Timothy J. Whyte puts it:

> [...] the Republic of Ireland remains an overwhelmingly Catholic State in terms of religious identification and the power of the church remains remarkably strong in terms of its influence on many political matters. This would seem to contradict the conventional wisdom that industrial high culture severs the historical link between faith and dominant national church (*I&C?*, p 250).

It seems that in Ireland, even though Catholic practice has stopped being synonymous with moral capital, it nonetheless remains one of the fundamental identity traits of the individuals it concerns, no matter where they stand on the continuum. And this fundamental trait remains a major source of influence on

---

24. Pierre Bréchon, 'Valeurs de gauche, valeurs de droite et identités religieuses en Europe', *Revue française de sociologie*, 47 (4), 2006, pp 724-754, p 726.
25. 'In the 1990 EVS data, Hardiman and Whelan found that "the Irish are distinctly less left-wing" than the European average and again noted that they has a particular tendency "to opt for a position just right of the political centre"' (*C&C*, p 142).

people's voting patterns and on the new legislation introduced by politicians.

Is it possible, in those circumstances, to view Ireland as a secular country? Judging by the persisting influence of Catholic practice on political practice in the country, we can say that Ireland is definitely not secular if by this term one means the marginalisation of religion in the public sphere. However, we also know that Ireland has become much more pluralist and open to foreign influences than it used to be, as Irish Catholics no longer accept blindly all of the teachings of their Church. Thus, according to Brian Girvin:

> If secularism is understood as a process by which the state and non-denominational agencies replace the church as the main provider of welfare, educational and health services, then Ireland has become somewhat more secular and is progressively more so. If secularisation refers to the beliefs and behaviour of individuals, the evidence is less clear. In comparative terms Ireland remains more religious than most other European societies, though this may not be incompatible with declining church membership. If secularisation involves political behaviour which does not reflect the influence of religion, the situation is even more complex. [...] Whyte argued that religion had little importance in Irish politics. The irony is that religion now plays a greater role than in 1969. But this is because the homogeneous society which characterised Ireland as late at the 1960s has disintegrated. Norms which have a religious origin have been challenged, and political conflict is often based on moral and religious issues. [...]. In a political sense Ireland is becoming more secular, while at the same time religion has become more central to its politics.[26]

This view is reinforced by Tony Fahey's recent study of values and attitudes in Ireland according to which the first factor of division in Ireland is a complex attitudinal spectrum 'characterised at one end by religious commitment, conservative moral

---

26. Brian Girvin, 'Church, State and the Irish Constitution: The Secularisation of Irish Politics?', in *Parliamentary Affairs*, 49 (4), 1996, pp 599-615, p 614.

views and a confessional attitude to politics and, at the other end, by a secular outlook, liberal moral views and a pluralist conception of politics' (*C&C*, p 22). Does this mean that secularisation entails a more leftwing outlook? Actually, things are a bit more complex than that, as Ireland's modern history (which was characterised by an alliance between Catholicism and nationalism and, later, Catholicism and the State) did not allow for a real rightwing/leftwing division, but rather a liberal/conservative one. As a result, the differences between leftwing and rightwing people in Ireland have more to do still, according to Fahey, 'with social and moral values than principles of economic organisation' (*C&C*, p 148). Thus, even though Irish left-wingers appear to be less religious than Irish right-wingers (85% of the former are regular churchgoers as against 53% of the latter), they remain particularly religious in comparison with their European counterparts. The fact that the majority of leftwing Irish people are Catholics, with probably more liberal views concerning morality, family and sexuality than their rightwing counterparts, disproves without doubt the theory that all Catholics share the same conservative outlook. How could it be otherwise after the Second Vatican Council? Indeed, with Vatican II the Catholic Church had embraced what it had always rejected on a political level, liberalism and pluralism. Forty-five years later, we can truly say that 'the Irish Catholic', understood as a prototype, has disappeared to give way to a myriad of Irish Catholics, whose definition of Catholic practice and identity can vary greatly. This must now be taken into account when one studies the influence of Catholic practice on political practice in contemporary Ireland, since this influence has now become as complex as the self-definition of Irish Catholics. All this appears to be proof positive that secularism – with the rise of individualism it entails – has definitely made its way into contemporary Irish Catholicism, thus redefining it – as far as the laity is concerned – in a more pluralist and, perhaps, more liberal way. The liberalisation and pluralisation of political practice amongst practising Catholics therefore explains why, even though postmodern Ireland is becoming more secular, religion is also becoming more central to politics. It also accounts for political parties such as Fianna Fáil, for example, recently redefining themselves along more liberal lines, as we noted earlier.

As a result, if, following French sociologist Danièle Hervieu-Léger, we redefine secularisation as a process of constant re-organisation of the work of religion in a given society, which implies that religious forces do not disappear in the wake of sec-ularisation but, on the contrary, infiltrate every level in society, then we can say that Ireland is well and truly secularised.[27] This process is, according to Hervieu-Léger, characteristic of what she calls 'ultramodernity' (*l'ultramodernité*). Indeed, she shows how the notion of postmodernity wrongly implies that modernity, understood as the era which separated man's various activities to ensure their autonomy in relation to others, and notably in re-lation to the religious norms that applied to society as a whole, is now over.[28] Whereas modernity shifted the source of legitimacy of political authority away from God to the State, ultramodernity takes this removal of political legitimacy from a transcendental to an immanent source even further by allowing individuals to find in themselves the source of legitimisation of the institutions whose authority they recognise (*CFM?*, p 88). In that sense, Ireland has therefore become ultramodern and not postmodern, which explains why Catholic practice never stopped influencing the nation's political practice after Ireland left modernity, but also why its influence has changed, as both have been redefined on a general, as well as on an individual level. Indeed, the per-sistent influence of an individual's chosen Catholic practice – or its chosen negation – on their political practice therefore seems to be a clear indication that contemporary Ireland is being secu-larised or, to put it another way, that religion is being rede-ployed in an ultramodern Ireland where every institution is in crisis and at a time when every individual claims his or her right to self-definition.

27. Danièle Hervieu-Léger & F. Champion, *Vers un nouveau christian-isme?* (Paris: Cerf, 1986), p 140.

28. Danièle Hervieu-Léger, *Catholicisme, la fin d'un monde?* (Paris: Bayard, 2003), p 85. Subsequent references will be to this edition and will be denoted in brackets by *CFM?*, followed by the page number.

PART TWO

Catholic Experiences

The New Prophets: Voices from the Margins

Catherine Maignant

In the words of Jean Vanier, the founder of L'Arche, 'a new spirituality is being born in the church today, flowing from the wounded hearts of the weak and broken who are crying out for friendship.'[1] This spirituality is a central expression of the deep changes which are currently taking place as a result of the disaffection towards 'traditional' religion as this concept is defined in the second half of the nineteenth century. It also bears witness to the vibrant desire to instil new life into the Church by showing the relevance of the Christian message in the contemporary world. In his prophetic 'dream'[2] about the Christian of the future inspired by the spirit of Vatican II, Karl Rahner saw a Church 'led by the Lord of history into a new epoch' in which the individual would be 'dependent in everything on faith and on the holy power of the heart' for he would 'no longer be able to draw any strength at all, or very little, from what is purely institutional'.[3] The contemporary dynamics of change is based on a similar analysis. Its agents throughout the world seek to reinvent catholicity from the margins, to reinstate what they consider to be true Christianity as symbolised by the love of Christ. In doing so, these movements go back to the origins of Christian faith and react to 'the signs of the time'. They also provide an interesting illustration of postmodern or late modern religious phenomena as analysed by such sociologists as Frédéric Lenoir, Danièle Hervieu-Léger or Michel Maffesoli.

The case of Ireland is particularly interesting in this perspec-

---

1. Foreword to *Spiritual Journeys*, edited by Stanislaus Kennedy (Dublin: Veritas, 1997), p 7.
2. Karl Rahner, 'The Christian of the Future', 1967 (http://www.religion-org/showchapter.asp?title=524&C=537), p 1.
3. *Ibid*, p 2.

tive for what is at stake is also the reinvention of national identity. D. Vincent Twomey suggests that 'the apparent collapse of the Catholic Church in Ireland' owes much to what he calls the 'false identification' of Irish and Catholic. Yet, to him, the ensuing dissociation of the two 'is not necessarily a source of regret', for a healthy reaction may eventually lead Ireland to grasp 'an opportunity for a new and vibrant Catholic Christianity that is life affirming and inspirational'.[4] Such appears to be the ultimate ambition of the Irish religious or lay men and women who seek to bring the margins into the centre of Catholic preoccupations. Indeed far from being inspired by mere charity, their commitment to the marginalised proceeds from the wish to labour for the advent of the Church of Christ, which, to them, is not fully embodied in the present Church of Rome. The movement is to some extent inspired by theology of liberation and it defends an alternative understanding of the Gospel from which a new Christianity may spring. It implies a denunciation of the past and present mistakes of the institutional Church, a reinterpretation of the Church and its mission, a redefinition of spirituality, and a re-evaluation of God. It also involves a new understanding of life, time and space, leading to a reinvention of the relationship with God and hence to a rebirth of Catholicism.

Karl Rahner claimed that he was 'no prophet'[5] and that his Catholic of the future had only seized the opportunity embodied in the teaching of the Second Vatican Council. Indeed, to him, 'the real seeds of a new outlook and strength to understand and endure the imminent future of a Christian way' had been 'sown in the field of the Church'[6] by Vatican II. However, the contemporary history of the institution is telling a different story. The option for the poor still seems to be defended by precursors on the margins of the Church and of society. It is still sowing time and, in the words of Stanislaus Kennedy, 'The business of sowing is like prophesying. Prophesying is about changing people's hearts, changing the way people think. This requires the courage to go alone on an unknown path, to make the

---

4. D. Vincent Twomey, *The End of Irish Catholicism?* (Dublin: Veritas, 2003), pp 20-21.
5. 'The Christian of the Future', p 1.
6. *Ibid*, p 9.

path by walking it.'[7] This analysis could be applied to the work of those who have willingly chosen a theology of struggle for justice and it might be argued that sowing the seeds of a new Catholicity *is* indeed prophesying.

Defining Hospice as a 'prophetic movement', Sheila Cassidy notes that 'prophets are individuals or groups of people who are called both to listen and to speak out.'[8] This corresponds to the etymological meaning of the concept: the prophet is not ahead of his time. He leads the way as he fundamentally voices the preoccupations of his day. He says out loud what people experience in silence.[9] To Sheila Cassidy, prophets 'must listen to God, to the signs of the time, and to the cries of the oppressed, and when they have understood the message, speak out, whatever the personal cost.'[10] Following the model of Micah in the Old Testament, the contemporary prophets fight against social injustice in the name of God. The Conference of Religious in Ireland (CORI) thus considers its core mission to be 'a prophetic voice in proclaiming good news for our time' because its members are 'aware of the hunger for God in our society.'[11] As all their predecessors since the time of Samuel, these men and women have the feeling they simply answered, 'Here I am, send me',[12] when God called them. This is how Stanislaus Kennedy explains why she once 'stumbled upon the Sisters of Charity' even though she 'did not particularly want to become a nun': 'What I didn't realise', she continues, 'was that this was God's way of calling me to walk with him and with the poor.'[13] In the same way, the St Patrick's Missionary Society (also known as the Kiltegan Fathers), reflecting on their task, state: 'Why would you want to do this? You have a call.' And this tells them to hear the

---

7. Stanislaus Kennedy, *Now is the Time* (Dublin: Town House, 1998), p 29.
8. Sheila Cassidy, 'Hospice: a Prophetic Movement', in *Spiritual Journeys*, p 159.
9. Michel Maffesoli, *L'instant éternel* (Paris: Denoël, 2000), pp 61-62.
10. 'Hospice: a Prophetic Movement', p 159.
11. CORI mission statement (http://www.cori.ie/general_info/mission.htm).
12. Isaiah 6:8
13. Stanislaus Kennedy, 'Moments of Grace", in *Spiritual Journeys*, p 86.

call of the most needy, the poor, the sick, the refugee, the marginalised. As a result, 'being a missionary means to be on the edge.'[14]

Indeed, siding with those on the margins almost necessarily leads to marginalisation because a prophet rejects conformity, fights against conventions and thus delivers an unpleasant message to his/her contemporaries who remain obstinately deaf to disturbing realities. Following in the steps of their biblical forebears, today's prophets are a threat to comfortable certainties even though distrust is naturally tempered by the tradition of Christian charity and the fashionable ethics of human rights. Some claim they have always been on the edge. Such is the case of Fr Joe Lucey, who sees himself as 'more tangential than centreline' as he has always found 'the centre claustrophobic'.[15] Dara Molloy, the unconventional ex-Catholic priest who runs a community on the Aran islands is another example. He defines himself as a fundamentally marginal person: 'I do not identify myself as someone who lives with the marginalised, or even as someone who works with the marginalised even though that is true also. My identity lies in being on the margins myself.'[16] Even more mainstream activists feel they are naturally 'frontier persons',[17] however influential they may be. Thus Peter McVerry, living with homeless young people as part of his Jesuit apostolate, acknowledges that the experience changed him: 'I had discovered goodness in those whom others thought evil', he recalls, 'and I was discovering evil in those who considered themselves good. My conventional values were questioned, sometimes rejected and newer, less conventional values replaced them.' He is also prepared to accept marginalisation in the name of God: 'He may ask me […] to become marginalised myself through the opposition and attitudes of those who are offended or upset at the stands I take, and thereby begin to share in some small way the state of marginalisation of those whose dignity I am defending.'[18]

14. St Patrick' Missionaries' web page, What is a missionary? (http://www.spms.org/stpatricksmissionarysociety/Main/WhereWeWork.htm).
15. Joe Lucey, 'The Time of the Clown', in *Spiritual Journeys*, p 165.
16. Dara Molloy, 'Hospitality on the Margins', in *Spiritual Journeys*, p 29
17. St Patrick's Missionaries' web page.
18. Peter McVerry, 'A Personal Journey', in *Spiritual Journeys*, pp 75, 83.

Living with those on the edge induces a leap into the unknown that goes far beyond a merely charitable commitment to
help the poor from above. It implies a transfiguration, of which
the social and geographical marginalisation is only the starting
point. It is true, in the words of Joe Lucey, that you become 'an
untouchable'[19] and the 'immersion' principle ensures that you
are required to dwell in initially unfamiliar territories far removed from centres of authority. But this also places you in a
privileged position to examine the mainstream worldview with
an acutely critical eye and to imagine a different future. Joe
Lucey thus understands the frontier as being 'a land of possibility',
'a place of blessing' and 'a threshold of hope.' He goes on to
state:

> When I move away from the centre and dare to live at the
> edge, I find myself living at a place where the system is not
> neat and tidy any more, but it is crumbling and even becom-
> ing meaningless. When I live at the edge, the chaos of the out-
> side begins to have as large an effect on me as the security of
> the centre. When I face the fears of the frontier world, when I
> realise that the story by which I have lived my life is not the
> only story, when I glance beneath the system and see how
> wobbly the foundations are, when I count the cracks that are
> appearing, when I dare to imagine that the centre may not
> hold, then perhaps the universe can begin again. On this
> frontier, everything is always in the throes of birth. It is the
> kingdom of midwifery and nurseries. Yesterday's alterna-
> tives have crumbled. Only the new remain.[20]

The new prophets are consequently somewhat critical of the
establishment in general and of the institutional Church in particular. They blame the authority crisis which the Church of
Rome is currently undergoing in relation to its own practices.
They denounce its excessive authoritarianism, its institutionali-
sation and its harmful clericalism. Donal Dorr reminds his readers that Jesus himself 'was particularly uncompromising in his
challenge to religious forms of domination, authoritarianism,

---

19. 'The Time of the Clown', in *Spiritual Journeys*, p 172.
20. *Ibid*.

and legalism.'[21] Sr Bernadette Flanagan, who studied the spirituality of the Liberties in order to suggest pastoral responses to present problems, echoes the hostility of the people to the Church's authoritarian attitudes. She quotes one of her interviewees as saying: 'I think people want God but they don't want a God that's kind of shoved down their throats.'[22] Denis Jeffrey argues that the rejection of any form of dogmatism, which is a central characteristic of the postmodern age, has effects on the perception of revealed truth as defended by the Church, which seems to stand in sharp opposition to the present ideal of the freedom of thought.[23] The notion that the Church may be the repository of absolute truth is thus denied, sometimes in vigorous terms. Stanislaus Kennedy makes the point very clearly:

> For years, centuries, religious institutions believed they had all the truth and all the answers. But the spiritual way is the way of the pilgrim and the way of the pilgrim is the way of continuous renewal, a way where there is no destination, only journeying, no answers, only questing.
>
> Arrogance dies slowly, but the way of the pilgrim is the way of humility, acknowledging that we have been and can be wrong. We can *think* that we are holy, we can *think* that we have the truth. We can *think* that we are different. We can *think* that we can judge others. But if we do, then we are unconsciously Pharisees.[24]

Many commentators note that the Church has made mistakes, misinterpreting the scripture in the name of Church tradition. The historical dimension of Church choices is exposed and confronted by the message of Christ. Particular criticism is addressed to the dualism which has led to the rejection of the body, and hence the denial of man's humanity, an unexpected

---

21. Donal Dorr, *Time for a Change* (Dublin: The Columba Press, 2004), p 16.
22. Bernadette Flanagan, *The Spirit of the City – Voices From the Liberties* (Dublin : Veritas, 1999), p 106.
23. Denis Jeffrey, *Jouissance du sacré – religion et postmodernité* (Paris: Armand Colin, 1998), p 47.
24. Stanislaus Kennedy, *Gardening the Soul – Soothing Seasonal Thoughts for Jaded Modern Souls* (Dublin: Town House, 2001), 8 November.

option in the perspective of the human nature of Jesus Christ. The disastrous effects of the rejection of, and unhealthy attitudes to, sexuality are analysed at great length. Donal Dorr thinks that 'one of the most urgent challenges facing spiritually sensitive people today is the development of a spirituality which values and respects human sexuality.'[25] To him, it is necessary to overcome dualism, to take account of gender differences and respect difference in sexual orientations. The attempt to cover up clerical child sexual abuse and the sexual abuse of nuns by churchmen has also been repeatedly denounced, for instance by Seán Fagan, whom Angela Hanley sees as a 'pastor to the alienated'.[26]

Besides, the most vociferous voices are deliberately silenced by the institution. Fr Fagan was thus reprimanded by the Irish Episcopal Conference in 2004, following a long investigation of his book *Does Morality Change?* by the Congregation for the Doctrine of the Faith. Angela Hanley and David Smith comment that 'this reprimand is a stain [...] on a church leadership who would seem to disdain the prophetic voices that seek to keep the church continually renewed so that it can speak the eternal truth of God's love to every new generation in a language it understands.'[27] A further problem is indeed what appears to reformers to be the incapacity of the Church – in fact its refusal – to adapt to a changing world. The official Church is seen as 'out of touch with reality',[28] because it has failed to acknowledge that 'truth is open and evolving'.[29]

The stress laid on obedience and the culture of silence protected the Church for as long as the legitimacy of its power remained unquestioned. Voices are now raised to say that this authority is in no way justified by the Gospel. Tony Flannery provocatively wonders if Christ ever founded a Church[30] and

---

25. *Time for a Change*, pp 44-45.
26. Angela Hanley, 'Seán Fagan – Pastor to the Alienated', in *Quench not the Spirit – Theology and Prophecy for the Church in the Modern World*, edited by Angela Hanley and David Smith (Dublin: The Columba Press, 2005).
27. Introduction to *Quench not the Spirit*, p 7.
28. Angela Hanley, 'Seán Fagan – Pastor to the Alienated', in *Quench not the Spirit*, p 23.
29. Bernadette Flanagan, *The Spirit of the City*, p 29.
30. Tony Flannery, *Keeping the Faith* (Cork: Mercier Press, 2005), pp 34-36.

Seán Fagan notes in his essay, 'Spiritual Abuse', that 'what many of the faithful experience on the part of church leaders is primarily a concern with power and control, with little reference to the gospel.'[31] Many elements that are central to Church teaching, including clerical celibacy and the ban on the ordination of women, have no firm grounding in scripture. Patrick Treacy goes as far as to suggest that 'the institutions of Christianity have declined greatly by placing a false God, namely the clerical power of these institutions, before the honouring of the movement of the Spirit.'[32] The meaning of the concept of Church itself has evolved. It now refers increasingly to the institution rather than to the People of God. As a consequence, the people have progressively been alienated from their Church, associated as it was with the denial of human experience, empty rituals and constraints, as well as with a certain element of fear. The new prophets denounce the official Church's inability to confront realities and urge its leaders to pick up the challenge of Vatican II's *Gaudium et Spes* 'to listen to the signs of the time'.

Frédéric Lenoir convincingly argues that the development of individualism and humanism have resulted in a dramatic evolution of people's attitudes towards structures of authority. Today, men and women can no longer be content with being passive witnesses. They need to question traditions and truths imposed from above. Ready-made answers have become unacceptable. Physical and psychological well-being has become a cause for concern and the world values emotions and imagination more and more. Rationality is consequently denounced as flawed or mistaken. Any analysis of contemporary religious phenomena, Lenoir says, must take into account this all-pervading context.[33] To 'Sr Stan', 'the prophetic people of our time' are precisely those 'who are calling us forth from the delusion of the rational world of the twentieth century'. They are those who 'are

---

31. Seán Fagan, 'Spiritual Abuse', in *Quench not the Spirit*, p 80.
32. Patrick Treacy, 'That all may be One', in *Credo – Faith and Philosophy in Contemporary Ireland*, edited by Stephen J. Costello (Dublin: The Liffey Press, 2003), p 167.
33. Frédéric Lenoir, *Les métamorphoses de Dieu – la nouvelle spiritualité occidentale* (Paris: Plon, 2003), pp 55-56.

about building up anew the broken humanity of the world'[34] be-cause, like artists, they are endowed with the gift of 'moral imagination.'[35]

By progressively drifting away from the recommendations of the Second Vatican Council, the official Church has become estranged from the People of God. John Waters once comment-ed that 'the Irish people did not so much stop believing in God as they came to believe God no longer believed in them'. This, to him, is the cause of the 'yawning chasm in the national soul' which may only be filled if God's faith in humanity is restored.[36] Beyond the mere collapse of the Church as a fully credible and trustworthy institution, the central relationship which seems to have been severed is indeed the one entered into with God. According to Patrick Treacy, 'we have lost the sense of the centre, where we can find the One who inspires us, cares for us and pro-tects us from being scattered. [...] We are not in touch with the centre which holds our lives together and which gives every-thing a sense of reference, meaning and purpose.'[37]

Religion should be the answer. For Hugh Cummins, it is in-deed 'a kind of binding that is also bound to its own unravel-ling', as is the earth that shall 'grow old like a robe' (Is 24: 18-20). Religion is therefore wound and bandage, existing on the edge of things, in a borderline region between the speakable and the unspeakable.'[38] It is time Christianity was reinvented from its own margins and from the margins of society to place Jesus Christ and his message of love once more at the centre. Recollecting her life dedication to the poor, Stanislaus Kennedy summarises her reaction and that of Bishop Birch in the follow-ing words:

> Bringing the periphery into the centre, creating services, ac-tivities, communities, touching the hearts of the rich and the poor alike, consoling the poor and disquieting the rich with

---

34. Stanislaus Kennedy, *Now is the Time*, pp 140-141.
35. Stanislaus Kennedy, *Gardening the Soul*, 27 October.
36. John Waters, *An Intelligent Person's Guide to Modern Ireland* (London: Duckworth, (1997) 1998), p 160.
37. Patrick Treacy, 'That All May be One', in *Credo*, pp 159-160.
38. Hugh Cummins, 'Beyond Belief and Unbelief : The God Question in a Time of Homelessness', in *Credo*, p 45.

the good news of the gospel, we set out to build a new model of church, vibrant, exciting, always changing, renewing, seeking, listening, searching, reading, waiting, speaking, campaigning, never satisfied.[39]

All people on the edge, whether religious or lay, whether activists or the marginalised, may be prophets in their own way. Tim Kearney, who works with the mentally handicapped, presents Danny, one of the inmates of l'Arche house in Cork, as a 'deeply spiritual person' who 'can be quite prophetic in what he says or does' even though 'he would not describe himself as a religious person'.[40] Many such examples could be quoted. They show that those who choose the option for the poor seek to walk in the footsteps of Christ. Jesus himself was indeed a prophet, he was homeless and marginalised; he was a friend to the lowly, the humiliated and the outcasts. Besides, the Good News he brought was that the Law was meant to protect the poor and that the weakest would be honoured in his Father's kingdom. Peter McVerry's idea of God is thus 'on the side of those who are unwanted, uncared for, despised, rejected and marginalised'. Consequently, he wants to devote his whole life to 'affirming the dignity of those on the margins', because as a good parent God has 'a special care or concern for those who are suffering or in need'.[41]

It could be argued that the way Peter McVerry understands his mission corresponds exactly to the present social teaching of Rome as expressed for instance in *Iustitia et Pax*, a document defining the Church's policy on homelessness, which was released by the Pontifical Commission in 1987.[42] In this document, homelessness is presented as 'a distressing sign of the time', which it is the mission of the Church to address. Quoting *Gaudium et spes*, it reminds the reader of the age-old teaching of the Catholic Church on the necessity to share goods fairly

39. Stanislaus Kennedy, 'Moments of Grace', in *Spiritual Journeys*, p 87.
40. Tim Kearney, 'The Saint and the song of Sixpence', in *Spiritual Journeys*, p 117.
41. Peter McVerry, 'A Personal Journey', in *Spiritual Journeys*, pp 83, 84, 82.
42. It is interesting to note that the Irish Episcopal Conference had produced a similar document as early as 1977.

'under the guidance of justice tempered by charity'. 'In each person or family lacking a basic good, and above all housing, the Christian must recognise Christ himself'; the text goes on to state: 'the Church, at the example of Jesus Christ, watches like a mother over her children and never tires of defending their individual and social rights.' Protecting human dignity and 'helping to make society more human' by supporting housing programmes, for example, are seen as part of the Church's mission. The official Church thus encourages the initiatives of local churches and organisations which provide shelter to the homeless, contribute to education and community development and engage in dialogue with authorities to promote legislation in favour of the poor.[43] Peter McVerry actually includes an element of discipline in his commitment. Contrary to Sr Stan, who joined the Sisters of Charity because she wanted to work with the poor, he only got involved at the age of thirty when the Jesuits developed a new approach to their mission, focused on the promotion of social justice. He also writes that he will devote the rest of his life to his work with young people in whatever way his 'life, health, energy *and provincial* allow'.[44] Individual itineraries are extremely varied and there is scope within the Church for a healthy plurality of opinions and approaches.

However, the question of the option for the poor is an excellent illustration of Church ambiguities. The very first encyclical on the social teaching of the Church, Leo XIII's *Rerum Novarum* (*On Capital and Labour*), issued in 1891, already pointed to some deficiencies in the commitment to the needy by the Church. All things considered, the recommendations of that time were strikingly similar to those of 1987 with regard to the alleviation of poverty, but the document warned Catholics against the revolutionary potential of social engagement. Its introduction summarised the nature of the problem as follows:

It is no easy matter to define the relative rights and mutual duties of the rich and of the poor, of capital and labour. And

---

43. Pontifical Commission, *Iustitia et Pax* (http://www.ewtn.com/library/CURIA/PCJPHOUS.HTM).
44. Peter McVerry, 'A Personal Journey', in *Spiritual Journeys*, pp 73, 84. My emphasis.

the danger lies in this, that crafty agitators are intent on making use of these differences of opinion to pervert men's judgement and to stir up the people to revolt.[45]

Socialism was therefore the primary target of the encyclical: the notion of class struggle was denounced as proceeding from a mistaken analysis of the situation and the remedies proposed by activists were rejected as being 'manifestly against justice'.[46] The same fear of social disruption was expressed decades later when it became clear that the liberation theology developed in South America somehow sought to reconcile Catholicism and socialism. Rome supported the defence of the poor but repeatedly condemned the political dimension of that theory. Both John Paul II and Benedict XVI are known to have expressed such extremely serious reservations that ensured the marginalisation of that approach, which has remained somewhat peripheral in geographical terms.

The new Irish prophets do not speak with one voice: rather, they echo the extreme polarisation of views in this area. There are obviously different ways of being on the margins, from outright eccentricity to what could be termed mainstream marginality. Account must be taken of this wide spectrum of approaches to assess the movement. The message of liberation theology has clearly influenced most of those under discussion, but to varying degrees. One can hear its echoes when Stanislaus Kennedy proclaims her anger at injustice in the following terms: 'This anger gives us the courage to speak and act for truth and justice, to turn the system upside down and to work for a different type of society, where all people can live in peace and justice.'[47] Donal Dorr for his part openly praises liberation theology which, he says, cast 'a whole new light on Christian spirituality – an active involvement in struggle on behalf of those who are victims of injustice'. 'This notion of spirituality of struggles', he claims, 'is something new; it contrasts sharply with the type of spirituality which most of us were brought up with.'[48] To him, it is an agent

45. Pope Leo XIII, *Rerum Novarum* (*On Capital and Labour*) (http://www.ewtn.com/library/ENCYCL/L13RERUM.HTM), par 1.
46. *Ibid*, p 2.
47. Stanislaus Kennedy, *Gardening the Soul*, 25 March.
48. Donal Dorr, *Time for a Change*, pp 40-41.

of change which will lead to the hoped-for rejuvenation of Christianity. Other statements are far less explicit and give the feeling that action is carried out within the framework of the inherited social teaching based on compassion and charity that is promoted by the official Church.

It can be argued, however, that all forms of poor-centred Christianity are an appropriate vehicle for transformation, if only because of their innate marginal position and critical dimension. Voices raised from these quarters are almost unanimous in their call for a renovation based on the fulfilment of a series of needs that are clearly identified. The need for a questioning Church, a 'listening Church', 'a Church of the grassroots' and a 'declericalised Church'[49] stands at the top of the list of priorities. An inclusive Church that rejects nobody is also desirable. The need to acknowledge the present and to reconcile human experience and Christian faith is no less important. Also mentioned is the need for society to recover a sense of community and to combine economic success with justice and spirituality. To these can be added the need to revise institutions, question beliefs, rethink obedience, re-evaluate the place of lay men and women in the Church. If the institutional Church were to lead the movement, it should enthusiastically seek to fulfil its prophetic mission, by placing spirituality at the centre of its preoccupations and recovering its 'secular voice'.[50] It should also be open to non-Christian experiences to confront ideas in an ecumenical spirit. All these needs are addressed by the experiments and proposals of those on the margins who are seeking to restore to Christendom what they hold to be true Christianity. They are prompted by this hope which is the central core of the Christian message. Indeed, as Karl Rahner once put it: 'Christianity is the proclamation of the absolute hope in the absolute future that is God himself.'[51] To Mary Redmond, there is

49. It was already identified by Karl Rahner in *The Shape of the Church to Come* (1967) in the follow up to Vatican II. Quoted by Cathy Molloy, 'A Search and Some Findings', in *Credo*, p 132.
50. *Ibid*, p 71.
51. Quoted by Michael McCabe, 'The Mystery of the Human: a Perspective from Rahner', in *Christian Identity in a Postmodern Age*, edited by Declan Marmion (Dublin: Veritas, 2005), p 57.

ground for hope today because 'soul' (understood as 'moral or emotional or intellectual life, spirituality') 'is alive and feeling in the voluntary and community sector.'[52] In the words of Sr Stan, such indeed is 'the work of the prophet – living in hope.'[53] 'People of hope', she adds, 'feel with the rejected ones of society'[54] since, according to Donal Dorr, they harbour 'the belief that new life can come through suffering and death'.[55]

This new life is certainly not any form of eternal life after death. To him, too much stress has in the past been laid by the Church on 'the other-worldly dimension of Christianity'.[56] New life will spring from the valuation of, and care for, people's everyday life in the here and there, here and now. It may be argued that the single most important characteristic of the movement in favour of the marginalised is its extraordinary vitalism. Worldly values are at the core of the new spirituality which is surging from the margins and which is resolutely man-centred. This is justified by the human nature of Christ and an understanding of his mission which places life at the centre of his message. Donal Dorr suggests that Jesus called himself 'the human one' and not 'the son of man', which he thinks is an inaccurate translation of the original. This in turn implies that not only was Christ a human being in the fullest sense of the term, but that 'his main concern was to help people live a fully human life'.[57] The anthropocentrism of the postmodern age has resulted in an overall celebration of life in all its aspects, especially in its emotional dimension. The French sociologist Michel Maffesoli thus explains that the Judeo-Christian legacy became outmoded because it imposed constraints like modesty and asceticism, preached patience and resignation and therefore neglected and even despised the throbbing heart of life.[58]

52. Mary Redmond, 'Social Entepreneurship – A New Authority?', in *Are we Forgetting Something?*, edited by Harry Bohan and Gerard Kennedy (Dublin: Veritas, 1999), p 152.
53. Stanislaus Kennedy, *Gardening the Soul*, 22 March.
54. *Ibid*, 25 March.
55. Donal Dorr, *Time for a Change*, p 41.
56. *Ibid*, p 186.
57. *Ibid*, p 14.
58. Michel Maffesoli, *Le rythme de la vie – Variations sur les sensibilités postmodernes* (Paris: La Table Ronde, 2004), p 45.

Today, not only is it legitimate to enjoy down-to-earth life and seek happiness, but it is meaningful from a spiritual point of view. Far from only focusing on an intellectual disembodied personal relationship to God, spirituality is now commonly interpreted as a quest for life through which God can be found in the innermost humanity of man or in nature. Such is clearly the postulate of the defenders of people on the edge in the Western world, whose actions seek to address immediate problems of everyday life. To them, spirituality is primarily life-affirming and it implies being 'in touch with the reality around us'.[59] The Franciscans who launched the Merchants Quay initiative as part of their action for social justice explained it thus:

> In Judaism, Christianity and several other traditions, spirit refers to the force, the basic energy of being. [...] Traditionally, this life force is seen in the passions and inspirations that draw us one way or another, connect us with the world and each other, prompt our choices, and empower our creativity and steadfastness. Spirituality is the wellspring of our sense of meaning and our will to live.

In the same way, spiritual life is 'a deep current, often unseen but always flowing through all our experience, moving us to seek connectedness and fulfilment, impelling us toward truth, goodness and beauty.'[60] The notions of 'connectedness' and 'interconnectedness' provide a key to understanding contemporary spirituality as expressed by the defenders of those on the margins. To start with, it affirms the primacy of the collective dimension of life and therefore interestingly combines individualism and community action.

The importance of relational experience, the need to recover a sense of hospitality and friendship, are stressed by all those involved in action in this area. Frédéric Lenoir suggests that the fragmentation of religious thinking which the distrust for institutions and individualism have engendered is limited by the hunger to belong. As a result, the quest for meaning often in-

---

59. Merchants Quay Ireland's webpage (http://www.mqi.ie/AU_Main.htm).
60. 'The challenge of Franciscan Spirituality' (http://www.mqi.ie/S_Main.htm).

volves a quest for social connectedness.[61] Community experiments are the most visible forms of this phenomenon. Religious and lay people placing the poor at the centre of their understanding of Christianity are generally committed to community experience based on the shared loved of Christ. Homes and shelters of various kinds have been created on that basis. Many welcome homeless people into their flats or houses for as long as they wish to stay and thus form new communities. Small structures of this type, often included in larger networks, have multiplied. Their inspiration is both archaic and new: indeed, they are reminders of the early Christian communities who progressively came together to form the original Church. Yet they are also clearly the product of our individualistic age: aware of their right to pursue their spiritual quest according to their own principles, these communities insist on the respect of individuals, which appears to be more important than conformity to a set of beliefs and rituals.

In his classic study of postmodernity[62] Jean-François Lyotard noted that our contemporaries favoured individual tales and disparaged mega-narratives. The new communities exemplify this analysis on the one hand by re-reading the Gospel in the light of individual experience, and on the other by calling their members to tell their own life-stories[63] in order to bear witness to the love of Jesus. Ours is an age of witnesses and the new communities share their own truth, based on shared suffering. The result is what Danièle Hervieu-Léger describes as an inversion of the traditional from-the-top-down Catholic pattern of authority. In modern democratic societies, she adds, legitimate power comes from the grassroots.[64] Irish examples of such an approach are numerous. Bernadette Flanagan thus seeks to apply 'a hermeneutic born of the experience of poverty to scrip-

61. Frédéric Lenoir, *Les métamorphoses de Dieu*, pp 104-105.

62. Jean-François Lyotard, *La condition postmoderne* (Paris: Editions de Minuit, 1979).

63. See for instance the Welcome Home Newsletter (Peter Mc Verry Trust) and its 'residents' testimonies' (http://www.pmvtrust.ie), which is but one example of what seems to be a common feature of all organisations working with the marginalised.

64. Danièle Hervieu-Léger, *Catholicisme, la fin d'un monde* (Paris: Bayard, 2003), p 90.

ture'[65] and the activists of the Society of St Vincent de Paul in Ireland base their social justice policy on their 'From the Ground Up' programme.[66] As for L'Arche Ireland communities of faith, they claim 'they are guided by God and their weakest members' in whom they find God.[67]

The respect of individual spiritual itineraries is emphasised by the recognition of our need for an individualised experience of the divine. Regeneration through communion with the Spirit is the way to an authentic spiritual experience. Personal commitment to God means going beyond conventional rituals and establishing an intimate link with the divine. The importance of a quest for a spiritual experience of that type is stressed by most prophetic voices in Ireland and in the remainder of the Western world. Prayer is especially valued as a means to that end and the frequent references to such medieval mystics as Meister Eckhart or Hildegard von Bingen further emphasise the contemplative dimension of action in favour of the needy. The interesting openness to Eastern practices expressed by some (Stanislaus Kennedy, for instance) can also be understood in that context. As Donal Dorr's references to John Main indicate, Buddhist and Hindu spiritualities may be a healthy source of inspiration since meditation and prayer go hand in hand.[68] The influence of Eastern philosophies, however, has more wide-ranging consequences, if only because it confirms rather than contradicts the striking connection between contemporary inner spirituality and the commitment to community experience.

Michel Maffesoli argues that the stress on communion – if not fusion – with others may actually in part be seen as a direct effect of the 'orientalisation' of contemporary Western culture.[69] The identity formation process which is central to the contemporary re-invention of religion involves what Maffesoli calls 'ecstasy', or coming out of oneself to fuse with the other. This implies that the individual both dissolves and finds himself in the group as a

---

65. Bernadette Flanagan, *The Spirit of the City*, p 122.
66. http://www.svp.ie.
67. http://www.larche.ie/charter.html.
68. Donal Dorr, *Time for a Change*, pp 68, 226.
69. Michel Maffesoli, *L'instant éternel*, p 203.

result of a process of identification with others.[70] Both the marginalised and the people who care for them find their true identity as a result of mutual recognition. Identifying with the group gives a status to those who had none and allows people who place them at the centre of their lives to find themselves as they 'are challenged to look at the masks' they themselves 'are hiding behind'.[71]

The re-invention of spirituality from the margins confirms the religious potential of social connectedness. The binding function of religion is thus emphasised. It is further developed by the many who consider that religion must also restore the weakened connection between men and God's creation as a whole. To them, the notion of interconnectedness implies that human beings are linked to all living things on the planet. Those who seek to reinvent Catholicism from the margins are often highly sensitive to ecological preoccupations. They see justice for men and the care of nature as one and the same thing since God is present in his humblest children as well as in his creation. Both must then be placed at the centre of today's spiritual quest. To the Roman Catholic Columban priest and missionary Seán McDonagh, the author in 1986 of *To Care for the Earth*, Jesus' life and ministry had 'a cosmic dimension': Christ was 'the centre of creation' and 'he entered into every dimension of earthly reality.'[72] Writing in the early 1960s, Mircea Eliade already underlined the cosmic dimension of the Christian liturgy as traditionally understood by the country people of Europe. Popular forms of Christian piety generally insisted on the connection between the mystery of Christ and the fate of the cosmos, the rebirth of nature and resurrection. Eliade, however, reminded his readers that 'the mystical solidarity with cosmic rhythms was violently denounced by the prophets of the Old Testament and hardly tolerated by the church, but remained at the heart of religious life in the countryside.'[73]

---

70. *Ibid*, p 67.
71. Stanislaus Kennedy, *Gardening the Soul*, 23 October.
72. Seán McDonagh SSC, 'Ecology and religion – a Green Christology' (http://www.sedos.org/english/mcdonagh_1.html).
73. Mircea Eliade, *Aspects du mythe* (Paris: Gallimard, 1963), p 211. My translation.

In the same way, the works of Seán McDonagh and other eco-theologians have not been warmly received by the official Church, but have found a significant echo among the people who work with the marginalised. Some actually openly defend popular piety and contribute to its re-invention. One peculiar example is that of Dara Molloy and the 'Celtic pilgrimages' he organises on Inismór. These illustrate the fact that a sense of an immanent God omnipresent in his creation is being recovered, which comes as a natural consequence of understanding ecological concerns in religious terms. Less eccentric activists also feel anxious about the planet and note a parallel between their action in favour of the poor and respect for the earth. For Sr Stan, 'we are interconnected not only with each other, but with the trees and the whales and the wolves and the flowers and with all living things that share the same space we do.' As a consequence, 'now is the time to revere the earth as our mother and the sky as our father. (…) Our challenge is to view the earth not as humanity's warehouse or playground but as God's creation.'[74] She also draws a parallel between 'gardening the soul' and being alert to nature's cycles through the seasons.[75] In his seminal analysis of what he terms contemporary tribalism, Michel Maffesoli notes that those who feel for nature suggest an alternative model that both signals the decline of a certain type of society and 'calls for an irresistible rebirth.'[76] Commenting on the will to survive at any cost, he further underlines that popular forms of religious piety can be understood as an expression of the need to belong,[77] which aptly symbolises the need for warmth and love that is the essence of life itself. As such they contribute to the restoration of a sense of community in the dehumanised late modern age. This only confirms the link between the care for the marginalised and the care for the earth as it is expressed by today's prophets.

In Ireland, it is best exemplified by the frequent connection between the option for the poor and the desire to revive the

74. Stanislaus Kennedy, *Now is the Time*, pp 21, 44-45.
75. See her *Gardening the Soul – Soothing Seasonal Thoughts for Jaded Modern Souls*.
76. Michel Maffesoli, *Le temps des tribus – le déclin de l'individualisme dans les sociétés postmodernes* (Paris: La Table Ronde, 1988).
77. *Ibid*, pp 109-110.

Celtic heritage of Irish Catholicism. It is interesting in several respects. To start with, early Irish saints and hermits are known to have had an intimate relationship to nature and they are just as natural reference points to proponents of creation-centred theology as Meister Eckhart and other medieval mystics. Praising the Celtic legacy is meaningful for other reasons, however. First of all, it implies the re-invention of a connection between the Catholic religion and the Irish territory that is different from the late nineteenth and twentieth century link between the Irish nation and the official Catholic Church. It can be argued that this corresponds to an aspect of what Michel Maffesoli identifies as the contemporary quest for an 'invagination of meaning'.[78] The new communities seeking new roots in the mother earth imagine new founding myths for themselves, and in so doing go back to origins. The social coherence they experience on an everyday basis is paradoxically justified and supported by long-standing traditions. The interpretation of the central notion of hospitality as a Celtic legacy, for instance, is significant in that respect. In his article 'The Celtic Church and the lessons for the future',[79] John Scally insists on the aspects of early medieval spirituality that to him are relevant to the contemporary situation: he thus stresses the link between aspects of spirituality we have noted before are emphasised by reformers, that is hospitality, generosity, the commitment to vulnerable people, the respect for all human beings including women, the belief in the holiness of nature, the value of scripture, creativity and imagination. What is new and what is traditional in that perspective is often difficult to distinguish. The new and the old seem to combine to create a feeling that some form of eternal truth – albeit different from Rome's – is at play. The re-birth from the margins is both creative and deeply attached to traditions or at least to the contemporary representation of traditions, Celtic or otherwise. Franciscans and the Society of Saint Vincent de Paul thus both insist that they are walking in the steps of their respective founders.

The intimate connection between past and present is in no way surprising. According to Stanislaus Kennedy: 'We are inter-

---

78. Michel Maffesoli, *Le rythme de la vie*, p 40.
79. John Scally, 'The Celtic Church and Lessons for the Future', in *Quench not the Spirit*, pp 164-176.

connected not only here and now, in this time and in this space, but with everything in the past and in the future and into that unknown dimension we call eternity'.[80] In such a perception, eternity is somehow subsumed in the present instant, which Michel Maffesoli describes as 'the eternal instant'. Presentism is a characteristic of our age. When understood in religious terms, it implies that the sacred is to be found in a sort of 'immanent transcendence' expressing itself in communion with others in a place the community calls home at the present moment, in its everyday life.[81] For Stanislaus Kennedy, life is thus but a circle: 'We live now, and now will soon be the past and the future now. All we have is a brief now and in now we are alone and yet we are not alone; we are accompanied in this circle, in this journey through life, by all life.'[82] If we accept the connection suggested by Hugh Cummins between religion and home, we may argue that, according to the new prophets, the official Church has become 'increasingly 'unhomely'[83] and that it no longer provides a fully acceptable identity for those on the edge. Through their actions, those who work with the marginalised seek to re-invent the Church of a true God of love which provides an access to a glimpse of eternity at the same time as an identity and a home. Providing a home is a *leitmotiv* of all those who seek to bring the Church of Christ back from the margins. Home is always the community, but it can also often be ancient Ireland and the planet earth. Through living their lives in these homes, the weakest members of our society and those who place them at the centre of their mission are given a chance to find God. They are also a model for an alternative Church that may in the future breathe new life into Catholicism.

80. Stanislaus Kennedy, *Now is the Time*, p 21.
81. Michel Maffesoli, *L'instant éternel*, p 67.
82. Stanislaus Kennedy, *Gardening the Soul*, 28 December.
83. Hugh Cummins, 'Beyond Belief and Unbelief: the God Question in a Time of Unbelief', in *Credo*, p 43.

Reporting Religion

Colum Kenny

What is the proper business of a journalist involved in writing or making programmes about religion? The question has a special resonance in Ireland, where journalism has played an important role in bringing to light the full extent of child abuse by priests and religious, and where some critics accuse the media of having actively fostered secular values.

There is no love lost between the Irish Catholic hierarchy, as a body, and even those journalists who most frequently write about religion in a serious way. While the hierarchy and some individual dioceses have resorted to normal institutional public relations by appointing official spokespersons to deal with media enquiries, Church leaders remain deeply suspicious of journalists and the mass media (or 'the commentariat' as Archbishop Brady dubs it).[1] A fuller understanding of the dynamics involved in reporting religion may enable the faithful of all persuasions to communicate more effectively their beliefs to a broad public, assuming that those beliefs themselves are founded in truth.

The journalist who is involved in reporting or writing about religion may work on a newsdesk or as a feature-writer, colum-

---

1. Archbishop Seán Brady, 'The Catholic Church in Ireland is experiencing the best of times and the worst of times' (Address to the 2007 Milwaukee Irish Fest at the Market Amphitheatre, University of Milwaukee, 17 August 2007, by the Primate of All Ireland). Brady said, 'The attitude to politicians, An Garda Síochána, financial institutions, the Church and other traditional sources of social and moral authority in Ireland has changed dramatically in recent years. This was a result, in part, of the multitude of investigations, many of them still ongoing, into how these institutions had managed their affairs. Nothing has yet emerged to replace the cohesion and stability that these institutions once brought. They have been partly replaced by the "authority" and influence of the "mass media" – the commentariat!'

nist, programme reporter or presenter. He or she will not always be a designated religious affairs correspondent or even be a person who considers him or herself to be religious.

Journalists need not necessarily confine their articles or reports to matters of uncontested fact, but may include their own ideas and the opinions of others. A journalist is likely to have a personal point of view on a story, perhaps expressing this only covertly (and even unconsciously) through the manner in which questions are asked or a report is structured. In any event, in every case, the moral obligation of a journalist is the same. It is to tell the truth and to be fair.

If a reporter believes that personal and social life are enriched spiritually or culturally by religious practice then, in my opinion and insofar as their work is concerned, the quality of their journalism should be sufficient to bear witness to their beliefs. However, others may feel that the best religious journalism is that which is a form of advocacy or public relations.

Modern Western journalism has grown out of an Enlightenment culture and has flourished within democratic societies. It is posited, generally, on the assumption that open and equal debate is a good thing. In practice, the paradigm of various religious organisations, including dominant Christian and Muslim groups, locates comment within a distinctly hierarchical and authoritarian structure which claims special privileges in respect of accessing or knowing such truth. Since this is so, leaders and spokespeople who struggle to hear or treat as equal the opinions of their faithful will not find it particularly easy to cope with any form of open media debate and may tend to resent it.

At the heart of the media's reporting of religion there is frequently a sort of 'clash of civilisations'. However, while it is evident that tensions exist, it is worth exploring bases of reconciliation between religious organisations and the media. One should not assume that differences of approach or perspective, such as those outlined by Cardinal Avery Dulles,[2] are set in stone. Both 'sides' may be enriched by being prepared to learn

2. Avery Dulles, 'Religion and the news media: a theologian reflects', in *America*, 171 (9), 1994, pp 6-9. Text at www.catholiceducation.org/ article/media/me0005.html (Aug 2007).

and by being open to change. Ironically, the gap between both sides has been explained in part by reference to the Churches themselves supposedly having internalised an Enlightenment view of what constitutes faith, '... so that other important expressions of faith such as everyday practices, visual and material culture are neglected'.[3]

We are concerned in this chapter primarily with just one aspect of the Church-media relationship, that relating to journalism. In my view, there are at least ten types of story about religion. The business of religious journalism, as categorised below, reflects the various functions of religious organisations. These functions are not confined to the private sphere but have a public dimension through the involvement of members of religious organisations in good works or social services, and through the intervention of religious leaders in policy debates and even politics. As the media is generally involved in reporting matters relating to the public sphere, it is not surprising to find in practice that the media's coverage of religion reflects principally those aspects of religion which are most public.

The ten divisions are:
1. Reporting the stated religious affiliation and beliefs of citizens.
2. Reporting the incidence of attendance at centres of worship.
3. Reporting the statements of religious leaders and organisations.
4. Reporting the behaviour of religious leaders.
5. Reporting disputes within and between religious organisations.
6. Reporting disputes between religious leaders or organisations and other citizens.
7. Reporting new developments in religious art, music and liturgy.
8. Reporting new thinking about theology and / or forms of religious organisation.

---

3. Peter Horsfield, 'Electronic media and the past-future of Christianity', at Jolyon Mitchell and Sophia Marriage (eds), *Mediating religion: conversations in media, religion and culture* (Edinburgh: T & T Clark, 2003), p 274.

9. Reporting spiritual experience.
10. Reporting the rejection of organised religion.

Before considering these categories further, it is worth bearing in mind that each of the ten will not interest every citizen to the same degree. This is partly due to human nature, in that a juicy scandal about a bishop is likely to generate greater curiosity that a calm consideration of the latest book by a great theologian. It is also due to the different levels of religious sensibility, education and experience that one finds even among those who are affiliated to a religious organisation.

In choosing what stories to write or publish, journalists often take into account the degree to which they believe a specific story will interest their publications' usual readers, listeners or viewers. A journalist's or editor's decision is also likely to be influenced, even unconsciously, by his/her own ideological dispositions and by social trends. These latter influences may be balanced to some extent by a process of engagement and persuasion on the part of religious organisations or individuals, which is a possibility that will be considered later. At that point, I shall discuss some of the barriers to the better reporting of religion. These include:

1. An absence of evident respect for the profession of journalism as a whole.
2. A failure to sustain dialogue with key media journalists.
3. The use of arcane or archaic forms of language by Church leaders.
4. Benign indifference by some to the very idea of communication through the media.
5. Humility on the part of some deeply religious individuals.
6. Cliché.
7. Prejudice on the part of some journalists and editors in respect to religion generally.
8. Indifference or disinterest among many citizens in respect of religious belief and practice.

There is no 'magic fix' or 'perfect fit' when it comes to reconciling the ambitions of a wide array of religious leaders and the perspectives of a variety of journalists. There will continue to be tensions between those with different outlooks, and that itself is not necessarily a bad thing. However, by considering the matter and by engaging in dialogue, all involved may learn something about their own limitations and prejudices.

Ten categories of reporting

Stories fall into various categories, some of which may be regarded by an editor as being most appropriately covered by a religious correspondent, if the media organisation employs one, and some of which will be assigned to journalists who have no great knowledge of religious matters. It does not follow from this latter eventuality that a journalist will necessarily be hostile or indifferent to religious organisations or to their members, and many will strive to be fair whatever their own opinions and whatever story they are covering.

1. Reporting the stated religious affiliation and beliefs of citizens

A census provides data on which the media can base objective stories about changes in society.[4] Are there more or fewer people describing themselves as Catholics or Jews than five years ago? What effect has immigration had on the relative number of Anglicans and Methodists? Answers to such questions lead to speculation about the cause of any change, as well as about the quality of belief of those who still declare themselves to be affiliated to a religious organisation. Such speculation will seldom be based on research data, beyond the headline information of a census itself, and so it is likely to be attacked as superficial and/or subjective by those who dislike a particular journalist's conclusions.

Apart from the official census, there may be research undertaken by academics or consultants that throws further light on religious belief. It is always relevant to ask who pays for any piece of research, as the objectives of those who fund it may influence at least the choice and framing of questions. This, in turn, can have consequences in terms of the answers that are given and may ultimately limit the value of the research.

---

4. Or, indeed, about how changes may not be as extensive as we assume. For example, see Suzanne Breen, 'After all these years, your religion still dictates where you work in the North [Northern Ireland]', in *Sunday Tribune*, 24 September 2006.

Unfortunately, journalists and other commentators are sometimes quite slow to interrogate the underlying basis of ostensibly objective research and may unintentionally mislead the public by seizing upon some startling conclusion or finding. While they may 'balance' this with a comment from a sceptic or critic, such balance does not fully discharge their ethical responsibility to check and even challenge sources.

One example of the way in which apparently objective research may be widely reported, and its methodology taken for granted, centres on the results of a survey that was undertaken into the levels of Irish people's knowledge of basic Catholic tenets and of biblical matters. The poll received extensive coverage in the Irish media. It had been conducted by Lansdowne Market Research, for the Catholic Iona Institute and the Evangelical Alliance of Ireland. On 9 April 2007, the *Irish Independent* headlined its report on this poll as follows: 'Steep decline in knowledge of Christian faith', while *The Irish Times* declared, 'Survey reveals low level of religious knowledge in young.' RTÉ ran a story on its main news bulletins, posting it to the RTÉ website under the heading, 'Ireland's Christian culture thing of past'. The *Irish Catholic* blogged the poll as, 'Shocking Survey of Irish Knowledge of Christianity.'[5]

Clearly stung by this coverage, two bishops questioned the survey's structure. At a press conference concluding the summer meeting of the Irish Bishop's Conference, at Maynooth, on 13 June 2007, Archbishop Dermot Clifford of Cashel and Emly said that he would like to see 'a critical study of the methodology' used in the survey. According to a newspaper report next day:

> He [Clifford] noted it allowed for one answer to each question, so that when it asked where Jesus was born, it accepted 'Bethlehem' but not 'a stable'. Similarly, he said those who answered 'consecration' as opposed to 'transubstantiation' when asked what occurred at the Eucharist Mass, were also discounted.
>
> Bishop [Martin] Drennan [of Galway] wondered whether those who commissioned the survey had 'an agenda against

---

5. http://www.RTÉ.ie/news/2007/0409/religion.html; http://irish-catholic.blogspot.com

the *Alive O* [religious education] programme'.

He pointed out that just 10 per cent of those surveyed would have been young enough to avail of the *Alive O* programme, introduced in 1996. Both bishops praised teachers of religious education as 'very competent' and 'extremely committed'.[6]

The bishops' defensive comments strengthened for some a perception that the Irish hierarchy is at sea in a storm of change and unable to face reality; but they also illustrate how the same data may be interrogated or interpreted in different ways. Journalists should always watch out for spin, from any quarter.[7]

2. Reporting the incidence of attendance at centres of worship

The observation of congregations can provide journalists with material for stories about religious affiliation and practice.[8] Shrinking congregations, a reduced numbers of Masses on

6. Patsy McGarry, 'Christian survey may have had agenda, say bishops', in *The Irish Times*, 14 June 2007.

7. Details of the survey, available on the institute's website (http://www.ionainstitute.ie/) show that the ninth question asked, 'Where was Jesus born', and the listed options for recording were 'Bethlehem', 'Any other answer' and 'Don't know'. The other relevant question was, 'Q.7 What name is given to the changing of the bread and wine into the body and blood of Christ at the mass?', and the listed options for recording here were 'Transubstantiation', 'Any other answer' and 'Don't know'. In each case, those conducting the survey were explicitly instructed, 'DO NOT READ OUT ANY ANSWERS'. One assumes that a person replying 'in a stable' or 'consecration' would have had their response not discounted as such but recorded as 'Any other answer'. The latter category is clearly so broad that it would be a reporting error to assume that it equates neatly to 'wrong answer', notwithstanding how significant or insignificant today are distinctions between 'consecration' and 'transubstantiation'. Incidentally, none of the four gospel writers states that Jesus was born in a stable, and his birth in a stable is not necessarily implicit in the account by Luke alone that Jesus was placed 'in a manger' after he was born (Luke 2: 7-16). For further on this see, 'Was Jesus born in a stable?', at http://www.christiananswers.net/q-abr/abr-a012. html (August 2007).

8. See, for example, 'Irish Mass attendance below 50%', at *Catholic World News* (www.cwnews.com/news/viewstory.cfm?recnum=44521 (1 June 2006), reporting an RTÉ survey; 'Mass attendance down by 27%' in *Irish Voice*, November 1995.

Sunday and the absence from pews of a proportionate number of young people compared to the population at large may be assumed to be measures of loyalty and fervour. This is especially so in the Irish Catholic Church, which traditionally insisted upon strict observance of the duty to attend Mass on Sundays and Holy Days of obligation. Based on past practice, it is evident that relatively fewer people now attend Mass than did so in former times. It may be asserted to journalists that the quality of faith or religious practice of those who still attend is high, and by implication even higher than the 'average' used to be, or that it is a mistake to make it 'a primary measure of religious fidelity',[9] but it is difficult to substantiate such assertions or to deny that the changes reflect a loss of interest in either the institution or in religion generally. Journalists are also likely to suspect that many of those older people who still attend do so out of habit or guilt or for social reasons – as much as they do out of a renewed sense of conviction.

Meanwhile, increased attendances at certain Protestant services are represented as being partly due to a switching of allegiance by some Catholics to a different Christian denomination, and churches generally have seen new faces in their pews because of the rising numbers of immigrants in Ireland. The establishment of entirely new congregations, be they in mosques or Orthodox churches, is also a source of interest and colour.[10]

3. *Reporting the statements of religious leaders and organisations*
Any analysis of media coverage of the statements of religious leaders and organisations would almost certainly find that they receive publicity in direct proportion to their perceived relevance to existing debates about politics and society. The media

9. Desmond O'Donnell, 'Faith is what really matters', in *Reality*, Jan 2003. Text at http://www.catholicireland.net/pages/index. php?nd=56&art=120 (on 10 Aug 2007).
10. See, for example, Stephen Breen, 'Ulster's Muslims to get first purpose built Mosque', in *Belfast Telegraph*, 30 Dec 2001; Helen Bruce, 'Huge growth in number of churches', in *Irish Independent*, 20 Oct 2002; Joe Humphreys, 'C[hurch] of I[reland] [Anglican] school opens in Dunboyne', in *Irish Times*, 16 Sept 2005; Cathy Grieve, 'Immigrants re-energise Irish Church', at news.bbc.co.uk/1/hi/world/europe/6639643. stm, 18 May 2007 (on 10 Aug 2007).

is comfortable with discussions about public matters, but distinctly uncomfortable with providing a platform to religious leaders for advice on how one ought to live one's private life. This is notwithstanding the fact that acres of 'lifestyle' pages and hours of broadcasting include many how-to tips on what one ought to eat or do in order to enjoy a healthy and a happy life. Clearly, if they ever had any, religious leaders have lost much of their currency in that respect. This is, to some degree, because the negative teaching of conventional religious organisations on matters such as contraception or homosexuality is now generally discounted by the population at large, and also because the dominant consumerist paradigm in respect to physical and material enjoyment is threatened by any advocacy of sacrifice or restraint, especially where this is not always matched by clear example on the part of those preaching it.

So when the Archbishop of Dublin condemns gang violence and calls for government action, he is widely reported.[11] If, with equal conviction of its great relevance, he calls on members of the public to commit themselves to daily prayer and fasting, he will receive far less attention from the media. This is partly because the media tends to report controversies, but partly because there is an underlying assumption in society about what can be most satisfactorily discussed in the public sphere. Similarly, if Muslims wish to stop and pray a certain number of times each day, that will be of no intrinsic interest to journalists: but if they wish to stop during work to do so, then journalists may soon become very interested in the reaction of employers and fellow workers to such practice.

Statements by religious leaders will generally be judged on the same basis as statements by other leaders, that is to say on their newsworthiness. Thus, because members of the Catholic hierarchy have had great power in certain areas of Irish life, their pronouncements on matters of sexual behaviour, education and health will be received eagerly by newsrooms that

---

11. For, example, 'Archbishop Martin condemns gangland violence' (RTÉ: www.RTÉ.ie/news/2007/0407/martind.html), 7 April 2007; Stephen Collins, 'Archbishop calls for action on crime as three die' in *The Irish Times*, 16 July 2007; John Cooney, 'Archbishop calls for summit on rise in violence', in *Irish Independent*, 18 July 2007.

regard these as political interventions: their pronouncements on consumerism or on war will be seen as less relevant because Irish bishops have wielded less power in such areas in the past (and also, perhaps, because their criticism of consumerism would not be popular with advertisers or readers).

The employment of press officers or of slick public relations companies makes little difference to how statements of religious leaders are received, except insofar as they elucidate the relevance of such statements to existing paradigms. Efforts to forge new paradigms are likely to be fairly fruitless. For one thing, 'The Goods News', alas, is not news by the standards of most newsrooms which are more interested in what *has* just happened than what *might* happen or is asserted. For another, journalists worth their salt will avoid being vehicles for spin and will see it as no business of theirs to facilitate public relations.

4. Reporting the behaviour of religious leaders

As in the case of the first three categories, many of these stories have little intrinsic spiritual content but principally address the social, cultural or political dimensions of religious affiliation or practice.[12]

Churches may actively encourage such reports precisely because they believe that members of the public are more likely to read or watch them than read articles or watch programmes about religious practices and experience. Such reports bear witness to the best values of religions being put into practice and, thereby, fulfil a sort of evangelisation function. They may be regarded as especially useful if Church leaders fear that people believe their religious organisations to be out of touch or out of date. It was partly for this reason, and partly because social activism was seen by some within the Catholic Church as a priority, that the *Radharc* series came to be made for Ireland's State-owned broadcaster by a special unit headed by priests. Its high production values and clear editorial judgements long made it

---

12. For example, Seán McCárthaigh, 'Church lends a hand to flood victims', in *Irish Examiner*, 8 February 2002; C. Kenny, 'Churches should beware of state', in *The Irish Catholic*, 20 April 2006, and 'When Bertie meets our various gods', in *Sunday Independent*, 19 November 2006 (both on the plan for structured State-Church dialogue).

popular with RTÉ audiences, while a more pious or preachy type of programme would have had less impact.[13] Yet, there is a danger that, in concentrating on their social activities, Churches will neglect the need for effective communication about the very fundamentals of religious belief and practice.

Secular journalists reporting stories of social activism quite often unintentionally reinforce stereotypes because of their conventional view of what constitutes religion in general and various religious traditions in particular, which are seen as fixed entities rather than evolving organisations or dynamic ways of life. However, in that respect, the journalists are representative of a community at large that was never greatly encouraged to reflect theologically or to treat organised religion as anything other than a fixed or given reality.

5. Reporting disputes within and between religious organisations
6. Reporting disputes between religious leaders or organisations and other citizens
Controversies provide subeditors with an opportunity to grab attention, but also reflect real divisions within churches or between churches and society. Thus, a headline that reads 'Founder of controversial religion to be canonised' undoubtedly elevates Opus Dei to a status that it has never claimed, namely that of being a religion in its own right, but the underlying story by a former RTÉ religious affairs correspondent (Kieron Wood) touches on tensions surrounding the actual status of that organis-

---

13. The Irish word 'Radharc' may be translated into English as 'sight', 'view' or 'vision'. For the Radharc archive see http://www.radharc-films.com/index.html. Also Joseph Dunn, *No Tigers in Africa: Recollections and Reflections on 25 years of Radharc* (Dublin: The Columba Press, 1986) gives an account by the priest most centrally involved. The conservative Archbishop of Dublin, John Charles McQuaid, supported the establishment of the Radharc team, and Catholic priests have continued to play a prominent role in determining the nature of RTÉ's religious programming. This institutional recognition of the significance of the electronic media may be seen, in the absence of dynamic forms of communication and dialogue between the faithful or between bishops and the public at large, to be intended as an expression of the evangelisation function of the Church.

ation within the Catholic Church.[14] And John Cooney deals with another divisive matter when he reports an intemperate attack by Senator David Norris on Benedict XVI, 'Pope's stance on gays "like Hitler".'[15] Notwithstanding quibbles that one might have with a headline, or even with what one sees as the sensational bent of a particular article, there is no denying that such stories are stories by any measure. The public are inclined to be interested in disputes, including reports of sexual abuse by priests or of a row over abortion advice involving the Catholic crisis pregnancy agency CURA – or reports of local bishops criticising a county council's treatment of nomadic Travellers or attacking the withdrawal of key services from a provincial airport.

Some Catholic bishops have been particularly irked by media coverage of the abuse scandals but their annoyance is generally misplaced. While mistakes have been made by journalists, the Catholic Church's handling of the scandal brought disgrace on itself. Repeated sideswipes at the media, in the absence of sustained analysis of any supposed shortcomings in media coverage, are at best futile and at worst counterproductive. If ever there were a case of trying to shoot the messenger then complaints of media coverage of the sex abuse scandal is it. Moreover, even if the incidence of abuse by priests is no greater than that by men in general, there is a special expectation of higher standards in the case of religious leaders. _yes !_

In respect of such stories as those under consideration in these three categories particularly, the new Press Council of Ireland will provide a useful function in that claims of untruth or unfairness may now be decided independently and in accordance with a code of practice.[16] However, there is little or no evidence of malice on the part of journalists who cover such stories and I believe that they simply take it for granted that the matters of which they write are proper food for thought in any demo-

---

14. *Sunday Business Post*, 29 September 2002. Opus Dei itself is associated with a significant number of the few events organised by Irish Catholics to consider the role of the media. These sessions at Cleraun in Dublin attract media speakers who have no other connection with Opus Dei.
15. *Irish Independent*, 27 March 2006.
16. For the new Council's code see www.presscouncil.ie/v1/codeof-practice.php.

cratic society. They are not out of step with the public in that regard. Moreover, by no means all reports of religious behaviour are negative. The Dalai Lama in Derry, in July 2007, received much publicity, partly (one suspects) because of the colourful personality of His Holiness and the contrast between his bright robes and the damp backgrounds of Derry. A bishop who feeds the poor may also get his picture in the papers. And, frequently, the role played by nuns, brothers and priests in providing various social services over the years in acknowledged.

7. Reporting new developments in religious art, music and liturgy
8. Reporting new thinking about theology and/or forms of religious organisation

These categories of story are less overtly anchored in the everyday life, practices and values of the public domain than are the six previous categories. One is getting closer here to the private sphere of belief, and to how individuals understand their lives and express their beliefs. For that very reason, and in the absence of a related controversy, it is not the news desk but the features editor who is most likely to run such a story.

But I fear that few editors will think these matters to be of great interest to the general public today, and they are probably right. To some extent, religious organisations themselves are to blame for that state of affairs. They have not always enthusiastically fostered understanding and discourse among their faithful in respect of such matters. The quality of liturgy, for example, is often quite unmoving if not downright embarrassing for people with a grasp of art or Church history, or even for the multitudes who now have ready access to the fruit of high production values through their experiences of concerts at big venues or when enjoying music on their iPods. Does anyone in authority, for example, listen to the words of some of those hymns still sung in Irish churches and *not* wonder what a modern, educated person could possible make of them? Apart from their bombastic or archaic wording, they reflect the imperial and theological outlook of the period in which they were composed. Not that one wants commercial production values in religious ceremonies, still less trendy, pop priesthood: but some greater sense of aesthetic and spiritual integrity would help people to relate to the liturgy.

Pope Benedict appears to be personally aware of this problem but his attempts to reinvigorate the liturgy may be defeated for many lay people by the ostensible reactionary agenda with which he is associated. One suspects that it is not so much a case of 'all is possible' as it is a matter of any change being possible only because and insofar as one man wants it in the context of a particular agenda. Hopefully such fears are misplaced.

Reporting theological trends is even more fraught than reporting on art or liturgy, where at least there is the incentive for an editor of reproducing visually or aurally attractive material. The media in general is not the best place for philosophical or academic discussions, which are ill-suited to articles of 800 or 1,200 words. However, that is not to say that journalists cannot alert people to interesting developments and debates through concise reportage or opinion pieces. Some people may criticise a journalist for being sensational or seeking conflict, whereas he or she is simply attempting to interest readers who perhaps 'should' be interested in such matters but frequently, in practice, are not. One example of a short piece on a complex topic that did work well, and that was not even written by a religion correspondent, was a report from Germany on significant changes in the thinking of the leading intellectual, Jürgen Habermas.[17] In writing of certain letters or declarations issued by bishops or the Pope, for a general readership of more than one million people, I personally try to give a flavour of the document and place it in context, flagging its title or place of origin so that those who are interested may follow up for themselves and read the original. This is so even if my commentary is critical.[18]

9. Reporting spiritual experience

With the best will in the world, an informed reporter writing for an informed readership about religious affairs will have great

17. Derek Scally, 'Religion on the rise in a secular world', in *The Irish Times*, 24 December 2005.

18. For example, 'Church report was not unanimously endorsed', in *Sunday Independent*, 6 March 2005 (on final report of working group on sex abuse); 'Pontiff, give up the auld sins of the Catholic Church' (Regensburg address) in *Sunday Independent*, 24 September 2006; 'This German pope is more Roman than the Romans' (*Motu proprio*), in *Sunday Independent*, 15 July 2007.

difficulty in discussing matters of spiritual experience. That relationship with the divine which is at the heart of religious experience does not lend itself to being properly described in public fora aimed at large and distant audiences. An opening declaration of the Tao Te Ching, 'The name that can be named is not the eternal Name',[19] springs to mind (as does the adage, 'Those who say don't know, and those who know don't say'). In February 2005, addressing a conference at the University of California, Zoketsu Norman Fischer, former abbot of the San Francisco Zen Center and founder of the Everyday Zen Foundation, began with a humorous anecdote about a newscast covering a blizzard:

> The reporter stood in the midst of it, saying, 'There is really a lot of snow out here, Bob.' Fischer paired this with a quote from Wittgenstein – 'Whereof one cannot speak, thereof one must be silent' – commenting that the unspeakable is the most salient reality, but it's unspeakable. From this perspective, Fischer stated that he tries not [to] mix up the world of media with the 'quiet, intimate world' in which he lives. He doubted that Buddhism could actually have a spokesperson in the media, or that Buddhism is determined by learned monastics or the media.[20]

This may well be so, but Buddhist organisations certainly can and do have their own spokespeople and they fulfil a useful social role. Moreover, when writing articles, there is surely a middle way for journalists between the 'quiet, intimate world' of monasteries and the frenetic, attention-seeking universe of newsrooms.

Insofar as one does 'say', direct interpersonal transmission or even a book may no doubt be a more satisfactory way of communicating about sensitive matters because such ways allow more space to explore complexity – and because there may be an intimate relationship created between a pupil and teacher or be-

19. Suzuki, Daisetz T. and Carus, Paul (translators), *The canon of reason and virtue: Lao-Tze's Tao Teh King* (Illinois: Open Court, 1913), 1:i.

20. See http://ieas.berkeley.edu/events/2005.02.08-09.html#panel3. The conference, on 8-9 Feb 2005, was entitled, 'Speaking for the Buddha? Buddhism and the media'.

tween a reader and author. Nevertheless, that ought not to stop journalists from attempting to convey or indicate in other ways and to a broader readership the reality of spiritual experience.

One of the best media modes of exploring spiritual experience is through documentary, although not all those who make documentaries see themselves as 'journalists'. Some, like Peter Gröning, are 'directors'. His recent German production, *Die Grosse Stille*, is an example of success.[21] Audiences have warmed to his slow, quiet exploration of daily life at the Grand Chartreuse, motherhouse of the Carthusian order. The BBC also tried a novel and fairly satisfactory approach for a mass audience by commissioning *The Monastery*, its recent television series about five men who decided to spend forty days and nights with the Benedictine community at Worth Abbey in Sussex.[22] The RTÉ television series *Would You Believe?* has had mixed success in trying to make many programmes which are interesting narratives and which also capture something of how an inner spiritual life influences the actions of those whose stories are being told.[23]

Even a journalist who normally finds him or herself confined to around 1,000 words must not spurn the challenge of communicating the essence of prayer and other spiritual experiences. If a poet can do so economically, in a Haiku, then why not a journalist in a short article? After all, when asked how to pray, Jesus himself responded in a few short sound-bites addressed to his heavenly Father!

---

21. English title, *Into Great Silence*, 2005. See www.diegrossestille.de/English (in August 2007). Available on DVD, but best seen in a dark cinema and without a break.
22. A US 'cloistered reality' series of the same name was shot for The Learning Channel, at Christ in the Desert Monastery, New Mexico. The BBC later provided gender balance in *The Convent*.
23. www.RTÉ.ie/tv/wouldyoubelieve/index.html. The current RTÉ radio series *Spirit moves* is another effort by RTÉ to serve those who are interested broadly in religious matters, including people who are not affiliated to any particular religious organisation. Such Irish media efforts are made in a context where, within or on the part of most such organisations themselves, there seems to have been little appetite for robust discussion or debate that might involve public dialogue between the faithful at all levels.

Yet, generally, in our hyper, multi-cut, sound-bite culture, meditation and contemplation may not make for arresting copy in the opinion of an editor, reader or viewer. Overt and emotional religious experience, on the other hand, is attractive for the media. The public dimension of crowds reacting to 'moving statues' or to people swooning at evangelical or Pentecostal meetings lends itself especially to television. While some people with a developed spiritual practice may cringe at such images and at what they say to a viewer about religion, others in positions of authority within a Church may be more ambivalent and regard that kind of publicity as being a form of crowd-pulling.

10. Reporting the rejection of organised religion

Evidence of the rejection of religion makes for interesting stories, not least in a society which, for a long time, was overtly very religious. For example, when people stop going to church, how do they constitute meaning? Are they still 'getting' their children baptised and getting married in church even if they have little belief, and are the Churches happy to oblige them in that respect? Does the incidence of suicide or substance abuse reflect a loss of faith? When it comes to atheism, in recent years, Richard Dawkins and his provocative books about God have on their own generated acres of newsprint.

It is also interesting for journalists, as it is for academics, to explore ways in which people piece together meaning, with or without a conscious transcendent dimension, even as they perhaps rely largely on television for their stories of life. If today, as Michael Warren bleakly observes, 'Many seem to be like the young man in Peter Shaffer's play *Equus*, who, in his madness, can only express himself in the jingles of TV commercials',[24] the level of cultural and psychological influence by the media is surely a matter of religious import that deserves attention from the media itself. The suggestion, admittedly, begs questions about the ability of the media to question or debunk itself as it does others.

---

24. Michael Warren, *Seeing through the media: a religious view of communications and cultural analysis* (Harrisburg, PA: Trinity Press International, 1997 ed), p 123.

Barriers to good reporting

Many journalists approach any story with a healthy scepticism, expecting vested interests to spin their actions and opinions in a way that is favourable to the organisation for which they work. The attitude of such journalists is based on their experience of human nature and is not necessarily as cynical as it may seem. Journalists will see bishops, for example, as being no different in this respect from other prominent citizens. Some reporters may of course be more than sceptical: they may be hostile to parties involved in a particular story, and such hostility can spring from a variety of sources. One is simple prejudice or ignorance. Another is their past experience of members of that organisation, either in a personal or professional capacity. Their initial antagonism could be justified, if in the past they have been lied to or misled by the same type of office holder, although hostility or other emotional states are always dangerous for any journalist who simply wishes to be fair and truthful or who wants to avoid trouble resulting from ostensible or actual bias.

That having been said, it is possible to adopt a policy that may improve the level of mutual understanding between religious organisations and the media. This is so particularly if people are prepared to consider the following barriers to effective communications.

(a) An absence of evident respect for the profession of journalism as a whole

It is futile and somewhat insulting to moan in broad terms about 'the media' (just as it also is about 'the Church' generally), and doing so tends to make one sound grumpy or old-fashioned. In common with some other elite groups such as academics, Church leaders may be carelessly dismissive of the media, and so slight all those who work for it. This is not a unique Irish phenomenon, and one Australian commentator has noted there

> a tendency ... to disdain electronic media as a lower form of culture that is unworthy of theological consideration ... Many church leaders tell me – sometimes proudly, sometimes dismissively – that they are too busy to watch television or go to the movies. Their major media activities are

reading books and journals, activities that put them out of touch with the most common media practices of people to whom they are supposed to be communicating.[25]

There is, quite obviously, much that is less than perfect about the media (and religions). On occasion, there will be specific errors that need to be corrected. It is quite reasonable to interrogate or even to lament certain broad tendencies, as Pope Benedict did on 20 May 2007 (World Day of Communications) when he remarked, 'programmes that instil violence or anti-social behaviour or vulgarise human sexuality are unacceptable', but one must also differentiate between media and between professional categories or individuals who work for it. One should not, for example, assume the worst of journalists.

Overall, the best way to respond to perceived problems is not by perpetual carping. It is better to attempt to speak in positive ways about what the media is doing and might do, rather than constantly lamenting its weaknesses or excesses as though all media workers were responsible for these. It is a mistake, and somewhat offensive, to assume that journalists are not 'among people to whom faith matters'.[26] Religious organisations might also put their own houses in order before they condemn others too sharply.

(b) A failure to sustain dialogue with journalists

Talk to journalists. Find out what interests them about religion. Raise criticisms and issues in a polite and open-ended way, without any expectation of immediate benefit. And do not try, if doing this, to groom some kind of elite inner core of approved 'sensible' journalists. Dare to talk to all who are interested! It is easy to do so from time to time on an individual basis, and a

---

25. Horsfield, 'Electronic media and the past-future of Christianity', p 274.
26. Breda O'Brien, 'Irish media and Irish religion', in *Studies*, 94 (2005), p 123, begins by asserting that, 'Among people to whom faith matters, there is a pervasive sense that Irish media are at best 'tone-deaf' or at worst, hostile to matters involving religion.' She admits that the charge is 'hotly denied' but her form of words expresses an exclusive, proprietorial and judgemental attitude that seems to be prevalent in some quarters.

great deal of very expensive PR misses this point completely. But you cannot fake this process, and if you are only going through the motions of dialogue and encounter then it will be both obvious and offensive to the media personnel whom you are meeting.

Unfortunately, there still exists for the Irish Catholic Church in this respect a fundamental problem that was eloquently identified by Fr Joseph O'Leary almost twenty years ago. Had it been then addressed, the Church might not face as many problems as it now does. He wrote prophetically:

> If the Irish Catholic Church could become a place of free exchange and communication, untold spiritual energies would be released. Free speech is the foremost clue to the solution of the malaise. The obstacles to it include the sense of inferiority induced in most Irish Catholics by the teaching of their church, and by the powerlessness and passivity to which its structures condemn the laity and the lower clergy; the cowardice and prudent trimming which are part and parcel of clerical culture; the lack of a secure perspective and an articulate theological language in which to identify the problems – because of this lack people fear to open their mouths lest they reveal their own confusion, making fools of themselves, and disturbing the faithful. The attack on the media conducted by conservative Irish Catholics often springs from a fear of free discussion. A phobic attitude to the media often stems from a fear of being honest, and of having to answer awkward questions. Irish clerical conservatism conceives itself as a bulwark of reason and common sense against the emotivism of the church's critics. In reality this is a deceptive self-image.[27]

There cannot be many Irish journalists who have encountered the Irish hierarchy during the past two decades who do not immediately recognise that malaise.

(c) The use of arcane or archaic forms of language by Church leaders
Reading letters by bishops or by the Pope, one is struck quite often by the form of language being used. What does it mean?

---

27. Joseph O'Leary, 'Religion, Ireland: in mutation', in Richard Kearney (ed), *Across the Frontiers* (Dublin: Wolfhound, 1988), p 240.

Does anyone really talk like this? It is not dumbing down to use clear modern English as normally spoken, and to use it transparently. Maybe if the Churches' own attempts at communication sounded less patronising than they sometimes do then Churches would engage the attention and interest of people more easily. One wonders if some of this language is like a wall behind which its authors hide from the threat of a wider dialogue that might stir up emotions or reveal weaknesses. One example, taken at random, is this from Pope Benedict's recent letter to his bishops, *Moto proprio* (7 July 2007):

> It is true that there have been exaggerations and at times social aspects unduly linked to the attitude of the faithful attached to the ancient Latin liturgical tradition. Your charity and pastoral prudence will be an incentive and guide for improving these.

In the absence of open press conferences at which such documents can be explored and their authors probed, a sentence like the one quoted retains a level of ambiguity that may be confounding even when read in its full context. It seems unreasonable to blame translators for this. In September 2006, on the occasion of the Pope's controversial address at Regensburg, ambiguity about the intent of his remarks referring to Islam led to speculation that he deliberately intended to be provocative. Greater clarity on the day would have either confirmed this or been more conducive to good relations between two great world religions.

(d) Benign indifference by some to the very idea of communication through the media
(e) Humility on the part of some deeply religious individuals
If the central purpose of religion is a relationship with the divine, or a personal understanding of the moral way of life, some of those involved in understanding the value of such practice may be so humble that they do not wish to talk publicly about it. They may be indifferent to the public sphere precisely because they feel that religious experience is primarily private or individual. If they seek their reward in heaven, they may not care about their reward in column inches. I am not suggesting that

they try to be other than who they are or that they be forced into a false camaraderie with the media, but if they hide their light under a bushel then it presents a challenge to religious organisations and to journalists as to how one can best tell the story of such experiences.

(f) Cliché

Journalists may be inclined to formulate stories about religion in ways to which they have become conveniently accustomed, lazily seeking out (for example) a predictable reaction whenever there is a possibility of sexual controversy. The 'usual suspects' can be called up to condemn something or other. For years, in Britain, Mrs Mary Whitehouse fulfilled that role. The purveyors of sleaze can depend on the media reaching for such critics and generating publicity for their productions. Clichés are frequently evident in television drama and film, too, when the 'religious nut' layman or 'Vicar of Dilby'-type clergywoman enters right on cue; and of course no self-respecting hero should be depicted having a serious spiritual moment.

Religious organisations play into this socially determined role when they reiterate the same types of opinion that challenge only certain sections of society to think radically about their behaviour. The support of the USA's 'religious right' for Republicans and a tendency on the part of the Roman Catholic hierarchy to be most explicit about sexual morality and abortion may be justified or not, but journalists are thus encouraged to equate religion with a very narrow range of perspectives on a limited number of matters. Those very media personnel who themselves are at least loosely affiliated to a religion may be the ones to baulk first at such a caricature of the spiritual life, while those least religious may embrace it as being both comfortable and convenient. While many callers condemned the BBC for broadcasting *Jerry Springer the Opera* in 2005, that Corporation's Director General, Mark Thompson, found himself defending the decision. Thompson was said to be 'a practising Christian'.[28]

---

28. Chris Frost, *Journalism Ethics and Regulation* (Harlow: Pearson, 2nd ed, 2007), p 169.

*(g) Prejudice on the part of some journalists and editors
in respect to religion generally
(h) Indifference or disinterest among many citizens
in respect of religious belief and practice*

People want to read what interests them, and editors want to give them what sells papers. A significant number of people have rejected religion as they understand it, and do not wish to be bothered with what they regard as exclusively religious stories. Nevertheless, among agnostics and even among atheists or opponents of religion, there is quite often a residual interest in spiritual matters, perhaps because such matters touch on a reality of some kind that people intuitively sense. Agnostics or opponents may serve a useful purpose for religious organisations and leaders by pointing out that the latter sometimes appear to be more concerned with social policy issues than with addressing in a communicative way the universal truths that are the very basis of their existence.

One ought to take with a grain of salt advice by columnists who tell bishops to stick to religion and to keep away from social or political issues, because the media itself actually likes those very stories that are generated when bishops mix it with society. Nevertheless, one may find in the words of one's critics a grain of truth, and when a columnist complains that both the Church of Ireland and Catholic archbishops of Dublin prefer to talk publicly about anything other than God it is worth asking why that columnist is so exercised. Perhaps he simply disagrees with their expressed points of view on a subject; or perhaps one may find validity in his criticism that they have not spoken often and loudly enough about that which is most relevant to them (Drumcree and child abuse instead of foreign policy, perhaps); or maybe he is also voicing a more widespread thirst among the public when he suggests that their graces' time 'would be much better spent helping to find our spiritual home again in a materialist world gone mad'.[29]

One moving and even shocking account of how a journalist became so disillusioned by his experiences of religious organisations that he lost his faith was published during 2007 by a senior

---

29. John O'Keeffe, 'We don't really like talking about God, anything else is fine', in *Sunday Independent*, 29 July 2007.

writer on a well-known Californian newspaper. Irish journalists may well recognise in his experiences some of their own.[30]

Of course, if members of religious organisations do not live according to their stated principles, and do not root out those who corrupt their organisations, then they can expect 'a bad press'. Moreover, there will be times when people simply disagree about what is appropriate, and no amount of cultural or social sensitivity can quite paper over the cracks. Thus, with Muslims in Europe being quick to complain when their faith is slighted, it was quite reasonable for an Irish journalist to raise a question about members of an Enterprise Ireland trade mission being advised to cover up Christian religious symbols on a visit to the Middle East.[31] Likewise, there is no good reason for journalists to avert their eyes from the brutal and undemocratic nature of some ostensibly Moslem regimes simply because of past or present Western imperialism.

However, the gap between the perspectives of secular society and religious organisations is exacerbated by sheer ignorance and insensitivity on the part of those media personnel who seem to believe that they are waging their very own Enlightenment crusade. This was evident in the crass provocation constituted by publication of offensive cartoons of the prophet Mohamed in a Danish newspaper, and in some subsequent coverage of that incident. Akbar Ahmed, writing of the tension between Islam and the West, does not sound very different from Cardinal Avery Dulles analysing tension between religion and the media in general. Ahmed states that:

> The perception of Islam as out of step with the West is at the heart of Western self-definition. The West believes it has successfully come to terms with and has balanced faith and reason, whereas Islam has not. It is this contradiction between the West, supposedly dominated by secularist and rational

---

30. William Lobdell, 'Religion beat became a test of faith: a reporter looks at how the stories he covered affected him and his spiritual journey', in *Los Angeles Times*, 21 July 2007. See http://www.latimes.com/news/local/la-me-lostfaith21jul21,0,3530015,full.story?coll=la-home-center
31. Kieron Wood, 'Saudi-mission delegates advised to cover crosses', in *Sunday Business Post*, 7 January 2007.

thought, and traditional Muslim society that is seen as the basis for friction and misunderstanding.[32]

Dialogue is better than condemnation when it comes to persuading the media why they may have caused offence. However, it is very difficult to persuade the media to adopt a less negative attitude if journalists share certain perspectives or prejudices with the bulk of society, for example, on the acceptability of 'artificial' contraception or on the wearing of particular forms of Muslim apparel (the *hijab*) in public institutions such as schools or courts. In these cases it may be necessary for the faithful to agree to differ with most journalists, and best to move on to more fruitful ground for dialogue.

Meanwhile, reporters and columnists would do well to take John Horgan's advice when he writes: 'We journalists should be the last to believe our own press notices, our big by-lines, our journalism awards, and should be the first to remember that our profession is primarily one of service, not of domination, influence or control.'[33]

Seven deadly sins?

In 1994, writing for the Jesuit journal, *America*, Avery Dulles identified what he described as 'seven points of contrast' between 'the nature of the Church's message and the communicative powers of journalism'.[34] His is an alluring schema that has much to commend it, but which may also seem fundamentally self-righteous and judgemental when viewed from the perspective of a journalist.

'First', he contends:

the content of the church's message is the holy mystery of

---

32. Akbar Ahmed, *Journey into Islam: The Crisis of Globalization* (Washington DC: Brookings Institute Press, 2007), p11. For Dulles, see below.

33. J. Horgan, 'The media and the enemies of truth', in Dermot Lane (ed), *New Century, New Society: Christian Perspectives* (Dublin: The Columba Press, 1999), p 100.

34. See n 2 above. I am grateful to the editor of *America* for permission to quote quite extensively from this article. In 2001, Avery Dulles SJ, Professor of Religion and Society at Fordham University, New York, was made a cardinal by Pope John Paul II.

God's presence and redemptive activity in Jesus Christ. This is a mystery of faith, to be approached in a posture of reverent worship. The press is by nature investigative and, one might almost say, iconoclastic. Far from being reverent, it revels in exposing what is pretentious, false and scandalous. The Catholic Church, with its exalted claims, is a particularly tempting target.

He does not acknowledge that it is reasonable for the media both to reveal what is 'pretentious, false and scandalous' in the Church and also to ask why the Church is not better at doing so itself in a transparent fashion. He also overlooks the fact that particular Church messages are frequently about more than just 'the holy mystery of God's presence': in their excess lies the seed of many a story that may fairly address what is not purely a matter of faith or worship but perhaps a question of politics or culture.

'Second', writes Dulles:

the essential message of the church is the one and eternal gospel. Convinced of the permanent validity of God's revelation in Christ, the church seeks to maintain continuity with its own past. It cherishes stability and shuns innovation. The press, by contrast, lives off novelty. It thrives on the ephemeral and panders to the 'itching ears' of its readers. In reporting religious news, it accents what is new and different, thus giving the impression that the church is in continual turmoil.

It is quite true that the essence of news is that which is new. However, it is not true to suggest that the press assumes that what is new is better. To say that 'it thrives on the ephemeral' is to imply that the many serious matters of lasting concern to people that the media addresses are somehow treated in a frivolous fashion, and that is too sweeping. To say that the Church by its nature 'shuns innovation' is highly debatable and, if correct, would surely not be a matter for self-satisfaction but for interrogation.

'Third', Dulles maintains:

the church seeks to promote unity and reconciliation, minimising discord and dissent. The news media, however, specialise in disagreement and conflict which evidently arouse greater interest and boost circulation. A story without a struggle between contending parties will frequently be turned down as dull. If 'no news is good news,' it follows that good news is hardly newsworthy. Understandably, therefore, the press tends to give the impression that the church is divided into warring factions and that every point of dogma is hotly contested within the church itself.

His assertions here about the media seem quite fair, in general terms, and most particularly when considering the news. However, the features sections of papers, as well as many broadcast programmes, frequently address matters where a struggle between contending parties is by no means paramount. The television documentary format, in particular, is comfortable with narratives of triumph, where good wins out over evil or effort over adversity. As regards the Catholic Church, in particular, it is all very well to say that it 'seeks to promote unity and reconciliation, minimising discord and dissent' but its aspiration in that respect is frequently confounded in practice when it sets itself against individuals or well-intentioned groups that it believes are harmful to society, be they (for example) campaigners for gay rights, contraception or liberation theology. And what self-respecting journalist could write seriously about Pope Benedict's speech at Regensburg or his *Motu proprio* on other Christian Churches without adverting to their actual or potential divisive effects? Besides, Jesus himself did not promise minimal discord, quite explicitly advising his followers, 'Do not think that I came to bring peace on earth …'[35]

'Fourth', argues Dulles:

the church seeks to dispose people to receive interior grace with a view to eternal salvation. These spiritual blessings, however, are not sufficiently concrete to make good copy. The press, therefore, tends to overlook the spiritual side of the church's mission and to concentrate on more tangible phenomena. Doctrinal pronouncements of the church are of little interest to the popular media unless they have a bearing

---

35. Matthew 10:34-39. Also see Luke 12: 49-53 and 14: 25-33.

on the usual fare of the press. Church teaching is very select-ively reported, often in such a way as to leave the impression that the Pope is chiefly interested in sex, politics and power.

What I have already written above tends to coincide with and explain this view to a great extent. I will only add, some-what mischievously, that long before the advent of modern mass media Rome had itself done quite a good job of appearing to be 'chiefly interested in sex, politics and power'.

'Fifth', declares Dulles:

the press in a democratic society tends to import democratic criteria into its assessment of any organisation. It has great difficulty in appreciating a hierarchical society in which the leaders hold their authority not from the people but from Christ, by apostolic succession. Any effort by the church to control the teaching of its own members is regarded as equivalent to censorship of the press by the state. Journalism, therefore, has a built-in bias against the authoritative teach-ing of popes and bishops, especially where that teaching runs against the ethos of contemporary democratic culture. The disobedient priest and the dissident theologian are lionised as champions of freedom.

As I pointed out earlier, the Western media belongs to a Western, democratic tradition and this is not necessarily a bad thing. Dulles does not allow that some other models of Church organisation might be preferable to the one he takes for granted, which he appears to regard as unproblematic. The phrase 'apos-tolic succession' also covers a multitude of debatable assump-tions. The assertion that 'any' effort by the Church to control teaching has been regarded as 'censorship' is an exaggeration. The phrase 'disobedient priest' begs a question as to whom the priest owes his primary duty of obedience.

On the other hand, journalists should not assume that they understand religious experience if they have neither had it nor studied it. They must be open to the possibility of a reality in which they have not shared. The *Qur'ân* teaches: 'Those who dispute about the signs of Allah without any authority be-stowed on them, there is nothing in their breasts but (the quest of) greatness, which they shall never attain to: seek refuge, then, in Allah. It is He Who hears and sees (all things)'.[36]

'Sixth', writes Dulles:

the teaching of the church on matters of belief and moral practice is frequently complex and subtle. As a result of hundreds of years of acute theological analysis, it deals with fine points that cannot be expressed without technical terms. The precise distinctions of dogma and moral teaching demand a degree of attention that cannot be expected of the average reader. The press and the electronic media are hungry for stories that are short, simple and striking. If they report doctrinal statements at all, they slur over nuances and qualifications that may be crucial.

There is certainly a time and a place for technical terms and textual complexity when it comes to theology or philosophy. However, in respect to religion and other areas, serious journalists spent much of their lives attempting to get to the heart of matters and explaining them to broad audiences. They may frequently fail but they are entitled to try, and in so doing fulfill an important public role – not least when 'matters of belief and moral practice' are of concern or relevance to people at large. I agree with Stewart Hoover when he writes that, '… the question of complexity seems to be tailor-made for good journalism rather than an excuse for avoiding it. As several informants said, in several different ways, if the world of religion seems complex and unexplainable, it is the role of the professional journalist to attempt to demystify and explain it.'[37]

'Seventh' and finally, Dulles maintains:

the church aims to persuade its hearers of the truth of revelation. It seeks to arouse a firm commitment to its creed and to the following of Christ. Journalism, by contrast, intends to report facts that are accessible even to unbelievers and to give an account that is acceptable to people of any or no religious bent. The secular press cannot presuppose or assert the truth

---

36. *Qur'ân* 40:56, as translated by Abdullah Yusuf Ali (1872-1953).
37. Stewart M. Hoover, *Religion in the News: Faith and Journalism in American Public Discourse* (Thousand Oaks: Sage, 1998), pp 218-9.

of revelation, especially as that revelation is interpreted in any particular community of faith.

It is the case that journalists working for most media in free countries do not see themselves as advocates of any particular religion, and I believe that most people in those countries would in that respect agree with his assessment of their professional role. Shortly after the collapse of the dictatorship in Czechoslovakia, I was invited to accompany some students from Dublin City University to Charles University in Prague to help in the process of restructuring some of their journalism courses there. In a cupboard in a room where we met, we found some English translations of abstracts of certain articles in an old communist journal for journalists. One abstract asserted that the primary role of the television reporter or presenter was to explain to viewers the teaching or position of the Communist Party. Fortunately, most journalists in Europe today do not have a similar burden to shoulder. However, in its understanding of how truth is best communicated, the Catholic Church historically may be closer to the communist model than to the liberal rationale favoured by journalists. The Catholic Church is essentially a teaching authority, as Ted Jelen remarks in his exploration of the distinction between the perspectives of Church and media. He notes that, '… the church seeks to maximise human freedom, understood as voluntary obedience to God's law as befitting creatures created in his image' and that 'church guidance has often been presented in a rather authoritarian form'. He adds: 'The Index of Forbidden Books as well as pronouncements from the National Office for Decent Literature have not typically been presented as suggestions.'[38]

From his seven-point consideration of the 'permanent inbuilt tension' between Church and media, Avery Dulles concludes:

> There is clearly a place for religiously oriented journalism that tries to offset the natural bias of the media to which I have called attention. The Christian press should consciously endeavor to present the church as it understands itself with

---

38. T. G. Jelen, 'Catholicism, Conscience and Censorship', in Daniel A. Stout and Judith M. Buddenbaum (eds), *Religion and the Mass Media: Audiences and Adaptations* (Thousand Oaks: Sage, 1996), p 49.

the emphases that flow from faith. The ecclesially responsible segment of the press, while trying to reach out to a broader public, will be on guard against the temptation to indulge in iconoclasm and to exploit the popular appetite for the sensational and the scandalous. While censorship by church authorities is not desirable, a measure of self-censorship on the part of editors and reporters may properly be expected.

This is yet another recipe for 'singing to the choir', or preaching to the converted, and both a morally questionable and not particularly engaging or fruitful one at that. Such 'a measure of self-censorship' can divert attention and resources from bigger challenges into activities that console those in authority that they are 'doing something about' communications while not actually communicating very much, if by communication we mean dialogue between two parties who are both listening.

If the Catholic Church and other religious organisations wish to address a broad public that depends on the media for much of its information then those organisations ought to do so in neutral terms, making the most of opportunities that present themselves while not compromising the dignity or truth that they believe they represent and teach. It is the case that much about the economics of global capitalism and the contemporary media landscape intrinsically militates against truth and justice, yet that fact simply highlights the benefits of some people being in the world but not of it. By entering respectfully into open dialogue with journalists, rather than assuming the worst, religious organisations and individuals may learn new ways of reaching the multitude and teaching all nations. In that respect, regardless of their personal outlook, those reporting on religion may be seen as potential allies of the wise rather than as adversaries of religious organisations.

In the case of Ireland, specifically, so much time and so many opportunities for renewal on the part of the Catholic Church have been lost that much of what I say may have little relevance now to the lives of most people. This is because much of the commercialised media do not give a toss about religion (and are sure that their listeners or readers basically do not care either), while the media that currently employ religious correspondents may not replace them as the state becomes more secular. A generation of journalists who were fundamentally well-disposed (if deeply frustrated) will pass on. They asked for bread and were given a stone. Now, serious journalists have their own institutional crises as globalisation accelerates a process of media trivialisation that sees their work undervalued and their professional role placed at risk.

The Irish Catholic Church is in a period of such far-reaching change, in terms of a loss of priests and church services that is only beginning to be fully evident, that there is a real possibility of its marginalisation. It seems to be retreating into a form of laicisation that has a very slender theological base, and that appears to be principally about parish management and the control of schools and hospitals. The narrow or nervous hierarchical mindset that helped to bring it to this point still shows little sign of being capable of fundamental self-criticism or reformation and the possibility of the institutional Catholic Church engaging mainstream journalists and their audiences in more imaginative ways than hitherto seems as distant as ever. In that respect, at least, the Irish Catholic Church is at one with the US 'religious right' and with the more orthodox forms of Islam.

Of Scribes and Pharisees

Patsy McGarry

My paternal grandmother Beatrice and her son, my uncle Matthew, have been much in my mind over recent times. In particular since it was officially announced by the Vatican in 2007 that limbo does not exist. But, in truth, they have been a more notable presence in my consciousness since it first emerged in recent years that limbo looked like going the way of all flesh. You will recall that on 20 April 2007 the Vatican consigned limbo to oblivion. For many centuries it was taught that limbo was where upbaptised babies, Socrates, Plato, Aristotle, and all good people who lived before Jesus went on death. There they languished for all eternity deprived of the Beatific Vision. When the long-awaited document, *The Hope of Salvation for Infants Who Die Without Being Baptised*, was released then in April 2007 by the Catholic Church's International Theological Commission, it concluded that limbo reflected an 'unduly restrictive view of salvation'. In 2005, while still Prefect of the Congregation for the Doctrine of the Faith, Pope Benedict expressed doubts about limbo. The concept should be abandoned, he said, because it was 'only a theological hypothesis' and 'never a defined truth of faith'. It was he who authorised publication of the April 2007 document.

The end of limbo had been expected and was well-flagged. Indeed, the *Catechism of the Catholic Church*, published in 1992, did not mention it at all. Limbo was never officially part of Catholic Church doctrine, although it was taught to Catholics at least until the advent of the Second Vatican Council. It evolved as a traditional teaching of the Church in medieval times. In his *Divine Comedy*, recently referred to also by some in the context of Pope Benedict's regrets that hell was not getting the attention it deserved, Dante placed virtuous pagans and the great classical philosophers in limbo. The April 2007 Vatican document on it concluded that 'there are theological and liturgical reasons to hope that infants who die without baptism may be saved and brought into eternal happiness, even if there is not an explicit teaching on this question found in revelation.' It continued: 'There are reasons to hope that God will save these infants precisely because it was not possible (to baptise them).'

The Catholic Church teaches that baptism removes the stain of original sin with which, as it also teaches, all of humanity is born since Adam and Eve fell from grace in the Garden of Eden. Pope Benedict's document stressed that its conclusions should not be interpreted as questioning original sin or be 'used to negate the necessity of baptism or delay the conferral of the sacrament'. 'People find it increasingly difficult to accept that God is just and merciful if he excludes infants, who have no personal sins, from eternal happiness, whether they are Christian or non-Christian,' it said. It added that a study of the matter was made all the more urgent as 'the number of non-baptised infants has grown considerably, and therefore the reflection on the possibility of salvation for these infants has become urgent'. You might conclude then that, due to the contingency that people now find the concept of limbo 'increasingly difficult' to accept and/or because 'the number of non-baptised infants has grown considerably', all has changed. Changed utterly.

Too late for my grandmother. And my uncle Matthew. She died in 1939 long before I was born. But I feel I got to know her through her four children: my two aunts, my uncle, my father. All deceased now. She had a powerful influence on them, especially the two boys. They grieved for her till they died, both in 1999. My uncle Sean, shortly before his own death and by then in his 80s, broke down and wept as he spoke of her and her long dying from stomach cancer. She was a strong and deeply devout woman. Another son of hers, Matthew, was buried in a field not far from the house in Mullen (north-west Roscommon) where he had been born, probably in 1915. I lived in that house until I was ten. It was built in the 1850s by my great-grandfather. Matthew died without baptism, shortly after birth, and so could not be buried in the graveyard. I know the patch of ground where he was laid in an unmarked grave. It is on a green height in an area known as 'the Hill of Lawn'. It had actually been the front lawn of an old Big House, long since gone. The area remained one of the more pleasant landscapes in the north-west Roscommon townland where I grew up. We were taught as children to approach it with respect, though it was years before I knew why.

I can only imagine what it did to my grandmother to lose Matthew. I cannot imagine what it did to her devout soul to believe, as she would have, that he was lost to limbo forever and that, unlike even the souls in purgatory, there was nothing she or anyone else in heaven or on earth could do to rescue him from that state. From that eternity of being without hope of seeing God. After all of which she had still to be 'churched' – as was my own mother after my birth – before she could resume being a normal member of the Catholic Church. She had to be ritually 'purified', because she had had such intimate contact with an infant soul marked with the stain of original sin.

No. It is not true to say I can only imagine what it did to my grandmother to lose Matthew so soon after his birth. I have witnessed what that can do to a mother. And, probably because the mother concerned was my sister Mary, it seared my soul too. My nephew, Sam O'Connor, would have been ten years old on 12 June 2007, instead of which he lived for just ten hours. He went from being a seemingly healthy nine pound ten ounce broth of a boy to his death with such speed, that no sooner were we aware of his arrival than we had to get used to the shock of his leaving. He had a rare blood disorder.

Despite a share of life's difficulties, we are a fortunate family. We have not known too much of death. And though all of my grandparents have passed on, as have my father and his siblings, those deaths have been in the order of things. No violation there. So when my mother rang on the evening of Thursday 12 June 1997 to announce Sam's safe arrival, I heard the news with a certain nonchalance. I had, after all, 20 nieces and nephews by then. When my sister Sinead, Sam's aunt, rang at 2.30 am the following morning to say he was very ill, I was jolted. When his father John rang at 5.30 am to say he had died, I was stunned. And as the events of his passing unfolded over the following hours and days, I began to realise that this ten-hour old boy would leave a mark on all of us such as we had never experienced before. It ensures he will always be with us.

My sister Mary and her husband John O'Connor live at Ballykelly, near Cashel in Co Tipperary. They have three other children, Roisin, Barney, and J. J. Earlier that year when Roisin, then four, became aware Mary was pregnant, she insisted the expected baby would be a girl. Her logic, as usual, was impeccable. God would not be 'so silly' as to send another one of 'them'. Roisin had a strained relationship with her brothers. She even picked a name for her new sister. It would be Sarah. As a precaution, and being more familiar with the silliness of God's ways, Mary and John asked her to choose a boy's name too. She chose 'Sam'. And when Sam was born at the hospital in Clonmel, John rang home to break the news, gently, to Roisin. She took it very well. No doubt this was helped by the fact that she was told Sam had brought presents with him for her, Barney, and J. J. He had brought Roisin a toy cat. She decided the cat was a girl and called it Sarah instead. A few hours later that evening, staff in Clonmel became anxious about Sam, and he was sent to Ardkeen Hospital in Waterford. By the time he got there he was seriously ill. John, who accompanied him to Waterford, realised he might not make it. So he returned to Clonmel for Mary. By the time they got back to Waterford Sam was dead.

Mary remembers he was still warm. They brought him back to the hospital in Clonmel, where he lay in a cot next to Mary's bed for the following two days. She found it hard to part with him, and wanted all of us to see him first. So we would remember him as Sam, and not just as 'the baby'. Lying there in his cot, he was perfect and still as a porcelain doll, his finely formed fingers interlaced. Strewn around him were a couple of stuffed toys and three red roses from Ballykelly.

'He's dead', announced Roisin, when she saw him. Then, examining him more closely she noticed how all his finger-nails had darkened. 'Why are his nails painted?' she asked Mary, 'Boy's don't have their nails painted.' Mary spoke to her about heaven.

My brother Declan drove my mother and sister there, along with his wife Eithne, instructing all of them forcefully en route that they were to keep a grip on themselves in front of Mary. But when all four arrived in the hospital room, it was he who was least prepared for the sight of Mary and Sam side by side. The worst moment was on the Sunday morning, just prior to Sam's funeral. John took him to another room to be coffined and Mary's heart shattered. I had never witnessed such heartbreak, though I had heard a mother ache like that once before.

It was in a graveyard in Dungannon, Co Tyrone, in February 1993. Mrs Chris Statham watched as her only child, Julie, was lowered into the earth. Julie was 20, and had taken her own life on 2 February. The previous evening she had attended a month's mind Mass for her boy-friend, Diarmuid Shields, and his father, Patrick, at their home near Dungannon. They had been murdered by a UVF gang, the first people to die in the Northern Ireland conflict in 1993. They were just Catholics, who loved Gaelic football and Irish music.

Little did Mary and John think they themselves would be facing into grief that week before Sam, when, so moved by pictures of another grieving Northern Ireland family, they had decided to invite them to Ballykelly for a break. Mrs Kathleen Taylor and her son Christopher (then ten years old), who has cerebral palsy, had been very distressed at the funeral of husband, father, and RUC officer Greg Taylor. He had been kicked to death by a mob.

'It's so cruel,' wept Mary, as her son was taken away. And it is. Life is hard on mothers. They suffer in our coming and in our going.

There were other bad moments. Mary being taken to the funeral in a wheelchair, still too weak to stand or walk. The sight of that small white coffin as it rested at an awkward angle on a trolley, inside a hospital corridor. Seeing it lifted single-handed by an undertaker, and placed on the back seat of Mary and John's car. The small opening cut into a corner of the grave where Sam would rest. Mary at the graveside in her wheelchair. The funeral Mass was brief. What Mary and John needed, the priest said, was 'Christ's touch, not Christ's teaching,' and he urged us all to embrace them. We followed Sam to the small graveyard nearby, where he was buried with his grandfather, Bernard (Barney) O'Connor. Over ten years later Mary still dreams about Sam and has the occasional nightmare. She still grieves for her lost boy.

I have never forgotten the priest's words at the Mass that day on what was needed – 'Christ's touch, not Christ's teaching.'

Because, as with so much else said and done in his name, limbo was never Christ's teaching. And I mourn for my poor grandmother and all those millions upon millions of mothers and family members who were put through so much additional and unnecessary grief by scribes and Pharisees past. It was 'so cruel', to use Mary's phrase.

Years after her own death, my grandmother Beatrice's piety would also be responsible for further additional and unnecessary grief. Though through no fault of her own. She developed stomach cancer and, in the 1930s when there was little morphine available, especially to poor people, her only consolation was that she could offer up her suffering for the benefit of others. She prayed constantly to St Philomena, to whom she had a lifelong devotion. In this she was not unique. A number of popes had shown similar remarkable commitment to St Philomena, believed to be a virgin martyr.

Very little was known of Philomena. She was allegedly martyred at the age of 14 in the early days of the Church. In 1802 the remains of a young woman were found in the catacomb of St Priscilla on the Via Salaria in Rome. It was covered by stones, the symbols on which indicated that the body was that of a martyr and virgin named St Philomena. The bones were exhumed and catalogued. Near her bones was discovered a small glass vial, containing the remains of blood.

In 1805, Canon Francis de Lucia of Mugnano, a small town near Naples, visited Rome. His intention was to obtain relics of a martyred saint and he was allowed visit the Treasury of Relics at the Vatican. It was a large hall where the exhumed remains of several saints were preserved. Standing before the relics of St Philomena he was filled with something akin to spiritual ecstasy and pleaded that he be allowed take them with him. Despite resistance, in August 1805 he brought them to Mugnano, where a shrine was erected to Philomena's honour. Miracles were soon being reported from the shrine and in a short time Philomena became the only saint to be declared so solely on the basis of miraculous intercession, as nothing historical was known of her except her name and the evidence of her martyrdom.

Pope Leo XII (1823-1829) gave permission for the erection of altars and churches in her honour. Gregory XVI (1831-1846) authorised her public veneration and gave her the title 'Patroness of the Living Rosary'. Pius IX (1846-1878) proclaimed her 'Patroness of the Children of Mary'. Leo XIII (1878-1903) made two pilgrimages to her shrine before his election to the papacy and, as Pope, approved the Confraternity of St Philomena which he later raised to the status of an 'Archconfraternity'. St Pius X (1903-1914) raised the Archconfraternity to a Universal Confraternity and named St John Vianney as its patron. He also donated expensive gifts to Philomena's shrine. St John Vianney himself called Philomena 'the New Light of the Church Militant', and had a strong devotion to her. Others saints devoted to her included St Anthony Mary Claret, St Euphrasia Pelletier, St Francis Xavier Cabrini, St John Nepomucene Neumann, St Madeline Sophie Barat, St Peter Chanel, St Peter Julian Eymard, Blessed Anna Maria Taigi, and Venerable Pauline Jaricot who was the subject of what became known as 'the Miracle of Mugnano' in which she was said to have been cured overnight of a severe heart ailment by Philomena.

So my grandmother, you would have thought, was in reliable company in her devotion to St Philomena. When she died she left her St Philomena scapulars to my father, her youngest child. He was an average Irishman of his generation in matters of religious practice. He made no great demonstration of it, but went to Mass every Sunday, usually with some of us kids in tow. That was until 1961. In August that year the Vatican announced that St Philomena was being removed from the Calendar of Saints. For my father this meant just one thing: St Philomena never existed and, for reasons that hardly need explaining, this had a powerful emotional impact on him. He stopped going to Mass, an extraordinary thing to do in the West of Ireland in the early 1960s. Thereafter and for the rest of his life, he continued to believe in his own way but would only go to funeral Masses and occasionally at Christmas. That was it. The scribes and Pharisees had struck again. Rather, they had been found wanting again.

Then there was my godmother's daughter. Her name was Mary and, as with the mother of Jesus, she was unmarried and with child. It was the early 1950s and she had arrived in London with her fiancé. They had left Roscommon because of her pregnancy. Neither had ever been in a city before, not even Dublin.

Both got jobs, she in a branch of WH Smiths on Oxford Street. Soon he was gone. He was not prepared to share her plight, regardless of his part in it. He fled to the USA. She was in despair. Forsaken. One day she lay down in a park, her big belly obstructing the sun, and pleaded with God to take her and her baby. But he did not. It seemed he too had forsaken her. Noticing her distress in the WH Smith shop one day, an older woman who worked there approached Mary and asked what the matter was. She told her sorry story. Deeply moved, the Englishwoman invited her to live in her family's large house in south London. The basement there was fitted out and turned into a home where Mary and her son lived for the best part of three decades. Mary worked all her life and paid an agreed rent to the kind Englishwoman, as she reared her son. She had little to do with the Irish community in London.

She attended Mass for the sake of the boy, though her own faith by then had been badly shaken. Soon she got a job in an art shop near where she lived. It was run by an unorthodox Irish couple. They did not judge. She liked them and the clientele who came to the shop who were mostly theatre people. Mary enjoyed those people's instinctive tolerance, penchant for gossip, and (by the standards of the time) their sometimes outrageous personal arrangements. Beneath all that 'luvvy' stuff she recognised a compassion and honesty which were lacking where she had been taught to most expect it.

Mary did not visit her family in Ireland very often, but kept contact with one brother. He was a businessman and a good man who helped her out and would come over to see her and her son. But even he was pushed to the limit when she visited Ireland. He used to ask her to hide in the back of his car, behind the front seats, so the neighbours would not see her and ask questions. Much worse was Mary's mother's attitude. At Mass on Sundays she would not sit in the same pew as Mary. There was a sense from Mary herself of accepting these humiliations as her due. For she had sinned against the moral template instilled in her. She was not worthy. A lifetime in exile was as it should be.

She did not blame her mother, her fiancé, the Church, or Ireland. At least not with any conviction. There was never self-pity, just suggestions of self-loathing. She was never with another man for the rest of her life after the father of her child disappeared to the USA (where he married and raised a family). How could she expect any man to take her on board and she with a child? How could she ever tell a man such a thing? How could she face rejection again? Better not get involved at all. She sent her son to Catholic schools in London and hoped he would be treated well. Her badge of shame. Her little star. She hoped all those kids from regular families would not humiliate him for her sin. She hoped he would not feel humiliated when he realised the truth. For his part he became very religious and, in his early 20s, worked for a time with Mother Teresa in Calcutta. He remains a devout Catholic. He married in the Middle East and now lives in North America. Far, far, away. In the early 1990s Mary returned to live with her brother in Ireland. She became ill, and over a period of years declined painfully. She died in 2000, as unobtrusively as she had lived. And as well-liked by all who got to know her. Loved even.

When I first met Mary, that student summer in London during the 1970s, her story was a great blow to my then green vision of Ireland. Our 'dreary Eden' as writer Seán Ó Faoláin described it. I was a little older than her son. The next summer I stayed with them throughout. She even organised a job for me. We grew very fond of one another. But our friendship had a deep impact on my attitude to her mother, my godmother. That lovely woman (my godmother) had spoiled me as a child. Even today, many, many years after she too has passed on, I remember the depth of the bond as she embraced me as a child. The deep affection. The timbre in her voice as she spoke. I could not feel the same about her again after hearing Mary's story. I could not reconcile the warm woman I knew with the one who refused to share a pew with her daughter. It did not fit. A wedge entered our relationship – my judgement. She died before it was removed. I will too before I forgive myself. Because I no longer blame her. She was just doing what she believed was right. What she was told was right. She listened to those scribes and Pharisees who taught her an interpretation of the words 'if thy right hand offend thee, cut it off, and cast it from thee ...' Who taught her that, because her daughter had a child out of wedlock, she had sinned gravely and deserved to be shunned.

In the Gospel of Matthew, chapter 23, we see Jesus at his most angry. He is addressing the people about the scribes and Pharisees: '... do not be guided by what they do: since they do not practice what they preach.' He continues:

> 'They tie up heavy burdens and lay them on men's shoulders, but will they lift a finger to move them? Not they! Everything they do is to attract attention, like wearing broader phylacteries (headbands) and longer tassels, like wanting to take the place of honour at banquets and the front seats in the synagogues, being greeted obsequiously in the market squares and having people call them Rabbi. You, however, must not allow yourselves to be called Rabbi, since you have only one Master, and you are all brothers. You must call no one on earth your father, since you only have one Father, and he is in heaven ... The greatest among you must be your servant. Anyone who exalts himself will be humbled, and anyone who humbles himself will be exalted. Alas for you, scribes and Pharisees, you hypocrites! You shut up the kingdom of heaven in people's faces, neither going in yourselves nor allowing others to go in who want to.'

It was the gospel reading at Mass on Sunday, 30 October 2005, in Rowe Street Church, Wexford town. That was the first Sunday following publication of the *Ferns Report*. Bishop Eamonn Walsh, then administrator of the diocese, celebrated the Mass. In his homily he spoke of how that gospel reading was 'so relevant for today'. The following Sunday another Bishop, Willie Walsh, asked whether an unhealthy or distorted understanding of sexuality might have contributed to the Church's clerical child sex abuse problems. Addressing the annual citizenship service at Dublin's Christ Church Cathedral and referring to clerical sex abuse, he said, 'We in the Roman Catholic Church must surely ask why such evil continued to go unchecked for so long.' He continued that it must also be asked why men who must have entered priesthood with high ideals could perpetrate such evil acts. 'Was it human weakness or was it an unhealthy or distorted understanding of the meaning and purpose of the gift of sexuality? Could our rule of celibacy have had a negative influence? Was the virtual absence of women in our decision-making processes a significant factor?' he asked. Those were 'uncomfortable, somewhat frightening questions for us to face. But not to ask them at this point is even more frightening,' he remarked.

It might be argued that the Catholic Church cult of virginity and chastity, with an emphasis on original sin and the general inferiority of the sensual and the body, as perpetuated by the scribes and Pharisees particularly in the nineteenth century, played no small part in perverting clerical male sexuality into the abuse of children, just as it punished mothers whose children were not baptised or were born out of wedlock.

The doctrine of the Immaculate Conception, that Mary was conceived without sin – and after which Wexford's Rowe Street Church is named – only became a dogma of the Catholic Church in 1854, for example. This emphasis on purity and the repression of sexuality by the scribes and Pharisees placed impossibly heavy burdens on priests and people alike. It meant that as I grew up in the West of Ireland there were almost as many bachelors as husbands. Most of the bachelors were shy men terrified into chastity by the Church. I saw them in our pub at home in Ballaghaderreen, where we moved in the 1960s. They were, in the main, inoffensive, lonely people, afraid of women and the damning temptation they represented. Most were on the road to alcoholism, if not already there. Or to suicide, though it was rarely recorded as such then. I knew some of them who took their own lives. One cut his throat with a slate. Another hung himself. Another drowned himself in a barrel of rainwater. Another in a drain. All single men.

For the women, life was no better. In general and apart from some teachers, their place was exclusively in the home, rearing the family, where they were totally dependent economically on the husband. It allowed for such horrors of abuse and drunken domestic violence which was borne in silence and with which no one intervened. In 2007 we celebrated the 200th anniversary of the abolition of slavery. For so many Irishwomen slavery was their condition until the current generation. And where were the scribes and Pharisees of the Church in those times? Predictably, they were bolstering the inhuman *status quo*. Some would suggest they were responsible for it and, in its interest, they advised terrorised wives and mothers to offer it up, to think of the children, to remember their marriage vows. To suffer on, as it was, after all, the will of God.

I had thought those days were gone until I visited Rome with an older relative in the Jubilee Year of 2000. She was on her first and only visit to the city. She had been going through a difficult time. Her husband had died shortly beforehand and her only sister was then dying and would pass away within weeks, the first of her siblings to do so. She was feeling put-upon and went to confession to a young Italian priest in one of the great basilicas. She had expected consolation, maybe explanation. Instead, she was told to stop feeling sorry for herself; accept what was happening as the will of God; and to get on with her life. She emerged from the confessional angry and upset.

Earlier, on a trip to the Sistine Chapel, and despite the prevalent nudity on the ceiling above, she was mildly rebuked by a priest there on that suffocatingly warm day for not covering her shoulders. She had forgotten. She had just climbed the 150-plus steps there with two artificial hips, as the priest was aware. Her generation of Irishwomen never knew much sympathy from the scribes and Pharisees. Many of those women lived lives of unrelieved despair, where lonely coping was their lot. And where the current Pope is concerned, as with his fellow scribes and Pharisees, such women's place remains back there in the home. In effect, one step behind.

In his *Letter to the Bishops of the Catholic Church on the collaboration of men and women in the Church and in the world* on 31 May 2004, less than a year before he became pope, Joseph Ratzinger made the Church's current position on women clear. Reflecting that 'recent years have seen new approaches to women's issues', he bemoaned the fact that 'in order to avoid the domination of one sex or the other, their differences tend to be denied, viewed as mere effects of historical and cultural conditioning'. He continued, 'This perspective has many consequences. Above all, it strengthens the idea that the liberation of women entails criticism of sacred scripture, which would be seen as handing on a patriarchal conception of God nourished by an essentially male-dominated culture. Second, this tendency would consider as lacking in importance and relevance the fact that the Son of God

assumed human nature in its male form. In the face of these cur-
rents of thought, the Church ... speaks instead of active collaboration between the sexes precisely in the recognition of the difference between man and woman.' Having taken the scenic route
to a predictable destination, the Pope made clear once more that
the Catholic Church is not about to allow women a role of
greater equality in Church liturgy particularly. Where women
are concerned the burdens remain *in tacta*.

Not least where abortion is concerned. How many tens of
thousands of Irishwomen have had abortions over the past
decades simply to escape judgement from a society dominated
by a distorted view of sexuality as taught by the scribes and
Pharisees? What a comfort it would be to those women, even
now, were they to know that the Church's teaching on when life
begins has changed again and again down the millennia and
that its current position is just 139 years old? And that it too
came about as much as a result of teachings on original sin as of
any changed understanding of when life begins.

In his 1869 document, *Apostolicae Sedis*, Pope Pius IX enacted
the penalty of excommunication for abortion at any stage of
pregnancy. For the previous 278 years, and following Pope
Gregory XIV's *Sedes Apostolica* document in 1591, such excommunication only applied where abortion took place after 'quickening', i.e. from those moments when a mother first detected the
foetus move. Pope Gregory determined quickening as beginning at just over 16 weeks (166 days) of pregnancy. Prior to
quickening, 'no homicide' was involved if abortion took place,
he concluded. In 1588, just three years previously, Pope Sixtus V
issued the Papal Bull, *Effraenatum*, which decreed that those who
carried out abortions at any stage of pregnancy should be ex-
communicated and should also be punished by civil authorities
(with the death penalty). For the 377 years previous to that, and
since 1211 when Pope Innocent III issued the decree *Sicut ex*, excommunication applied as it had before 1869 – when an abortion
took place after 'quickening'. So, for the greater part of the last
millennium the Catholic Church did not hold that human life
began at conception – its current teaching.

Indeed its adoption of that teaching in 1869 was dictated, not
so much by a decision on when human life began, as by the

dogma of the Immaculate Conception promulgated by Pius IX in 1854. In 1701 Pope Clement XI had declared the Immaculate Conception a feast of universal obligation. He settled the feast date at 8 December, exactly nine months prior to the feast of Mary's birth on 8 September. It meant the Church believed Mary's sinless soul came into being at the moment of her conception. When in 1854 Pius IX proclaimed the Immaculate Conception as a dogma of the Church, he stated that Mary had been free from sin 'in the first instant of her conception'. Fifteen years later, in 1869, he was therefore being consistent with that teaching when he revived the penalty of excommunication for abortions at any stage of pregnancy. Among those who disagree with the teaching that human life begins at conception are some of the most eminent thinkers in Catholic Church history. These include at least three of the 33 Doctors of the Church – St Jerome, St Augustine, and St Thomas Aquinas.

Women, of course, remain excluded from the Catholic priesthood. They are women. That is that and there is to be no further discussion about it. In an article in *The Tablet*, published on 15 March 1997, President Mary McAleese, (though not yet nominated for election to that office) writing on this issue, said: 'Within the Irish Church as elsewhere there is a nervous deadlock between those who believe in the God-ordained equality of women and those who do not. It has never been just a debate between men and women. Rather, it has been a debate between the rigid, conditioning forces of an old world and the challenging, insistent voices of the new emerging world.' She quoted Pope John Paul II, who said: 'In every time and place our conditioning has been an obstacle to the progress of women. Women's dignity has often been unacknowledged, they have often been relegated to the margins of society and even reduced to servitude ... If objective blame especially in historical contexts has belonged to not just a few members of the Church for this, I am truly sorry.' President McAleese continued: 'Most intelligent men and women can recognise sexist cant, no matter how nobly dressed up, no matter how elevated the speaker, from miles away. So when the Holy Father admits the Church just might have been a teensie-weensie bit sexist at times, we wait for the next obvious statement – that the Church is going to take a long, hard, scholarly look at itself. It is going to try to understand how its own thinking, its very own understanding of God, has been skewed and damaged by 2,000 years of shameful codology dressed up as theology and, worse still, God's will. But the statement does not come. Instead the big guns, the howitzer of infallibility, is armed and aimed.'

Those 'rigid, conditioning forces of an old world' remain in the ascendant among the Church's scribes and Pharisees today. They show no sign whatever that they will lift any of the current burdens where women in the church are concerned. Nor where the current male-only priesthood is concerned either. There is to be no relaxation of the mandatory celibacy rule, a tradition without even the backing of 'shameful codology dressed up as theology'. There is no doubt this is a particularly heavy burden for very many priests, pushing some into double lives. Just the other evening I was speaking to a young couple who have three children and had become particularly close to a dynamic young priest who in a recent move-around was transferred to another parish. They recalled his visits to their house and his open expressions of envy at their having children and his baleful comment that he would never have a home. The emotionally desiccated lives such good men are forced to lead is a crime against their humanity. And if some become involved in irregular arrangements, it is not they who are to be blamed.

The hypocrisy of the scribes and Pharisees, however, is most evident where homosexuality – prevalent within their own very ranks – is concerned. In that same article in The Tablet Mary McAleese said: 'The dynamics of priesthood have altered radically along fault lines some of which have yet to be openly acknowledged and explored. Women have observed the enormous drain of heterosexual males from the priesthood and the growing phenomenon of gay priests.' She continued: 'They (women) are quietly asking what is happening at the core of the call to priesthood that attracts homosexuals in much greater numbers than their population distribution would explain. These questions are not being raised in any homophobic way but are among the raft of questions bubbling to the surface as we struggle to come to terms with the manifest demise of the model of priesthood on which the priest-mother alliance was once founded and is now foundering.' Yet, outside the Muslim world, there are few international institutions as virulently opposed to homosexuality as the Catholic Church, which it sees as a lifestyle choice rather than as a 'discovery', as President McAleese described it more recently. Speaking at the 24th world congress of the International Association for Suicide Prevention in Killarney on 31 August 2006, she said: 'Homosexuality is a discovery, not a decision and for many it is a discovery which is made against a backdrop where, within their immediate circle of family and friends as well as the wider society, they have long encountered anti-gay attitudes which will do little to help them deal openly and healthily with their own sexuality.' There is no doubt that the Church's attitude to homosexuality as 'objectively disordered' and as an orientation which tended towards the 'intrinsically evil' – to quote words of Joseph Ratzinger (before he became Pope Benedict) from 1986 – has contributed enormously to the distress and anxiety suffered by gay priests and to the deep insecurity of gay lay Catholics.

None of which was helped when in November 2005, seven months into his papacy, Benedict issued an instruction banning homosexuals from becoming priests, while seminarians with so-called temporary homosexual tendencies must be free of those for three years before ordination. All based too, many would argue, on what Mary McAleese referred to in her 1997 article in *The Tablet* as further 'shameful codology dressed up as theology'.

Meanwhile, what of our homegrown scribes and Pharisees? Most play the safe, orthodox, career game. With some outstanding exceptions, they are an unremarkable lot. A pale cast indeed. Included would be many of our younger theologians, from whom more gusto might be expected when it came to the theological liberation of priests and people from unnecessary burdens. No lions among them, either. None, for instance, have tackled the 'uncomfortable, somewhat frightening questions', that Bishop Willie Walsh raised in Dublin's Christ Church Cathedral on 6 November 2005 and which he said it would be 'even more frightening' not to face. Through torpor, inertia, or fear they have opted for the 'even more frightening' scenario. Maybe they have been cowed by the Vatican's brute treatment of their peerless seniors, men such as Fr Enda McDonagh and Fr

Seán Fagan, to mention just two of that great generation which has such brave men and women of deep compassion and integrity, lay and clerical, in it. And possibly that timidity among our younger scribes and Pharisees was reinforced by what happened to Fr Iggy O'Donovan after he, with a fully informed conscience, concelebrated the 2006 Easter Sunday Mass at St Augustine's in Drogheda with Rev Michael Graham, a Church of Ireland priest of equally informed conscience. Subsequently Fr O'Donovan was made issue a statement by Rome saying he had done wrong. He was then silenced and stopped from teaching Church history in Rome. They have such gentle, Christian ways!

So, while their counterparts in Rome continue to 'tie up heavy burdens and lay them on men's (and women's) shoulders', what of our homegrown scribes and Pharisees? '… will they lift a finger to move them? Not they!' Yet still they retain an extraordinarily high opinion of themselves. Some like to remind us they are now responsible for approximately 26 institutions which teach theology in Ireland. That in the process they have become 'defenders of the Vatican line, who sound more and more like Communist Party apparatchiks hawking redundant clichés' – to quote from Mary McAleese's article in *The Tablet* again – seems neither here nor there with them. Some too like to criticise the media – which is easy, as the media is never above criticism – for the lack of sophisticated debate on theological matters here, compared to France for instance, where such debate is lively. They, however, fail to acknowledge that theological debate was suppressed by them in Ireland for so long it forestalled any such tradition emerging here.

There is also the situation that what many of them instance as debate appears to most of the rest of us as little more than the absurd 'sound' of one hand clapping. How can there be real debate when one side is clearly not open to any different point of view on women priests, mandatory celibacy or homosexuality, for example? What is the point of 'debate' in a context where what you get from one side is little more than mere exposition of an immovable position? Instead, many of our native scribes and Pharisees pass their time attending and/or hosting conferences. Lots of conferences. I have been to enough over the years to be able to say with some conviction that their main purpose appears to be about no more than perpetuating the reputations and careers of speakers. Rarely do they concern themselves with issues of relevance to the broad mass of people, such as read newspapers.

One such conference I attended last year provided just 300 words of a news report and then only because the speaker, Bishop Donal Murray of Limerick, made a typically interesting observation (on Europe). However, a 60-line news report hardly justified the day spent at that conference. Indeed the liveliest part of that day was when it looked likely two participants might come to blows over their differing interpretations of the work of German philosopher, Immanuel Kant! A talk at a more recent conference was on 'A pneumatological Christology in the service of ecumenism: A case of neglect?' The man who presented the paper is among the more lucid of communicators, but try selling that title to a news editor! Or what of the rightly respected theologian who last year wrote a *Rite and Reason* column for me which began with a paragraph that was 182 words long, broken only by semi-colons. That paragraph alone would take up 36 lines in an *Irish Times* report. As time was short and I knew the paragraph as written had not a hope of getting into the paper, I broke it into shorter sentences while attempting not to violate a heavily nuanced point. The choice was as stark as do that, or allow a sub-editor 're-arrange' it. Or not publish it at all. I have not heard from its author since. Draw your own conclusion. So be it. My conclusion is that the author was not so much interested in communicating with readers, as with fellow theologians.

Such people then should stick to academic journals. Yet they demand (some, almost as of right) a wider audience. Which is fine. But if so, then they must deign to leave behind a style and language the public do not know.

What is particularly fascinating though about our current crop of scribes and Pharisees is their preoccupation with the arcane and obscure while the Catholic Church in Ireland faces its greatest crisis since penal times. Indeed, probably its greatest crisis ever. Nero fiddled while Rome burned. They talk cant while Catholic Ireland heads the way of O'Leary in his grave. To put it at its mildest, this is irresponsible, indulgent, and short-sighted, while the very edifice on which they have constructed their lives, identities, and careers declines all around them. There is more than an echo here of the band playing 'Nearer My God to Thee' as the Titanic sank beneath the waves. That, at least, had meaning. It is time they woke up to the Ireland around them and the needs of its people.

But, for now it is 'alas for you scribes and Pharisees ... Alas for you, blind guides ... straining out gnats and blind camels! ... In truth I tell you, it will all recoil on this generation ... Your house will be deserted ...'

Articles consulted in preparing this chapter

The Hope of Salvation for Infants Who Die Without Being Baptised, published 20 April 2007, by the Vatican's International Theological Commission.

Articles on St Philomena in the Catholic Encyclopedia, www.catholic. org, and at www.saintphilomenal.com

The Gospel of Matthew, Chapter 23.

The Irish Times, 31 October 2005, 'Comiskey now being unfairly scapegoated, says victim.'

The Irish Times, 7 November 2005, 'Church view of sexuality queried.'

Letter to the Bishops of the Catholic Church on the collaboration of men and women in the Church and in the world, by Pope Benedict and published on 31 May 2004

'It Won't Wash With Women', Mary McAleese, *The Tablet*, 15 March 1997.

'President Highlights Links between Sexual Identity and Suicide', delivered at the 24th world congress of the International Association for Suicide Prevention in Killarney on 31 August 2007. Available at www.president.ie

Instruction concerning the criteria for the discernment of vocations with regard to persons with homosexual tendencies in view of their admission to the seminary and to Holy Orders, published in Rome on 4 November 2005 by the Congregation for Catholic Education.

CHAPTER EIGHT

Devotion to Dissent: Irish-American Catholicism, 1945-2006

Lawrence J. McCaffrey

Looking back, I see that it was religion that saved me. Our ugly church and parochial school provided me with my only aesthetic outlet, in the words of the Mass and the litanies and the old Latin hymns, in the Easter lilies around the altar, rosaries, ornamented prayer books, votive lamps, holy cards stamped in gold and decorated with flower wreaths and a saint's picture. This side of Catholicism, much of it cheapened and debased by mass production, was for me, nevertheless, the equivalent of Gothic cathedrals and illuminated manuscripts and mystery plays. I threw myself into it with ardor.[1]

Tom Hundley opens his 9 July 2006 *Chicago Tribune* article, 'How Catholicism fell from Grace in Ireland', at 8:30 am Mass in Dublin's pro-Cathedral. To him, the celebrant, Father Remegious Owuamanam, a Nigerian priest, symbolises fading Irish Catholicism; a nation that once covered the globe with nuns and priests has become mission territory. Perhaps Hundley would also be surprised by priests saying Mass in Evanston, Illinois. The last three associate pastors at Saint Mary's, its oldest parish, once Irish, have come from Africa, Poland and India. Another priest from India is pastor at St Nicholas, the neighbouring parish. Foreign priests serving in the United States also indicates declining enthusiasm and loyalty in American Catholicism.

***

Early nineteenth-century Irish immigrants, the first large group of Catholics to enter the United States, arrived impoverished, often illiterate and strange to urban living, causing massive social

---

1. Mary McCarthy, *Memories of a Catholic Girlhood* (New York: Harcourt and Brace, 1957), p 18.

problems. Anglo-Protestant Americans detested them more for their religion than their anti-civil behaviour. Increasingly, priests from Ireland came to preserve and strengthen their faith. The educational and social institutions they established, as well as the messages they preached, constructed familiarity bridges between old and new worlds. In time, local seminaries and novitiates provided home-grown priests and nuns for the American Church.

While lacking competitive economic talents, Irish newcomers possessed some survival skills. In addition to strong backs for hard work, they usually spoke English and knew about Anglo-Protestant laws and political institutions. As Alexis de Tocqueville noted during his 1835 Irish journey, clergy in Ireland, unlike the Continent, enthusiastically endorsed popular sovereignty.[2] Since a majority of bishops, priests, nuns, and brothers were Irish, American Catholicism developed a distinctly Hibernian flavour.[3]

Irish American Catholicism resembled the Irish variety. Both served as essences for cultural as well as spiritual identities. To quote Patrick O'Farrell, Catholicism was 'a set of values, a culture, a historical tradition, a view of the world, a disposition of mind and heart, a loyalty, an emotion, a psychology – and a nationalism.'[4] Unlike other Catholic immigrants, the Irish came from a land where believer generosity, not the State's, financially endowed their Church. They followed that tradition while also proudly contributing some of their best and brightest sons and daughters to religious life. Irish Puritanism also travelled over

2. Emmet Larkin (editor and translator), *Alex de Tocqueville's Tour in Ireland, July-August, 1935* (Washington DC: Catholic University of America Press, 1990), pp 39-47, 61-67, 78-80.
3. According to Charles R. Morris, *American Catholics: The Saints and Sinners Who Built America's Most Powerful Church* (New York NY: Random House, 1997), p 52: 'The ethnic background of American bishops consecrated between 1850 and 1910 clearly shows the rise in Irish influence. From the 1850s through the 1900s, the Irish, including native priests of Irish descent, accounted for half the consecrations, rising to 60 percent in the 1890s, and to 75 percent by the early 1900s, where it remained until the 1960s.'
4. Patrick O'Farrell, *Ireland's English Question* (New York: Schocken Books, 1971), p 306.

the water. Men and women often married late, if at all, but once wed had large families. Puritanism encouraged gender segregation and male comradeship in pubs and saloons, breeding alcoholism.

There were differences as well as similarities between Irish and Irish-American Catholicism. Although Catholics in Ireland suffered through a long history of British and Anglo-Irish oppression, they had the consolation of being a majority in their own country and defining its personality. And since Irish nationalism blossomed in the struggle for Catholic civil liberties, and bishops and priests were influences in agitations for Repeal and Home Rule, sovereignty came in the form of a Catholic confessional state.

In contrast, for a long period Irish Americans were an unwelcome minority in an Anglo-Protestant nation. Nativist hostility tightened Irish and Catholic bonds while fostering persecution defensiveness, often reaching paranoia. With Protestants viewing their religion as an alien, authoritarian, anti-intellectual, subversive threat to American institutions and values, Catholics tried to balance religious and national loyalties, often an illogical task. Authoritarianism in the American Church pragmatically was less visible than in Ireland with many Catholic politicians trying to avoid appearances of subservience to clerical dictation.

Although Irish Catholics were mostly rural and Irish-Americans usually urban, the latter's city parishes functioned a bit like villages in Ireland, serving as educational and social centres as well as faith sanctuaries. In Ireland, bishops had more unified agendas than American prelates who had to adjust to a variety of regional experiences. In eastern cities, Anglo-Protestant discrimination and aloofness plus their own defeatism cultivated Irish mental as well as physical isolation from the main stream. Sharing and promoting lay insecurities and fearing Protestant encroachment, the hierarchy distrusted and resisted Americanisation. In the Midwest and West, where Irish settlers confronted less hostility and had more economic opportunities, the hierarchy tended to embrace and endorse many American values and institutions.

In general, American Catholic bishops and priests, usually from working-class homes, were politically and socially more liberal than those in Ireland. In the 1920s, Monsignor John A. Ryan, Head of the National Catholic Welfare Conference, authored a social justice agenda anticipating President Franklin D. Roosevelt's New Deal. Roosevelt awarded American Catholic Democratic Party loyalty with 25% of government appointments, most of them Irish.[5] He had cordial relations with members of the hierarchy, especially Chicago's Cardinal Mundelein. Irish Catholics fit well into the alliance that formed the 1932-1968 Democratic Party. Their communalism shaped its social welfare policies.

***

From early nineteenth century arrivals to early decades of the twentieth century, Irish-American Catholics advanced from mostly unskilled to skilled workers, with significant penetrations of the middle class, and moved from turbulent inner-city neighbourhoods to more pleasant urban and suburban dwellings. Surging occupational mobility owed something to the Devotional Revolution, which post-Famine Irish priests brought to the United States. Its discipline improved immigration quality and reduced destructive conduct hampering the progress of Irish America. Negatively, it imposed an authoritarian, puritanical, relatively joyless, simple-minded, rules and regulations form of Catholicism on the American Church, which more integrated generations later rejected.[6]

Irish religious and secular experiences established a model and set a pattern for Eastern and Southern European immi-

---

5. George Q. Flynn, *American Catholics and the Roosevelt Presidency* (Lexington KY: University of Kentucky Press, 1968), pp 50-55, 98-99, 230, 234, 237 details Roosevelt's rewards to Catholics.

6. In 'The Devotional Revolution in Ireland, 1850-1875,' *American Historical Review* 77, 1972, pp. 625-52, republished in Lawrence J. McCaffrey (ed), *The Historical Dimensions of Irish Catholicism* (New York: Arno Press, 1976), revised and republished Washington DC: Catholic University of America Press, 1984), Emmet Larkin first traced the beginnings and character of the Devotional Revolution. In his latest book, *The Pastoral Role of the Roman Catholic Church in Pre-Famine Ireland, 1750-1850* (Washington DC: Catholic University of America Press, and Dublin: Four Courts Press, 2006), Larkin expresses reservations on its merits. He now believes it imposed a dour religious perspective on a bawdy, jolly people.

grants following them into urban America. They too, not always happily, became part of the Irish spiritual empire. Irish-American politicians took care of their worldly needs and Irish priests and politicians mediated between them and the Anglo-Protestant Establishment. Because they led an expanding and powerful Church, politically controlled numerous cities, and were a major force in organised labour, Anglo-Protestant nativists continued to despise Irish Americans.

After a bitter no-popery campaign, Herbert Hoover defeated New York's Irish-American Governor Al Smith in the 1928 presidential election. At a time of national prosperity, it was unlikely that a Democrat would prevail over a candidate from the incumbent Republicans. Still, religious prejudices widened Hoover's majority, while shattering Catholic hopes of full acceptance in a nation they loved.[7]

After the 1928 heartbreak, life for Irish-Americans and other Catholics improved. Common misery during the Great Depression, which began in 1929 and lasted until the United States entered World War II, reduced ethnic and religious conflict. Compared to many other Americans, the Irish endured the nation's economic collapse relatively well. Those employed in such largely Irish occupations as policemen and fireman, railroad and transport workers, nurses, teachers and civil servants, continued to draw salaries. World War II, and the Cold War that followed, joined Americans in patriotic fervour and sacrifice. From 1941 to 1945, combat in Africa, Europe, and the Pacific theatres provided Catholics with courageous and dangerous opportunities to demonstrate love of country.

During the 1930s, 40s, and 50s, movies presented positive Catholic images, especially those featuring popular actors – Spencer Tracy, Pat O'Brien, Bing Crosby, Barry Fitzgerald, Karl Malden – as Irish-American priests. Roman collar movies drew large audiences and earned critical reviews and prizes, particularly Leo McCarey's 1944 *Going My Way*, which captured seven academy awards, including best actor and supporting actor for Crosby and Fitzgerald, and set a box office record. The follow-

---

7. Alan J. Lichtman, *Prejudice and the Old Politics; The Presidential Election of 1928* (Chapel Hill: University of North Carolina Press, 1969)

ing year, with Crosby reprising his Father Chuck O'Malley role, *The Bells of St Mary's* attracted an even larger audience.

Irish-American movie priests were manly specimens, functioning more as social workers than agents of religion. They did not say Mass or hear confessions. Tracy impersonating Father Edward Flanagan rescued troubled youth in two Boys' Town movies; O'Brien's Father Connolly did the same in *Angels With Dirty Faces*; his Father Francis Duffy, an actual Hell's Kitchen cleric, comforted World War I soldiers in *The Fighting 69th*; and Crosby's fictional Father Chuck O'Malley saved boys from delinquency. In *On the Waterfront*, Malden's Father Barry battled communists and gangsters attempting to control the dockworkers' union. These admirable, do-good Irish-American priests indicated to non-Catholic film goers that Catholicism was a benign, civilising force.[8]

On-screen, George M. Cohan, who wrote songs Americans sang in two World Wars, epitomised Irish-Catholic patriotism. In 1942, Warner Brothers released *Yankee Doodle Dandy*, a fictionalised biography of Cohan. In the film, when Franklin D. Roosevelt (Captain Jack Young) presented Cohan (Jimmy Cagney) with the Congressional Medal, he commented: 'That's one thing I've always admired about you Irish Americans. You carry your love of country like a flag, right out in the open. It's a great quality.'[9] *The Sullivans*, later renamed *The Fighting Sullivans* (1944), another tribute to Irish American patriotism, was a true story of five Waterloo, Iowa brothers who enlisted in the navy following Pearl Harbour and died together when a Japanese submarine torpedoed their cruiser, the *Juno*. *The Fighting 69th* (1940) and *Guadacanal Diary* (1943) presented two non-fictional, heroic Irish-American Catholic chaplains, Fathers Francis Duffy and Ignatius Donnelly.

8. Joseph M. Curran, *Hibernian Green on the Silver Screen: The Irish and American Movies* (Westport CN: Greenwood Press, 1989); Charles R. Morris, *American Catholic*, pp 196-200; Lawrence J. McCaffrey, 'Going My Way' and Irish-American Catholicism, Myth and Reality,' in *New Hibernian Review* 4 (3), 2000, pp 119-127; Lawrence J. McCaffrey, 'Catholic Irish America: Drifting Into The Mainstream,' in *Irquas* 3, 2006, pp 3-4. *On the Waterfront*'s Father Barry is based on Father John Corridan SJ, an active labour priest.
9. Curran, *op. cit.*, p 87.

In addition to elevating Catholic images, World War II reduced their social isolation. Those in military service met and co-operated with a variety of ethnic and religious comrades. Servicemen often returned home racially prejudiced but with good will in regard to once ignored whites. Catholic women, less culturally and socially affected by the war, did establish connections with other-faith co-workers in offices and defence plants.

Perhaps even more than World War II, the 1944 Servicemen's Readjustment Act (GI Bill) speeded Catholic integration into the general population. This generous and grateful legislation offered veterans many benefits, most important an expense-paid college education. Campuses quickly filled with ex-soldiers, sailors, and marines. No group profited more from the GI Bill than Irish Americans. Rigorous Catholic secondary education prepared its graduates for higher education challenges. After earning BA and BS degrees, many proceeded to graduate and professional schools. In numerous ways, the GI Bill created a social revolution. It certainly resulted in an essentially middle-class Irish America.

'White Flight', as well as prosperity, motivated Irish-American migrations to 'safe' urban and suburban neighbourhoods. Joining other whites, they either abandoned old residences or stayed and opposed integrated racial education and housing for African-Americans, attempting to escape overcrowded, poverty- and violence-loaded ghettoes. In *Parish Boundaries: The Catholic Encounter with Race in the Twentieth-Century Urban North* (1996), John T. McGreevey describes the transition of parishes from psychological shelters for depressed and oppressed Catholics to defensive garrisons, defying Christian charity in efforts to protect white ethnic interests.[10]

Racism and militant, often irrational, irresponsible anti-communism, reflected in support of Senator Joseph McCarthy's 1950s witch hunt for communists in government and later support for the disastrous war in Vietnam, revealed lingering Irish-

---

10. John T. McGreevey, *Parish Boundaries: The Catholic Experience with Race in the Twentieth-Century Urban North* (Chicago, Il: University of Chicago Press, 1969).

American status insecurities. Still, at the same time large numbers of Irish Americans were marking the nation's political, social, and cultural landscapes, and in businesses and professions that once excluded them. While still a significant force in urban governments, increasingly Irish-American politicians were influential in Washington DC. John F. Kennedy's election as the 35th American President, and his post-inauguration American and world popularity, enabled Irish Americans and other Catholics to shed lingering anxieties. Film director, John Ford, wrote to a friend that Kennedy's victory made him for the first time feel like a 'first-class' American.[11]

Prior to the election, some Irish-American political leaders feared Kennedy's candidacy would revive 1928 style anti-Catholic ranting and raving. It did, affecting a number of Protestant voters, but not enough to impede a Democratic win. President Kennedy was just one example of Irish-American power and influence. During and after his brief administration, the chair of the Democratic National Committee, John Bailey, was Irish Catholic; so was Mike Mansfield, Senate Majority Leader; John McCormack, Speaker of the House of Representatives; Richard J. Daley, Mayor of Chicago, head of probably the most efficient and powerful urban political machine in American history; and George Meaney, President of the combined American Federation of Labor (AFL) and Congress of Industrial Organizations (CIO).

Post-War times also shed good fortune on Irish-led American Catholicism. A booming economy encouraged early marriages and large families. Population increase and new homes in expanding suburbia required additional churches and schools. Thanks to the GI Bill, enrolments in Catholic colleges and universities rapidly increased. To keep pace with these trends, Irish-America continued to supply the Church with priests, religious sisters and brothers and funds for bricks and mortar. Quite a few young men choosing religious life were former servicemen, spiritualised by war-time experiences.

College and university education, professional success, political power and prestige not only freed an overwhelming majority

---

11. Curran, *op. cit.*, p 133, n 4.

of Irish-American Catholics from ghetto mentalities, it also, for a time, liberated their Church from antagonism toward American ways. Priests and religious sisters were highly visible in campaigns for inter-racial justice and world peace. North and South, they marched for civil rights and against the Vietnam War, which resulted in some cases with imprisonment. Catholic institutions of higher learning intellectually moved beyond medieval style neo-Thomism to confront modern realties, gaining respect throughout academia. In general, Catholic clergy and laity extended hands of friendship and co-operation to other Americans. Not particularly astute in theological intricacies, Irish-American representatives at Vatican II (1962-65) led their Church in accepting ecumenical dialogue, and liberal democracy with its separation of Church and State principles.

Architecturally lavish Churches and schools, over-flowing with worshippers and students, a large supply of religious vocations, high status and social standing for Catholic priests and people, and liberal views evident in colleges, universities and clerical circles, obscured trends that eventually challenged Church authority and doctrine, reducing lay loyalties. What happened to the Church since the mid-1960s gives strength to an old cliché that a candle burns brightest before going out.

Vatican II excited hopes that the Church was going to catch up with history, to migrate from the Counter-Reformation to the twentieth century, and respond to the desires and needs of a laity that no longer were rural peasants or urban immigrants. But Vatican II results were more shadow than substance. Liturgical changes camouflaged a determination to resist theological modernisation. Tedious sermons and unpleasant music took the place of the history and mystery of discarded Catholic rituals, transforming for many, especially the young, religious services into boring experiences.

Post-Vatican II disappointments instigated dissent on a number of issues, especially contraception. Shortly after the Council adjourned, Pope Paul VI appointed a commission of distinguished clergy and laity to examine the question and make recommendations. In 1967, commissioners advised parental discretion in regard to family planning. Rejecting their decision, Paul VI issued *Humanae Vitae*, insisting the rhythm method was the only legitimate means of family limitation. Most Catholics made it clear that calendars and thermometers ('Roman Roulette') were not going to govern romance between husbands and wives. A large number of priests agreed with an angry laity. Critics have described *Humanae Vitae* as a time bomb, the Vietnam of Roman Catholicism, the beginning of a religious revolution.[12] Certainly, it aroused challenges to Vatican authority on more issues than just contraception. The majority of American Catholics approve a married clergy, women priests and a return of divorced people to the fold. There are those who believe certain circumstances can render abortion a lesser evil than bearing a child. And some Catholics are certain embryonic stem-cell research reaffirms rather than denies life.[13]

Not only does an American Catholic majority reject the Church's position on contraception because it unnaturally interferes with married romance and reflects neurotic sexual opinions of a celibate clergy, but also fears that it jeopardises their middle-class status. In the United States, raising and educating children and keeping them healthy is expensive, forcing family size to conform to financial resources.

Humanae Vitae proved cataclysmic. Mass attendance began, and continued, to drop. Many priests, sisters and brothers, in-

12. 'Catholic Freedom Versus Authority,' in *Time*, 22 November 1968. For a discussion of the contraception issue and defence of *Humanae Vitae* see W. Bradford Wilcox, 'The Fact of Life & Marriage: Social Scientists and the vindication of Christian Moral Teaching,' in *Touchstone Magazine*, Jan/Feb 2005.
13. A number of polls exist concerning American Catholic opinion on moral and social issues. A September 27-29, 1995 *Time/CNN* survey appearing in the October 9 issue of *Time* indicated 70% favoured married clergy, 60% approved ordaining women, 69% thought divorced people should be able to marry in a religious ceremony, only 20% disapproved of pre-marital sex, 79% viewed contraception as a matter of private conscience, 59% practised birth control, and 80% believed that their disagreements with the Pope did not disqualify them as good Catholics. According to a May 2002 *Newsweek* opinion poll on American Catholic viewpoints, 50% felt at odds with Rome on sexuality, 59% did not think screening gays out of the priesthood would make much of a difference in reducing sexual abuse, 51% had no qualms attending Mass in a parish with an openly gay priest, 73% would accept married priests and 65% ordained women (*Newsweek*, 6 May 2002).

cluding some of the most talented, have abandoned vocations. Throughout the 1970s, 80s, 90s, into the early years of the twenty-first century, clergy numbers have continued to decline. Too many surviving nuns, priests, and brothers are old or aging, with few replacements. Irish Americans who supplied their Church with so many religious no longer do so; their names infrequently appear on ordination lists. Formerly, bright Irish-American males, confronting Protestant prejudices, had few opportunities outside the Church, politics or the labour movement. Women, interested in more than marriage, could be nuns or lay equivalents, teachers or nurses. Now both sexes have multitudes of possibilities.

On 20 September 2006, Chicago's archdiocese, the nation's second largest, announced a June 2007 closing of Quigley preparatory seminary. In the 1950s, it enrolled about 1,300 high-school age students. Now there are only 183, few intending to become priests. During the last 16 years, just one Quigley graduate has done so. In 1967, there were 171 American preparatory seminaries with 16,000 students; in 2006 there are five with 763.[14] Clerical quality as well as quantity is also a problem. While intelligence is not necessarily a vocational qualification, sermons and/or homilies are mandatory, giving an importance to what priests say and how they say it. In 2005, the Chicago archdiocese ordained just twelve men, four from Poland, three from Mexico, two from South America, one each from Africa and Asia and only one from the United States.

Foreign clerics fulfil a definite need but cultural gaps and language barriers can and do hamper communication between altar and pew and in confessionals. Seminaries are featuring late vocations, which is all for the good if life experiences have taught candidates that the religious life is truly for them; it is a disaster if viewed as a refuge from personal problems or world realities.

Despite priest shortages, Sunday Masses still attract many worshippers but on weekday mornings only the elderly usually appear. Unlike former times, lines for Saturday confessions are

14. On the closing of Quigley Preparatory Seminary see *Chicago Tribune*, 20 Sept 2006, pp 1, 15. On recent ordinations of foreign priests in Chicago see *Chicago Tribune*, 23 Sept 2006, editorial, p 18.

small or non-existent. Since Eucharist recipients are numerous, today's Catholics obviously have different notions of sin than did their parents and grandparents. Quite a few inner-city parishes, victims of suburbanisation, have vanished or are disappearing and parochial schools in cities and suburbs have merged or closed, particularly those providing chances for African-American children, usually Protestant, to obtain a decent education when public schools fail to supply same. With few sisters and brothers available to teach, Catholic elementary and secondary schools have raised tuitions, often beyond family means, to pay lay teachers. Large numbers of Catholic parents prefer to take advantage of culturally rich and varied public school programmes that they pay high taxes to support.

Have the lures of materialism and secularism seduced Catholic loyalties in the United States and elsewhere? 'Yes', said Pope John Paul II and other Church leaders, predicting that Africa and other underdeveloped countries are Catholicism's future. Did they and do they mean that it is a religion best suited for the poor and ignorant? But blaming worldliness on lost or disappearing Church allegiances is too facile. Religion is significant for most Catholics but less so than in the past because much of its message seems unimportant and at times a bit silly.

Actually, religious slippage began ages ago. Since the eighteenth century, cultural and social trends have detached people from religious commitments. Enlightenment rationalism appealed to upper- and middle-class intellectuals. Following the Industrial Revolution, Christianity slowly and inadequately responded to working-class problems. For unique reasons, Catholicism managed to retain Irish loyalties. Until recently, the bulk of Ireland's population was rural, lightly affected by industrialisation and urbanisation. Catholic and Gaelic-Ireland nationalism, and World War II neutrality kept it fairly well isolated from outside 'pagan' influences. Like the Irish in Ireland, those in America tightly hung on to their religion as a foundation of their identity and psychological comfort and security.

Tourism, movies, television, books, returned immigrants, plus membership in the United Nations and European Union and post-DeValera industrialism, accompanied by urbanisation, ended Ireland's cultural separation from the rest of Europe. In the United States, patriotism during World War II, followed by acceptability and respectability, immersed the Irish in America's mainstream. As Irish Catholics in both countries adapted to general Western values and conduct, they doubted the Church's ability to interpret and express God's word in meaningful ways.

In pre-1960s Ireland, literary artists such as Seán O Faoláin, Frank O'Connor, Mervyn Wall, Patrick Kavanagh, Austin Clarke, James Plunkett and others blamed Irish-Catholic Puritanism, authoritarianism, and anti-intellectualism for their country's cultural retardation. Irish-American writers made similar charges. Devout Catholic, J. F. Powers, talented novelist and short story writer, lamented priests who neglected their vocations to focus on golf and rectory comforts and limited their reading to *The Reader's Digest*. Thomas Fleming, whose novels have covered America's wars from the Revolution to Viet Nam, also discussed Irish-American politics and Catholicism. He lacerated the latter's irrelevant defensive posture and intellectual medievalism, denying post-World War II Catholics admittance to American opportunities. Fleming believed *Humanae Vitae*-style puritanism destroyed married joy, passion, and love.[15]

Suburbanisation substituted multi- for single-ethnic parishes, gradually lessening connections between religion and group identities. Theologically this was positive, insisting on Catholicism as universal rather than tribal, but for many ethnics it eliminated a major source of who they were, or at least how they thought of themselves. College, university and suburban experiences resulted in communication, friendship, and frequent intermarriage between Catholics and other Americans, reducing religious faith as a distinct aspect of individual lives. Parish activities took second, sometimes third or fourth place, behind various non-sectarian social events. Higher education resulted in situations where lay people were more knowledgeable than priests and bishops, leading to critical judgements of what

---

15. Lawrence J. McCaffrey, 'Fictional Images of Irish America,' in Tom Dunne (ed.), *The Writer as Witness: Literature as Historical Witness* (Cork: Cork University Press, 1987), pp 227-244. For an excellent survey of Irish-American literature, see Charles Fanning, *The Irish Voice in America: 250 Years of Irish-American Fiction* (Lexington: University Press of Kentucky, 1999).

was heard and read. Since the Irish tended to be more sophisticated than other American Catholics, they have led and still lead much of the dissent.

Tom Hundley attributes much of Catholicism's decline in Ireland to sex abuse, which has damaged reputations of clerical perpetrators and bishops who enabled and covered up molestations of children and adolescents. Similar crimes and sins have occurred in the United States, branding the Church in both places as morally hypocritical and insensitive to abuse victims. Since so many American bishops and priests have been Irish, it is hardly surprising that they have been numerous among offenders.

Newspaper and television journalists exaggerate paedophile dimensions of sexual abuse. Most victims are adolescents, not children. And too many Catholics mistakenly link paedophilia and homosexuality. But the disproportionately high numbers of homosexuals in the clergy – estimated at twenty-five percent and over – troubles the laity.[16] Many fear that gays culturally dominate a number of seminaries, monasteries, friaries and other religious residences. Because priests have lost much of the admiration and respect they once enjoyed, their sexual problems are more obvious today than yesterday. Without that something-to-live-up-to prestige they once enjoyed, some probably find it more difficult to summon courage, pride and will to resist temptations. On the homosexual issue, the Church faces a dilemma. It now wants to exclude gays from the priesthood, but current low-status clerical life has little attraction for talented heterosexuals, and while there is considerable tolerance for homosexual clerics, lay people in general oppose designating religious life as a priestly profession.

Press and television reports of priestly misadventures have

16. A.W. Richard Sipe, a former Benedictine monk, and a psychologist, estimated that about 30% of priests have homosexual orientations. Father Donald Cozzens, former rector of the Cleveland seminary has written that approximately 50% of seminarians he knew were probably homosexual in tendencies. Sipe, Cozzens, and Eugene Kennedy, former priest and psychologist, evaluate a large percentage of the clergy as psychologically immature. In many places, Charles R. Morris' *American Catholic* intelligently discusses sexual problems in the American Catholic clergy.

seriously wounded the Church, particularly in Ireland and Irish America, where it has stressed sexual purity and clerical celibacy. Scandal, not only sexual, but financial as well, has dimmed the luster of what was a once celebrated vocation. In a 26 April 2002 *Chicago Tribune* 'Tempo' section essay, Julia Keller predicted that cinema would no longer feature admirable, manly priests such as Fathers Chuck O'Malley and Edward Flanagan.

Media exposures of disgusting clerical sexual frolics have created financial crises in numerous dioceses. Needed funds for educational and social services have gone to victims and lawyers. At present, four dioceses have declared bankruptcy – Portland (Oregon), Spokane (Washington), Tucson (Arizona), Davenport (Iowa) – and others have had to sell valuable property to compensate victims.[17]

In addition to Rome's long-time indifference to clerical sexual abuse, its hierarchical appointments have widened divisions between the institutional Church and the laity. Frequently, John Paul II's choices have been inflexibly conservative. Without appreciation of America's separation of Church and State principles, in 2004 a few prelates boldly advised voters to reject presidential candidate John Kerry, a Catholic, because he supported freedom of choice on abortion. Bishops, priests and lay conservatives, so militant in opposing contraception, abortion and stem-cell research, and so apparently indifferent to the unjust war in Iraq and poverty issues, leave an impression that a right to life emphasis ceases with birth. A large shift of Irish-American Catholics from politically Democrat to Republican suggests that for them individualism has replaced social justice communalism.

---

17. On 10 Oct 2006, Davenport became the latest diocese to file for bankruptcy. A relatively poor diocese in eastern Iowa with 84 parishes and approximately 105,000 Catholics, Davenport has paid out about $10,500,000 dollars in abuse claims since 2004. The most infamous abuser was Lawrence Soens. As principal of Regina High School in Iowa City, he victimised many students. He then became Bishop of Sioux City, Iowa. For at least fifty years bishops in Davenport have moved priestly abusers from parish to parish, a frequent occurrence in the American Catholic Church. Many wealthier archdioceses and dioceses, such as Boston, have sold considerable amounts of property to settle abuse claims. For the bankruptcy story in Davenport see *The DesMoines Register* and *Iowa City Press Citizen*, 11 Oct 2006.

Concentrating on *Humanae Vitae* and sex abuse fallouts to explain Catholicism's 'fall from grace' only scratches the surface. Is a Church grounded intellectually in the thirteenth-century equipped to communicate with the twenty-first? Can a rigidly authoritative religion adapt to liberal-democratic political environments? Eugene O'Brien argues that a Church frozen in a pre-eighteenth century God-centred atmosphere cannot speak to desire-motivated twenty-first century Catholics.[18] While deconstructing Catholicism's symbols and vocabulary, he pleads for its reconstruction rather than its destruction.

The Church's increasing irrelevance has as much to do with structure as message. In Ireland and Irish America, Catholics have shared contradictory loyalties to a despotic religious system and liberal-democratic political opposites. With contemporary Ireland politically sovereign, prosperous, and culturally, economically and politically integrated into Europe, and Irish America comfortably sailing in its country's mainstream, both, emancipated from past doubts and anxieties, prefer freedom of conscience and opinion over Vatican intellectual and theological despotism.

In 2002, Dublin Cardinal Desmond Connell described Ireland as post-Catholic. The next year, his successor, Archbishop Diarmuid Martin, opened a discussion centred on whether Irish Catholicism would survive another 30 years. In the United States, where belief in God and Church attendance are strong, the situation appears more promising. However, it is true that most American Catholics, conservative as well as liberal, take a casual approach to their religion, choosing and rejecting items on the papal menu to suit individual beliefs and values.

Irish America has profited from mainstream membership and a casual approach to the official Catholic bill-of-fairs, both liberating it from a ghetto mentality and religious authoritarianism, enriching its intellectual and creative contributions to national culture, and opening once-closed doors of opportunity. Still, for

---

18. Eugene O'Brien, 'Kicking Bishop Brennan up the Arse ...: Catholicism, Deconstruction and Postmodernity in Contemporary Irish Culture,' in Louise Fuller, John Littleton and Eamon Maher (eds), *Irish and Catholic? Toward an Understanding of Identity* (Dublin: The Columba Press, 2006), pp 47-67.

some there have been losses. Mental ghettoes offered psycholog-ical security, the comfort of a clear identity in a multi-cultural, multi-ethic, multi racial America, constantly in flux. For the am-bitious and bright, gains outweigh losses.

Archbishop Martin insists that the Church in Ireland must become less authoritarian, reach out and listen to lay voices. No American prelate has been that flexible or perceptive. However, it must happen here as well as there for Irish Catholicism to sur-vive in a relatively healthy form. Of course, much depends on Rome. Common sense dictates an increase in the quantity and quality of the clergy, necessitating ordinations of married men and women, and intelligent approaches to sexuality, marriage, family planning, health and medicine, and gender equality.

***

The Church has become just another fallible, sometimes corrupt and intellectually irrelevant institution. For most Irish Americans Catholicism now constitutes merely one aspect of their ethnicity; for a few it does not matter at all. Those concerned about being Irish find it in history, literature, music, theatre, and compiling genealogies as well as in Catholic worship and tradition. Obviously the Irish-American Catholic candle has dimmed but some flame remains. 'Once a Catholic always a Catholic,' at least culturally, is a saying with merit. In his 2006 published memoir, *All Will Be Well*, the late John McGahern, who abandoned Catholicism, like Mary McCarthy in the opening quote, beauti-fully expressed how much its devotions brought to his life: 'In an impoverished time they were my first introduction to an in-door beauty of luxury and ornament, ceremony and sacrament and mystery.'[19] Gary Wills, perhaps America's leading, certainly one of its most versatile intellectuals, has also hailed the ele-gance and spiritual comfort that Catholicism and its sacraments had in former times: 'Moments of purity remembered, when the world seemed fresh out of its maker's hands, trees washed by some rain sweeter than the world's own.'[20]

---

19. John McGahern, *All Will Be Well* (New York: Alfred A. Knopf, 2006) p 213. McGahern had a Catholic funeral and burial.
20. Gary Wills, *Bare Ruined Choirs* (Garden City NY: Doubleday and Co, 1972), p 37

Perhaps Catholicism can no longer offer what it gave to McCarthy, McGahern and Wills at various stages of their lives, but it will remain an important, if not essential, portion of Irish-American existences. American Catholics will continue to respect the papacy, though wishing, like the British monarchy, it would reign, not rule. They remain excited about papal visits, deaths, funerals and elections. Vatican pageantry and ritual command audiences, giving colour to otherwise colourless lives.

If not necessarily an essential element in their ethnic identity, Irish-American Catholics will continue to practice their religion as part of family heritage, a need for beauty and the stability of tradition. They will baptise children and see that they receive First Communion and Confirmation. Most marriage ceremonies will be at an altar and funerals and burials in Catholic Churches and cemeteries. Religious ceremonies will continue to mark Irish-American life passages. Irish-Americans also will continue wearing green and often drinking too much alcohol on St Patrick's Day. Quite a few over-imbibers will think this more Irish than attending Mass or saying a Rosary.

PART THREE

Artists, Poets and Writers on Irish Catholicism

Sites of Worship, Sites of Desire:
Catholicism and Dorothy Cross's Stabat Mater

Eóin Flannery

[W]hat is most relevant here is to consider the tombs as a link between everyday life, ever visible in the landscape, and the sacred, marked by ceremonies at the sites which emphasised the continued link between the past and present, between ancestors, the dead and the living community.[1]

I

Pope Pius XII's encyclical letter *Fulgens Corona*, published in 1953, proclaimed 1954 to be the Marian Year, in order to commemorate the centenary of the definition of the dogma of the Immaculate Conception. And subsequently a statement was issued by the Irish Bishops on this matter, which encouraged the community of Catholics in Ireland to undertake the task of financing and producing statues of the Virgin Mary at a local, parochial level.[2] The institution of the Marian Year in 1954 was politically and culturally consonant with the temper of Irish society both during and prior to this period. The De Valerean social vision had been legislatively enshrined in the 1937 Constitution, as well as in his famous 1943 St Patrick's Day speech, both of which endorsed the primacy of the nuclear family and confirmed the passive domesticity of Irish womanhood. As has been well documented in recent Irish feminist historical and cultural studies, the female body was legally and morally sequestered within a battery of theocratic ideals and injunctions. The recalcitrant sexuality of (Irish) femininity is also a matter that has been productively addressed in discourses such as literary theory, women's studies, national history and visual culture.

1. Gabriel Cooney, 'Sacred and Secular Neolithic landscapes in Ireland', in *Sacred Sites, Sacred Places*, David L. Carmichael *et al* (eds), (London: Routledge, 1994), p 35.
2. On the Irish Bishops' statement see *The Furrow*, 4 (11), 1953), pp 666-668.

In adjacent fields of Irish history we witness a similar objectification of femininity: Irish nationalist literary history and popular cultural history. Throughout the protracted, and by no means homogenous, history of Irish anti-colonial nationalism, the figure[s] of Irish femininity was at the forefront of the nationalist symbolic armoury. From the verses of the Gaelic 'Aisling' tradition, to Thomas Moore's *Melodies* and James Clarence Mangan's 'Dark Rosaleen', and on to Yeats's *Countess Cathleen*, the desire for Irish national autonomy has been figured in terms of a violated and/or incarcerated female. Yet the sanctity of the metaphorised female has been too frequently in inverse proportion to the actual agency afforded to Irish women in daily social and political life. The symbolisation of Irish femininity effectively disabused women of such agency and precluded ideas such as female desire or volition from the public sphere.

In light of much revisionist social commentary, and equally cultural criticism, in recent times, the affective relationship between the majority of Ireland's population and the Catholic faith would seem to be approaching the nominal and the residual. It is, perhaps, no less true to state that the sites of religious worship, both Catholic and Protestant, in Ireland have undergone a transformation in the shadow of Ireland's contemporary cultural economy. Even at a superficial level the deferent attitudes of Irish people walking by Churches, shrines, grottoes, even graveyards, are assuredly performances of the past at this juncture. Indeed a cursory survey of popular culture points to a secularisation, or at times an ironisation, of the sites of both Catholic and Protestant religious worship. In a number of instances we have witnessed the conversion of Churches from decorous spaces of prayer and veneration to scenes that act out the rituals of capitalist modernity; there has been a widening of the uses to which such sacred spaces have been put. Such a transformation is evident in the re-deployment of erstwhile Churches as postmodern public houses, a phenomenon also apparent in the United Kingdom; the opening up of cathedrals and other religious sites as financial resources as part of the global/national tourist economy. Once dominant monumental symbols of a resolute political-cultural landscape, these religious spaces have become attuned to the newly forged political-cultural configurations of contemporary Ireland. Indeed one highly successful instance of this broadening of the performative space within a site of worship took place in December 2006 in St James' Church in Dingle. As part of the RTÉ television programme *Other Voices ... Songs from a Room*, 20 musicians, from Ireland and abroad, gathered at this venue to participate in a musically eclectic series of performances. In a further venture the space of St James' Church was also used as one of the venues for the Dingle Film Festival in September 2007.

For many this process of secularisation has an air of welcome inevitability; it is wedded to the desirability of modernisation and is complicit with the further de-mystification of authority and the increased landscapes of consumption. In other words, Marian grottoes are further facets of this (Catholic) religious imprint on the Irish landscape. The grottoes are features of the cognitive maps of most Irish citizens no matter how devoted to the Catholic faith they might be. The Marian grotto is a local, communal manifestation of the Catholic seizure of public space in Ireland, yet there is a sense in which the Marian grotto, and the figure of the Virgin Mary, skirts the public and private, the wordly and the domestic. Images and reproductions of the Virgin Mary have long been part of the popular aesthetic of Catholicism. Indeed Marina Warner has written an extensive history of the devotion to the Virgin Mary in her book, *Alone of All Her Sex: the Myth and the Cult of the Virgin Mary*.[3]

As mentioned above, the independent Irish State subscribed to a homosocial national narrative, one founded on, and adherent to, a Catholic moral economy. Within such a moral nexus, sexual morality became the sustaining force of these co-operating social institutions. Sexuality, female sexuality, is the absence that announces its presence at every juncture; it is submerged, policed, harangued and demonised – it is excoriated yet desired all the more for that very reason. The volatility of the corrosively sexual female body, and perhaps mind, in effect became the *agent provocateur* of important strands of Catholic moral instruction – this sexual absence/presence is the moral abyss that

---

3. Marina Warner, *Alone of All Her Sex: the Myth and the Cult of the Virgin Mary*, (London: Vintage, 1983).

threatens but that also lures. It is a return to archetypal desire and loss, blindness and vision, masculinity and femininity, a return to the myths of Edenic origin at the core of Christianity's foundations. And this is precisely where the significance of Dorothy Cross' aesthetic becomes apparent. As the director of the Irish Museum of Modern Art (IMMA), Enrique Juncosa remarks in a catalogue essay entitled 'A Theory of Seeing':

> Cross' works seem to analyse emotions like desire, while urging the viewer to question appearances, stereotypes and the social conventions and superstitions that are associated with them. Cross' work tackles the rigidity of socialisation, she unravels the codes of acceptable desire that frame human behaviour and she exposes the ways in which 'surrendering to desire can take us with astonishing speed to unexpected places'.[4]

Devotion to the Virgin Mary, indeed Catholic devotion broadly speaking, has both verbal and non-verbal registers. Catholic devotees enunciate devotion to the Virgin Mary through the verbal recitation of the 'Hail Mary', while Marian grottoes bespeak of a non-verbal manifestation of maternal devotion, most often in tandem with the Holy Mother's prayer. Verbal and non-verbal discourse, then, are not mutually exclusive; the two coincide in the ritual 'performance' of Marian devotion at such designated Marian sites. The verbal and the non-verbal combine in a form of consecrated theatre, in which the devotee submits to the 'represented' embodiment of the Virgin Mary and beseeches this physical incarnation of the numinous through prayer. Importantly such 'performance' establishes a sense of stability in both spatial and temporal terms, a point that will become important when we discuss Cross' work. In other words, the statue of the Virgin concretises a stable physical image of pure womanhood in space, while the 'Hail Mary' is a verbal act over time; it is sequential from present to future and it does not sanction any sense of ambiguity. Furthermore the physical 'representation' of the Virgin Mary is a non-verbal catalyst for devotion; her image is projected and protected in a realistic aesthetic form. There is

4. Enrique Juncosa, 'A Theory of Seeing', in *Dorothy Cross Exhibition Catalogue* (2005), p 11.

no sense of aesthetic ambivalence intended in such creative pieces of statuary; the artistic form, then, is an accomplice of the theology, or ideology, from which it emanates and these are issues that are challenged, as we shall see, within Cross' appropriation of Catholic sites and icons.

This chapter, then, concentrates on the Irish dimensions of Catholic Marian devotion and how it has been simultaneously challenged and expanded through contemporary visual culture. Specifically, it looks at the work of the Irish artist Dorothy Cross, who has long been fascinated by, and interrogative of, naturalised notions of femininity in Irish culture. Likewise, Cross' work has consistently been concerned with, and has drawn on, the feminine imagology of 'Irishness' – a battery of visual codes that includes Catholic marriage rites; the Virgin Mary and the debilitating reification of male and female passion. In what follows I will, firstly, summarily, treat of some of Cross' earlier works and discuss how they pertain to the issues just cited. However, this chapter will pay most attention to an explicit engagement by Cross with a specific site of Marian veneration in her 2004 site-specific work, *Stabat Mater*, a piece that introduces a dissonance of sensual experience to the tempered veneration typically associated with sites of Catholic worship. In addressing the *Stabat Mater* site-specific project I allude to an important concept that is relevant to the ritualistic economy of Catholicism and its pre-eminence in Irish cultural history. Namely I will introduce the concept 'performativity'; I do so in order to highlight the subversive aesthetic and political assertions of Cross' work. Integrated historical narratives safely house volatile memories, and conservative artistic forms are often complicit in such processes of historical manipulation. Cross' work undermines the safe complacency of received historical knowledge and, likewise, troubles the rigid lineaments of a dominant aesthetic, which simultaneously idealises and dis-empowers. As Cross' aesthetic challenge contends, art is not created to smooth out the rough edges of history, but in order to unsheathe the incendiary residues of the past, of the unconscious and of the body.

II

The provisionality of spatial political and cultural identities, together with the intersection of mythology, memory and history have been consistent concerns of the multi-media aesthetic of Dorothy Cross.[5] In her one-minute DVD loop, *Endarken*, she presents an image of a gutted cottage, which has been thoroughly overgrown by foliage and that barely retains its edificial integrity. An absolute darkening of the screen gradually eclipses the image of the cottage. Notably, the 'endarkening' emanates from the centre, or the heart, of the screen; the darkness issues from the cottage itself rather than descending from above or from any external source. By the end of Cross' short loop the cottage has been blotted out from the field of vision of the viewer, but returns again as the loop continues. So in a way it is not entirely obliterated, as there is always the prospect of return. Taken in the context of many of Cross' other installations, video presentations and staged events, *Endarken* is part of her challenge to the historical use of space, including grottoes, handball alleys, cottages and quarries. Cross' work foregrounds the contingency of our spatial orientations and alerts the viewer to the sterility of the habitual. Social and natural spaces demand, and service, divergent forms of veneration, production, violence, neglect and pleasure. Cross juxtaposes the ends to which spatial locations and their attached meanings are put and is most accurately seen as an 'artist of dispossession'.[6] Combining the visual and the aural, Cross' layered pieces dramatise the intense somatic generation of meaning and attachment that adhere to our individual and collective spatial maps. The experience of loss is a primary generative force in her work; the losses attached to the repres-

5. A selective exhibition of Cross' work was held at the Irish Museum of Modern Art, (IMMA), during the summer of 2005. See Dorothy Cross, 'Stabat Mater', *Dorothy Cross Exhibition Catalogue*, (2005), p 48. See Robin Lydenberg, *GONE: Site-specific Works by Dorothy Cross* (Boston: McMullen Museum and University of Chicago Press, 2005) and 'Contemporary Irish Art on the Move: Home and Abroad with Dorothy Cross', *Eire-Ireland* 39 (3 and 4), 2004, pp 144-166; and also, Marina Warner, 'Passionate Cruces: The Art of Dorothy Cross', in *Dorothy Cross Exhibition Catalogue* (2005), pp 25-48.
6. Robin Lydenberg, 'Dorothy Cross and the Art of Dispossession', in *Circa*, 112, p 24.

sion of unfulfilled desires, or of forgotten individual and communal memories.

In one of her recent site specific exhibitions, *Chiasm*, Cross juxtaposed and entwined the redundant space of handball alleys in Galway with the natural beauty of a similarly proportioned space carved into the coast of Inis Mór: the Worm's Hole, a limestone tidal pool. While projecting a film of the Atlantic Ocean crashing onto the rocks of the Aran Island onto the walls of the handball alley, Cross employed a tenor and a soprano to perform sections of ten tragic romantic operas in this radically transformed spatial location. The 'ruin' of the defunct playground was thereby re-energised by the presence/absence of the cinematic western seascape and by the classical tones of operatic performance. The discarded handball alley stands as a testament to the speed with which cultural practices can be jettisoned once they have outlived their usefulness. Such monuments to the vagaries of modern culture litter much of the inner cityscapes of contemporary Ireland. However, it seems that Cross' exhumation of this cultural space is not an exercise in nostalgic retrieval; rather, she dissolves the neat dichotomies of the 'traditional' and the 'modern'. Through the visual, edificial and aural hybridity of her artistic performance, Cross suggests that these cultural spaces are still very relevant to our contemporary spatial and temporal cartographies. Further, Cross created a striking contrast between the rigid man-made structure of the handball alley and the unrestrained violence of the natural thrashing force of the ocean. Such juxtaposition has clear resonances in the capacity of individuals and communities to structurally prohibit volatile sources of cultural and political contraband.

In her earlier work, Cross also mined the corridors of unfulfilled and unrecognised desire, and did so through re-deployments of the mythical and the religious – most often in terms of the feminine. In works such as *Virgin Shroud* (1993), *Bible* (1995), and *Mategna/Crucifix* (1996), Cross anatomises the relationships between the mythic, the religious and the aesthetic in her treatment of gender and sexuality. All three have clear roots in the idioms and iconography of Christianity, yet all subvert the complacent acceptance of such sign systems. For instance, in

Mategna/Crucifix we see the prostrate figure has been altered in gender to that of a female body; equally, *Bible* deploys a familiar material artefact of Christianity, its textual sourcebook that textually verbalises the enunciations of the divine. However, Cross' version of the *Bible*, the physical book on show, has a hole cut out of its centre. These two works, then, can be read as uncompromising interrogations of doctrinal beliefs; furthermore they are also symptomatic of Cross' suspicion of the ways in which mainstream religious doctrine merely services power, in effect disabling, and disqualifying, the pleasures of unfettered desire. There is, of course, a disturbing quality to Cross' work as she brings subjects such as the unconscious, desire, death and loss into focus. Yet part of her success is that she opens her art, indeed all matters of creativity, to manifold interpretation. Her aesthetic strives towards an egalitarian cultural politics, as she critiques aesthetic and value systems that have historically retained positions of aesthetic and political authority. This is made obvious not only in her more 'secular' works, but also, as we have seen briefly, in her engagements with the semiotics of mainstream religion – this is a matter that we will turn to in more detail in the next section when we look at her most recent, and ambitious, engagement with Catholicism.

The aesthetic philosophy outlined and exhibited above is important when considered in the light of contemporary Irish Catholicism and the emerging revelations and histories about the institution in Ireland. It is a truism to assert that the Catholic Church not only plays a significant part in the narratives of modern Irish history, it is also apparent that the institution has been instrumental in the authorship of specific prominent narratives about Ireland; the Church is both participant and author in relation to the narration of Irish history. As with any skein of local and national narratives, dissonant voices are registered but not always welcome, or heeded, and it is only recently that such dissonance has been permitted its say in the construction of the narratives of Irish Catholicism. While much of this historical, and ethical, re-writing is available in the public sphere as a series of traumatic personal histories and cruel institutional hypocrisy, my focus is on the manner in which a visual artist can participate in this re-scripting of what it means to be a Catholic in contemporary Ireland. In other words, what is the nature of our relationship to spaces of Catholic worship and ritual in the light of such legal and public discourse? I do not suggest a causal relationship between Cross' work and the unseemly revelations about the Catholic Church, but I do suggest that the two processes are not unrelated. Both reflect and enable a re-assessment of the political and moral power of the Catholic Church in today's Ireland.

III

Stabat Mater [7]

In her catalogue for Cross' GONE: Site-specific Works by Dorothy Cross at the McMullen Museum of Modern Art at Boston College, the literary critic Robin Lydenberg suggests that 'Cross' art reveals the complex ways in which loss obstructs and animates desire, history, religion and language'.[8] In addition, according to Lydenberg, 'in many of her sculptures, videos, and site-specific projects, Cross succeeds in making loss palpable, productive, even playful; as she transforms death and absence into art, she conjures up the poignant beauty not of any specific object, but of ephemerality itself'.[9] Judging by Lydenberg's comments on Cross' aesthetic, there are explicit intersections between the underlying principles of religious faith and her own sensual aesthetic philosophy. The beauty, indeed, the allure of the Christian faith is its transcendent afterlife, its promise of a life after death, which makes the transience of the material physical life sustainable. Such faith evacuates physical death of its sublime terror. Purged of this sense of oblivion, the Christian death is differentially beseeched and embraced with equanimity. In Cross' aesthetic there is no consolation in nostalgia, no romantic celebration of that which has passed; contrarily there is a process of implied resurrection, or perhaps retrieval, through which that which has been destroyed, forgotten, superseded can re-live as a vibrant memory in the present.

Cross continued and extended this series of preoccupations

---

7. For a discussion of Stabat Mater see Julia Kristeva, 'Stabat Mater', in The Kristeva Reader, Toril Moi (ed), (Oxford: Blackwell, 1986), pp 160-186.
8. Robin Lydenberg, GONE: Site-specific Works by Dorothy Cross (Boston: McMullen Museum and University of Chicago Press, 2005), p 77.
9. Ibid., p 77.

in her site-specific work, a performance of Giovanni Battista Pergolesi's eighteenth century masterpiece, *Stabat Mater*, which was held on three consecutive nights in late August 2004 on Valentia Island off the coast of Co Kerry.[10] For this event Cross employed a slate mine, which is now used as a Marian grotto as her spatial canvas. The mine was part of the long tradition of slate-mining on the island of Valentia that stretches back to the nineteenth century. Indeed the slate extracted from the site was put to use in such venerable architectural projects as the British Houses of Parliament in London and the Paris Opera House. However, mining work was discontinued at the site in 1911 subsequent to the collapse of its stone wall. In 1954, the Marian Year, a grotto was installed at the site, as both a devotional gesture to the Virgin Mary, but also as a token of remembrance to those workers who lost their lives in the operations of the slate mine. Even at this popular level, these aggregated motives combine the secular and spiritual experiences of loss and desire; a sorrow at intimate individual and communal loss but also a desire for redemption through memory and faith. In fact, the grotto is widely acknowledged as one of the most impressive of the slew of such sites of Marian worship erected during 1954, a point alluded to by Louise Fuller in her study of Irish Catholicism in the twentieth century. Fuller remarks in her discussion of the Marian celebrations: 'In parishes throughout the length and breadth of the country, grottoes and statues were erected to celebrate the Marian Year, 1954. One of the more impressive of these grottoes was built by the people of Valentia Island in Co Kerry, on the site of a disused slate quarry'.[11] The slate mine at the site is no longer defunct, however, and has been operating in this capacity again since 1998; at the moment the cave is both a space of religious performance, a site of industrial labour, and of course it is a place of remembrance, within which the memories of the deceased miners are entombed.

Working in association with The Dublin Opera Theatre

---

10. For an extended critique of Cross's *Stabat Mater* see Brian Hand, 'Mining a Quarry: *Stabat Mater* by Dorothy Cross', in *Circa* 112, 2005, pp 34-37.
11. Louise Fuller, *Irish Catholicism since 1950: The Undoing of a Culture* (Dublin: Gill and MacMillan, 2002), p 25.

Company, Cross convened a baroque chamber orchestra and two opera singers, counter-tenor Jonathan Kenny and soprano Lynda Lee, to perform within the hat-shell theatre of the cave's entrance. In addition to this cast of players from 'high' secular culture, Cross also constructed a metal scaffold structure, which was used to support and to transport a large video screen from the rear to the front of the cave. This screen, projecting an image of a singing mouth, provided a backdrop to the performance of the musicians during the initial movement of the set-piece, but once the musicians and singers retired to the back of the cave the screen literally took centre-stage. Once centre-stage, as Lydenberg describes:

> The video screen and soundtrack suddenly spring to life with the chaos and cacophony of industrial machinery digging, cutting and polishing stone ... The video details not only the industrial production now brought back into production, but also the natural surroundings. Rain sweeps over workers, sparse vegetation, and the Virgin alike ... The camera travels inward to cave's hidden depths where the singers sit by an internal pool, evocatively lit from below, a space of contemplation surviving within the industrial clamour.[12]

But if we return to the opening of the performance, with their emergence from the interior of the cave, attired in the clothing of miners, the musicians' and singers' entrance reconfigures the space of the cave's interior as a bustling back-stage. Together the garments of industry and the tones of classical music engendered an aesthetic that recalled early twentieth century *avant-garde* aesthetics, such as the Italian Futurists, with an alignment of technology, labour and art. In many ways Cross' project brought a suite of aesthetics into chafing proximity – the intimacy of 'high' art and technology, as cited, clearly recalls twentieth century Modernism. While the sublimity of the natural surroundings bear close affinities with the dramatic visual and aural canvasses of German Romanticism. Notwithstanding the obvious Freudian and Platonic resonances of the cave as a site of performance and origin, Cross united the natural, and, of course, prehistoric, space of the cave with the sheer somatic ecstasy of

12.Lydenberg, *GONE: Site-specific Works by Dorothy Cross*, p 102.

classical instrumentation. 'Things begin in caves', according to Brian Hand's reading of *Stabat Mater*, 'the stone rolls away, stories emerge, witches gather, precious seams are discovered, accidents happen, visions occur.'[13] This feeling of sensual rapture spilled over into the cave's conversion from a space of intense physical labour to a site of religious veneration, and at the same time draws the viewer's attention to the politics of desire that adhere to gender, sexuality and spirituality.

Cross' interrogative appropriation of a Catholic site of worship cannot be figured as part of the arid de-spiritualisation of Irish society over the last 15 years. As a consequence of our financially 'feline' economy, consumption, speed, and utility have become the watchwords of a newly cast Irish cult of wealth. Looking at the irresistible digestion of the outlying natural landscapes of our urban centres by property developers, it is obvious that the Irish landscape is being neutered of its affective currency. Commuter belts, ring-roads, and suburban ghettos evacuate the topography of any sense of transcendent worth; the entire landscape is transformed in a wholesale process of mechanisation. And while Cross does deploy the site, sound and materials of industry in her *Stabat Mater* piece, it is not at all in sympathy with the crass fetishisation of technology that is in the ascendant in contemporary Ireland. In this contemporary Ireland, as we have seen, Catholicism is alternately viewed as an anachronistic eccentricity of a bygone era, which is unable to bear the freight of a modernised society. It is adjudged as a morally corrupt institution that can no longer be relied upon as an ethical or spiritual compass for guidance; or most cynically, the sites and rituals of Catholic doctrine and practice are commandeered as part of the consumer economy. In particular, the landmark rituals of Catholic belief such as baptismal ceremonies, holy communions, confirmations and weddings are transformed into spectacles of wealth. These life rituals of Catholicism have been assimilated into the consumer economy, and are now, in many cases, showcases for the financial success of their participants. In this way the rituals and ritual spaces of Catholicism are hijacked into a spiritually devalued network of material exchange. The rituals and ritual spaces of Catholicism are, then, little more than

13. Brian Hand, 'Mining a Quarry', p 35.

saleable objects, necessary commodities of a specific type of lifestyle. And this is perhaps where the value of Cross' work is evident; she does not deny the need for some form of spirituality in contemporary Ireland, but she does try to forge a more spiritually affective engagement with these ritual spaces of Catholicism. While capitalist consumerism stimulates vacant, superficial desire, Cross attempts to unearth the vibrancy of unconscious desires through her re-configured spiritual aesthetic.

Cross does not simply present a passive space of faith but a Marian shrine, sites which hold particular significance within Irish social, religious and gender history. In a sense the ossified contours of the cave are no limit to the meanings or performances that can be generated within its viscid interior. In Cross' site-specific performance we see the chafing of sounds, touch, sights and sites. During the performance rain began to fall and the performers were forced to move further and further into the interior of the cave. However, this did not stop the performance, but merely changed its sound effects. Like a deranged conductor, the natural rainfall itself became a participant in Cross' narrative, as it extracted tonal and positional changes from the musicians. The cave's echo, classical timbres, Marian devotion and the memory of disbanded mining labour register as a disturbing chorus, a choric emission that issues from the craggy sub-strata of an Atlantic island. Cross' radical artistic performances, then, bear witness to the unharvested yields of seemingly defunct spatial locations and she attends to their accumulated and repressed 'social, mythic and symbolic functions (sic)'.[14] Her site-specific theatre acts as a form of historical echo chamber, through which unrealised spatial, historical and cultural potentialities are unleashed. The uterine space of the cave and the grotto can be read as a space of re-birth from which these possibilities bloom; but just as easily the uterine space can be read as a space of death, a grave, a tomb – a space of resurrection akin to that of Jesus' tomb. In making such implicit allusions, Cross is, again, aware of the importance of the rituals of birth, baptism, and death within the Catholic faith – she is conscious of the notion of performance as a stabilising agent within a ideological faith, but

---

14. Hand, 'Mining a Quarry', p 37.

she is equally aware of the contradictory impulses of her own art as a series of explicit and oblique performances. The cave is a dark netherworld of possibilities; it is differentially a metaphor for the unseen, the unknowable, the repressed and the unconscious and, as such, is both a space of positive change, but also a threatening location. Indeed in his seminal text on the nature of religion, Mircea Eliade refers to the metaphysical and spiritual qualities of these subterranean haunts. Eliade suggests that 'caves are *secret retreats*, dwellings of the Taoist Immortals and places of *initiation*. They represent a paradisal world and hence are difficult to enter (my emphasis)'.[15] It is significant that Eliade highlights the performative in his assessment of the features of the cave – they are spaces of seclusion but importantly of transition and of potential transcendence.

In her use of a site of Catholic devotion, Cross is keenly sensitive to the 'performative' aspects of Catholicism, whether this relates to the Mass, the celebration of the Eucharist, or more private acts of ritual devotion. The politics of performance as an element in the gradual construction of cultural identities is a topic that has been broadly addressed, notably in work by Peggy Phelan and Richard Schechner.[16] And it is telling to refer to Phelan's comments on the importance of performance in the evolution of cultural, gendered, national or ethnic identities. Drawing on Derrida, Phelan's work highlights the core provisionality of performance; too often in the enactment of theatrical, ritual, religious or cinematic performances, the performer is identified with that which is performed – yet, as Phelan contends, there is a gap between the performed and the performer. Because the physical body of the performer is present in action, it is assumed by the viewer to correspond to an external reality, but this is not the case; performance is representation, and therefore as contingent as any sign system. For Phelan, performance is entirely transient; no single performance can ever be repeated. Once it is performed, it is obliterated, it can only exist in the present, and so can the audience's relation to, and experience of,

15. Mircea Eliade, *The Sacred and the Profane: The Nature of Religion* (New York: Harvest Books, 1959), p 153.
16. See Peggy Phelan, *Unmarked: The Politics of Performance* (London: Routledge, 1993).

that performance. In terms of Cross' approach to the performances of Catholicism, then, how can we relate such notions of the
performative? In the first instance, from an ideological position,
the built-in acts of performed devotion within Catholicism are a
blend of the verbal and non-verbal – they combine the ritual
enunciation of prayer with the decorous disposition of the body.
In these circumstances the devotee is tethered to a strict repert-
oire of performative indices; the performance of such devotion is
designed to police the performance of the body, which by its
nature is capable of immorality, violence, self-abuse. The devotee
in private prayer or in public communal celebration is part of a
performative economy, which denies the provisionality spoken
about by Phelan. Performance, then, becomes identified with
reality and loses its 'represented' qualities; in other words, the
devotee urgently believes in the reality of his/her performative
bond with the divine. This is taken a step further in Marian devotion; in committing the image of the Virgin to a 'represented'
form in statuary, the performative options of femininity are radically reduced to a 'representation' that is now read as reality.
From a Catholic perspective, the squalor of the real is displaced
by the contained representation of the Virgin. The volatility of
the gross reality of sexuality, gender and class are bypassed by
the idealised incarnation. Thus, the performance of femininity is
strictly reduced to the limits of an ossified artefact; the contingency of representation, then, is ignored as the female body is
entombed in the concrete and ideological limits of a theocratic
aesthetic.

The natural epic proportions of the cave, which typically resonate with the clamour of labour and technology as well as the
hushed tones of prayer, are put to full use as now they house the
rousing, emotive timbres of Pergolesi's masterpiece. The setting,
the music, the voices all combine with the verbal evocation of
the aria to summon the transgressive non-verbal corporeality of
the Virgin and of idealised womanhood. The thrilling reverber-
ations of sound electrify the senses and the emotions, recalling
the Virgin in agony at the foot of her Son's cross. The swell of the
music matches the swell of feeling aroused in the audience as
Pergolesi's aria verbalises the somatic trauma of the mother in
agony at the sight/site of her son's crucifixion. Cross' work

takes a dominant ritual performance and refracts it through an interrogative prism, during which the volatile material femininity of the Virgin is uncovered. The cacophony of sounds and sites, then, constitutes a cumulative subversive performance on Cross' part. *Stabat Mater* re-introduces the somatic materiality of the Virgin; it weds this corporeality, which is marked by suffering and sexuality, to her Son's anguished and prone body and corpse. It retrieves the repressed memory of flesh from the ossified metaphor that is planted at the cave's entrance. Crucially, the site-specific *Stabat Mater* accords with Liam Greenslade's recent comments on the incendiary, yet revelatory, voltage of art. Greenslade contends that 'all art attempts to record or escape the limitations of the solipsistic consciousness, of unitary things'.[17] Simply, Cross' work defies the consolations of aesthetic distance and of viewerly composure; the audience/viewers are not permitted to retain a disinterested posture in relation to the work; it is an experiential jolt in as much as it is an aesthetic triumph. Like all powerful artistic pieces, *Stabat Mater* provokes out of oneself unyielded responses, and it disinters the buried life of repressed memories and desires. It explodes the steady continuum of history and memory and, likewise, fractures the composure of aesthetic form, laying bare the provisionality of the dominant or canonical forms of representation. Similarly, as Lydenberg concludes, Cross' work reaches out beyond the limits of representation to grip its viewers: 'in her sited works the experience of time and the effects of the unconscious go public, and place is transformed into a staging ground where viewers are engaged at the level of memory, desire and anxiety'.[18]

Religious iconography, statuettes, grottoes, holy-water receptacles, back-lit wall decorations of religious figures, were all constituent elements of the visual economy of Catholic ideology in Ireland. Such physical objects were equally part of the material culture of Catholicism in Ireland, offering an aesthetic extension of the doctrinal teachings of the Church. And one of the most noticeable features of such material culture was the manner in which it became part of the domestic sphere in Ireland. The aes-

---

17. Liam Greenslade, 'A Complex Kind of Joy: Art Diaspora Identity', in *Contexts: Arts and Practice in Ireland*, 4 (4), 2005, p 45.
18. Lydenberg, *GONE: Site-specific Works by Dorothy Cross*, p 15.

thetic of Catholicism, thus, became a reassuring and guiding presence within the familial, the local and the private spheres through the accumulation of these artefacts. And in this way a degree of uniformity of belief is established; we see the mass dissemination of religious objects by the Church and religious retailers. The uniformity of the aesthetic form, its inherent conservatism and instant familiarity are indices of the uniformity of belief, as the bland homogeneity of the art works forecloses any inclination toward individual scepticism. Indeed, as David Lloyd affirms, this is not only characteristic of religious iconography in Ireland, but is equally true when one looks at the visual history of Irish nationalism. Lloyd captures a crucial point when he argues that such visual agenda merely seek to draw attention to surfaces; these aesthetics are essentially superficial and stylised. In the case of nationalism, for Lloyd it 'requires a certain homogenisation of affect, a requirement served not so much by selection as by proliferation, the dissemination of countless ballads, newspaper articles, symbols and images which are virtually indistinguishable ... stylistic idiosyncrasy would be counter-productive; stylisation is of the essence'.[19] In other words, the aesthetic style is limited in its range in order to prevent misunderstanding and to re-enforce the import of the uncomplicated message of the ideology. Yet Lloyd's discussion does allude to the possibility of a subterranean, and subversive, suite of meanings emerging from beneath the surface stylisation of visual icon.[20] Despite, or perhaps because of, the emphatic dedication to the surface meanings of the visual, with their attendant conservative political impulses, contradictory political messages can be discerned when one interrogates even the most reproduced and seemingly inert images or visual reproduction, just as Cross has consistently done in her artwork and site-specific projects.

In summarily considering Cross' work it is clear that the secularisation of Irish society extends beyond declining vocations,

19. David Lloyd, *Ireland After History* (Cork: Cork University Press, 1999), p 90.
20. Lloyd discusses the subversive nature of such cultural artefacts in relation to the concept of 'kitsch'. See 'The Recovery of Kitsch', *Ireland After History*, pp 89-100.

falling attendances at Mass, and widespread public cynicism regarding the moral values of the Church as an institution. Yet while each of these areas represents an area of crisis, and are also based on a flat rejection and/or contradiction of Catholicism, it is perhaps viable to suggest that Cross uses the artefacts of Catholic ideology and of its corresponding aesthetic in an enabling fashion. That is not to say that hers is an affirmation of Catholic teaching or its conceptualisations of femininity and sexuality, but merely to suggest that she rouses the somatic from the abstract; her work locates a submerged and vibrant spirituality. Her viewer is excited into a confrontation with desire in the most unusual of locations and by the most familiar of visual representations: the Marian image. The language of every ideology has a sell-by-date and the Catholic Church is no different; its tenets and idioms are under immense strain to evolve or perish. Cross' work is not Catholic; it troubles the stale certainties of its theology and its aesthetic, allowing the viewer to experience a re-configured species of the numinous in a transformed spatial setting. Ritual is transfused with ambiguity, uncertainty, and it now accommodates the unpredictability of unconscious desire, something that was driven from view by Catholic theology but was never destroyed. Whether we look at Cross' earlier works, or at her most recent site-specific works, there is an acute understanding on her part 'that no site is neutral, that our perception of space is always shaped by ideological forces. Her site-specific projects often render that process visible and explicit, revealing selected locations as an intersection of multiple and even conflicting systems of knowledge and authority.'[21]

---

21. Lydenberg, *GONE: Site-specific Works by Dorothy Cross*, p 16.

CHAPTER TEN

Secularising the Sacred:
Dermot Bolger and the Problem of Catholic Nationalism

Damien Shortt

Dermot Bolger is a contemporary Dublin poet, playwright and novelist; since 1985 he has published some nine novels, twelve plays, and seven collections of poetry. His work is predominantly set in Dublin, and usually depicts young people in conflict with a politically and culturally moribund society. The conflict that most often provides the dramatic force in Bolger's work usually occurs between tradition and modernity. On the side of tradition he presents nationalism, Catholicism, homogeneity, conservatism, middle/old age; on the side of modernity he presents youth, radicalism, heterogeneity, secularism and cosmopolitanism. While this is not unique to Bolger, the way in which he juxtaposes and combines these threads is worthy of closer analysis.

As will be shown below, Bolger is not alone in seeing Catholicism and nationalism as forming a cultural and political duopoly whose origination in colonial Ireland, and perpetuation into the independent State, restricted the capacity of Irish society to create a fertile space in which the concept of Irishness could evolve in a fashion similar to that of its continental neighbours. In plays such as *Blinded by the Light* (1990)[1] and *The Holy Ground* (1990)[2] the reader can detect an authorial critique of the spiritual sterility of a society in which the alliance of nationalism and Catholicism promoted the glorification of homogeneity. In the novels *A Second Life* (1994)[3] and *The Family on Paradise Pier* (2005)[4] Bolger delves into Irish history, something he usually avoids, in

1. Dermot Bolger, *Blinded by the Light* collected in *Plays: 1*, (London: Methuen, 2000), pp 127-210.
2. Dermot Bolger, *The Holy Ground* collected in *Plays: 1*, (London: Methuen, 2000), pp 101-125.
3. Dermot Bolger, *A Second Life*, (London: Penguin, 1995).
4. Dermot Bolger, *The Family on Paradise Pier*, (London: Fourth Estate, 2005).

order to reinforce his critique. Ultimately, Bolger's work often seeks to show that there has always been a counter-culture, concurrent with the dominant hegemonic ideology, which provides a counterpoint and space in which Ireland and Irishness may be re-imagined without the elision of spirituality.

The result of this re-imagining is a stripping away of the sacrosanctity that is sometimes traditionally ascribed to Ireland's fight for, and achievement of, independence. In Bolger's view of Irish society and its history, the sacred is secularised, the provincial is pluralised and the national is made international. Bolger's politics may thus, perhaps, be best described as trans-national socialism, in that its portrayal of young, working-class characters at odds with a failing political and economic system goes beyond the Irish paradigm. However, the peculiarity of Bolger's work lies in the way in which he approaches the question of the function of religion in Irish politics and culture – an approach, coupled with international socialist politics, which positions his writing as postnationalist.

Considering Bolger is an author who questions the relevance or usefulness of nationalism in contemporary Ireland, it may seem surprising that he names members of the clergy as deserving of admiration for their social work, especially given Irish nationalism's strong association with the Catholic Church.[5] By emphasising this, he seems to confirm that such socialist leanings are usually seen as being at odds with traditional conceptualisations of Irishness, its associations with nationalism, and the important role the Church has played in the formation and evolution of the State.[6] This apparent mutual incompatibility of socialism, on one side, and Irish nationalism and Catholicism, on the other, has lead to a somewhat uneasy relationship in Bolger's writing between his working class characters and the Church.

In order to analyse the way in which the clergy and Church function in Bolger's writing, it is vital to understand how the

5. In interview with this author: Damien Shortt, 'An Interview with Dermot Bolger', *Irish Studies Review*, 14 (4), 2006, pp 465-474.
6. Richard English, *Radicals and the Republic: Socialist Republicanism in the Irish Free State 1925-1937* (Oxford: Clarendon Press, 1994) pp 212, 253.

Church came to perform such a pivotal role in Ireland's affairs. Ernest Gellner argues that modern/developed societies are characterised by 'occupational instability and the semanticisation of work' which 'require people to be socialised into a standard and codified idiom so that they can understand each other's messages, and replace one another in any given slot', and hence, in such societies, education is very high on the political agenda.[7] Thus, in a bid to secure for itself a continuing influence on Irish life, the late nineteenth-century Catholic Church, along with the other Churches in the British Isles,[8] sought to gain control of the education system to the exclusion of all other potential providers – even going so far as to make it a mortal sin for Catholics (up until 1971) to send their children to non-Catholic schools.[9] The role of the almost exclusively Catholic education system would be to 'keep alive and to renew the culture of the sacred in a profane and secular world' and to develop 'an influence and moral control over the future dominant class and political elite'.[10]

Considering that the Catholic Church got more favourable terms 'than were achieved by any other denomination' in controlling education in nineteenth-century Ireland, it is unsurprising that this domination 'carried over into Independent Ireland'.[11] In *The Ex-Isle of Ireland* (1997) Fintan O'Toole provides a succinct analysis of the role played by the Catholic Church in the formation of ideas of Irish nationalism in the nascent state:

[...] in the Easter Rising, the Jesuit Belvedere College (who

7. Ernest Gellner, 'Nations, States and Religions', in *State: Historical and Political Dimensions*, Richard English (ed), (London: Routledge, 1998), p 236.
8. David Hempton, *Religion and Political Culture in Britain and Ireland: From the Glorious Revolution to the Decline of Empire*, (Cambridge: Cambridge University Press, 1996), p 85.
9. Tom Inglis, *Moral Monopoly: The Catholic Church in Modern Irish Society*, (Dublin: Gill and MacMillan, 1987), pp 53, 55.
10. Gerald Grace, *Catholic Schools: Mission, Markets and Morality*, (Routledge, 2002), p. 5 and Tom Inglis, *Moral Monopoly: The Catholic Church in Modern Irish Society*, (Dublin: Gill and MacMillan, 1987), p 58.
11. David Hempton, *Religion and Political Culture in Britain and Ireland: From the Glorious Revolution to the Decline of Empire*, (Cambridge: Cambridge University Press, 1996), p 92.

imagined themselves as a ruling class in waiting) supplied five ex-pupils to the ranks of the rebels; the Christian Brothers O'Connell schools supplied 125. Seven of the 14 men executed as leaders of the Rising were Christian Brothers boys. Three of the five members of the IRA executive elected in 1917, including the chief of staff Cathal Brugha, were in the same category. Of the seven-man Cabinet appointed by the Dáil in 1921, five – Kevin O'Higgins, Austin Stack and Arthur Griffith as well as de Valera and Brugha – had spent their schooldays praying for the beatification of Edmund Rice.[12]

The impact of Catholic education on the formation of Irish nationalism as it manifests itself in contemporary Ireland is also made by Conor Cruise O'Brien, who argues that 'the combination of Catholic and nationalist ideology [was] systematically inculcated by the Irish Christian Brothers' in the late nineteenth and early twentieth centuries.[13] Cruise O'Brien also accredits the Brothers with making the terms Irish and Irishness synonymous with Catholicism not only in Ireland but also in the rest of the English-speaking world, and that they have been the 'indefatigable and explicit carriers' of this erroneous assumption.[14]

While the Catholic Church used its control of education to foment nationalist uprising in the late nineteenth and early twentieth centuries,[15] the two-tier class system that was inherent in the school system[16] planted the seeds of a type of social revolution that was unintended. The pupils of the working class schools, whom James Joyce refers to as Paddy Stink and Mickey

---

12. Fintan O'Toole, *The Ex-Isle of Ireland*, (Dublin: New Island, 1997), p 76.
13. Conor Cruise O'Brien, *Ancestral Voices: Religion and Nationalism in Ireland*, (Dublin: Poolbeg Press, 1994), p 9.
14. *Ibid*, pp 9, 10.
15. Fintan O'Toole, *The Ex-Isle of Ireland*, (Dublin: New Island, 1997), p 77.
16. Whereby the pupils of the poor were to be educated by the Christian Brothers, and those of the wealthy by other religious orders such as the Jesuits and Franciscans. See Marcus Tanner, *Ireland's Holy Wars: the Struggle for a Nation's Soul, 1500-2000*, (London: Yale University Press, 2001), p 272.

Mud[17] (and who people Bolger's work), would go on to form a culture which countered that of the nationalist/Catholic hegemony. The existence of this counter-culture goes on to debunk the dominant ideology in Bolger's writing, which had assumed the characteristics of what John Smith terms a 'quasi-religion' where 'the ultimate objects demanding absolute loyalty are finite and conditional realities [and are] elevated to the status of an absolute'.[18]

In *The Holy Ground* Bolger explores the potential problems that might stem from the way in which the family was a core component in the conceptualisation of Irish identity as articulated in the Constitution. It depicts how a couple comes together and marries, only to see their dreams for the future dashed with the discovery of their inability to have children. In the Irish Constitution the family is identified as the atomic social unit of the state, and Bolger explores this presumption of the importance of family; he questions perhaps not only the place of family in Irish society, but also the notion that any general concept can be used to define satisfactorily the heterogeneous groups classified under the umbrella-concept of Ireland. The entire play is narrated by Monica, and she describes her life with her husband Myles. Through her narration Bolger gives voice to a character doubly removed from hegemonic influence: as a woman she is considered less important than her husband, and this point is made especially clear in the discussion of how even the feminine side of Christianity, as manifested in the devotion to the Virgin Mary, is denied her by Myles's influence in the Legion of Mary; as a childless woman she is further removed from inclusion in society since she has patently failed in the eyes of her husband, and his religious associates, to fulfil even the most basic task expected of women – to produce a child.

Monica knows that it is her husband who is infertile; however, his refusal to confront his infertility and his complete turning away from her leaves her isolated from society. Myles disapproves of her going out to socialise, or even watching TV or

17. James Joyce, *A Portrait of the Artist as a Young Man*, (London: Penguin, 2003), p 74.
18. John E. Smith, *Quasi Religions: Humanism, Marxism and Nationalism*, (London: MacMillan, 1994), p 134.

reading magazines, and she is consequently perceived as existing in a liminal zone – represented on-stage by the house and its
décor that is overtly anachronistic. To understand the theme of
this play it is vital to be aware that Monica is the only character
to actually appear in the play, and perhaps Bolger is implying
that, to the private individual, the world of religion and politics
only impinge on that individual's existence in the most abstract
of ways, and that it is only experienced through a process of
mediation and interpretation. The almost infinite possibilities of
interpretation, as indicated by the manner in which Monica experiences life, questions the validity of a monologic ideology,
such as Catholic nationalism, in the contemporary Irish context.
It is an obvious problem with framing constitutions, and similar
social framework documents, that they invariably fail to meet
the expectations of all factions within society, and are consequently viewed by some groups as being unnecessarily restrictive and by others as being unnecessarily vague. Bolger appears
to argue that in the Irish case it has indeed been restrictive, and
unfortunately has had the worst effects on the most disadvan-
taged sections of the community, and that, ironically, the aspect
of the Irish Constitution that endeavoured to foster a sense of
community (namely, the promotion of the family) could actually
result in further increasing the alienation of the individual.

The discovery of the infertility of Monica's husband, Myles
Hurley (who later changes his name to an tUasal Ó Muirthile),
causes him to abandon practically all social contact with the outside world and become an embittered religious nationalist – he
changes his name to its Irish version, stops playing and supporting soccer, and refers to the doctor who diagnosed his infertility
as an 'Oul Jackeen, trained in England. A West British pup!'[19]
Myles becomes increasingly estranged from his wife, and puts all
his energy into Church societies such as the Legion of Mary and
the Men's Confraternity. Membership of a society such as the
Legion of Mary for a man like Myles is something Gerry Smyth
sees as inherently ambiguous, since 'the Rosary was always an
ambiguous weapon for an Irishman' because 'it constitutes a

---

19. *The Holy Ground*, p 115.

tacit acknowledgement of the power of women and their centrality to patriarchal discourse'.[20]

Myles rails against all efforts at the modernisation of morality in Irish society by organising protests against theatre plays, the divorce referendum and the availability of contraception. It is significant that, in order to ensure his campaigning letters to the newspapers get published, he signs them 'Cork Mother of Five' or 'Dublin Mother of Seven', and orders Monica to re-write them so that his handwriting will not become too familiar to the newspaper editors.[21] Myles's aggressive assumption of the female voice is perhaps symbolic of a belief by Bolger that this is the manner in which religious nationalism often appropriates femininity in order to achieve its goals, while giving scant regard to issues of importance to women. Yet it is possible that Bolger is also appropriating the female voice, but for different reasons.

The deconstruction of the manner in which gender and sexuality are traditionally envisaged is something Bolger foregrounds in his texts. His central characters all contain a certain fluidity of identity that underscores the central themes of the relativity of perspective and the importance of the allowance of autonomy of opinion. By voicing the oppressed female in a play almost totally concerned with Catholicism, it seems clear that Bolger is seeking to deconstruct the patriarchal structure of the Church and, in so doing, is highlighting the interdependency of both gender binaries in defining the self.

In *Blinded by the Light*, written in the same year as *The Holy Ground*, Bolger adopts a different approach in deconstructing Catholic-nationalist ideology when he humorously depicts the battle between the Catholic Church and the Mormon Church for the soul of Mick Flaherty, whom Fintan O'Toole describes as 'a Dublin Canute, trying to staunch the flow of the sea as it pours across the threshold of his bed-sit in the form of Mormons, Legionaries of Mary, interfering landlords and would-be friends'.[22] Mick simply wants to be left alone, and ultimately

20. Gerry Smyth, *The Novel and the Nation: Studies in New Irish Fiction* (London: Pluto Press, 1997), p172.
21. *The Holy Ground*, p 120.
22. Fintan O'Toole, *Critical Moments: Fintan O'Toole on Modern Theatre*, Julia Furay and Redmond O'Hanlon (eds) (Dublin: Carysfort Press, 2003), p 92.

barricades himself into his bed-sit with the head of St Oliver Plunkett that his friends, Pascal and Ollie, have stolen from St Peter's Church in Drogheda. It transpires that the head is in fact that of a Scottish greengrocer, George MacSpracken, executed on the same day as, and mistakenly believed to belong to, St Oliver. As his name suggests,[23] MacSpracken's disembodied head has the ability to speak and, over the many years confined within the Church and being read to by a Marxist sacristan, he has become a communist. This carnivalesque play utilises satirical humour in order to suggest that for a young man like Mick, organised religion can no longer provide a satisfactory philosophical paradigm through which he can live his life. The persistence of the Catholics and Mormons in trying to save Mick's soul forces him eventually forcibly to eject them from his bed-sit and shout:

> If you want to do me good then leave me alone. Can't you see that all I want is to be left by myself ... to eat scuttery kebabs, white bread and scabby packets of soup with E's in them, to read books in Latin and watch Open University programmes at five in the morning about frogs fucking and the homosexual tendencies of the ten-spied stickleback. To do ... I don't know ... anything except be a part of whatever the hell you're all into.[24]

The light mentioned in the title of the play is evidently supposed to be the light of faith, or of religious conversion and zeal. However, Mick is metaphorically 'blinded by the light' when these missionaries squabble less for his soul than for the glory of beating the opposition to the prize. The fanatical scramble by the religious characters for the credit of saving his soul disgusts him, for it is through his realisation that the arch-symbol of Christianity in Ireland in this play – the head of Oliver Plunkett – is a fake, that he realises no one has a monopoly on the truth. Mick opts to withdraw from the society he has grown to hate, and looks forward to living life following his own rules and desires; he embraces the counter-cultural and rejects the ideals of the outside community that values conformity to such a high

---

23. From the German verb *sprechen*, meaning 'to speak'.
24. *Blinded by the Light*, p 205.

degree. He intends removing himself from society, creating his own small world in the company of MacSpracken's head, locked away in his bed-sit. Mick's reaction is undoubtedly extreme, but it is the sort of psychological reaction that Carl Jung claims is typical in such a situation:

> Just as the arch-Bolshevist revels in his unshaven appearance, so the man who is bound in spirit finds a rapturous joy in saying straight out for once exactly how things are in his world. For the man who is dazzled by the light the darkness is a blessing, and the boundless desert is a paradise to the escaped prisoner.[25]

In this play Mick may be interpreted as representing a section of Irish society that has totally rejected the tenets of its parents' generation, going to the opposite extreme in a bid to find his own integral identity. Throughout the majority of the play Mick is portrayed as a rather typical young man of his time who has been socially formed within the parameters of the hegemonic system – in this case the symbiosis of religion, education and nationalism, but who evolves a personality that resists complete interpolation into what he sees as the herd-like community, opting instead for the uncertainty of individual existence. Through the characterisation of Mick, Bolger portrays a version of Irish youth eager to reject all-encompassing ideologies. Mick is an educated individual, but his is a type of education different from that normally provided in the predominantly Catholic Irish school system. He is largely self-taught through reading an eclectic blend of books that he steals from the mobile libraries in which he works. His collection of books include Caesar's *Gallic Wars*, Arthur Schopenhauer, *Churchill's History of the Second World War: Volume Six*, and *Winnie-the-Pooh*[26] – presenting a paradox of sorts by implying that Mick is more educated than the other characters, yet refuses to take life as seriously as they do.

When Mick eventually decides to keep the head, he pretends to Ollie and Pascal that he has burned it, prompting Ollie to rant:

25. Carl Gustav Jung, *The Spirit of Man, Art and Literature*, (London: Ark, 1984), pp 121-2.
26. *Blinded by the Light*, p 144.

You bad bastard. We were always going to put it back, no matter what […] Have you not got a tad of respect for anything? Have you no respect for culture, for the past, no respect for your heritage? If it's one thing I hate it's you city slickers with your pluralist society, kinky sex and rock and roll. Well I'm proud to be an Okie from Muskogee. That's my culture you're burning.[27]

Of course the irony Bolger perhaps wishes to transmit to the audience here is that the head, such an icon of Irish history, culture and religion, is not what Ollie thinks it is – it is a fake. Ultimately Mick is left alone with the head, which delivers possibly the most crucial line of the play, encapsulating Bolger's theme: 'We're two of a kind, Mick. The little men of history, unimportant, overlooked, just getting on with living as best we can.'[28] Mick and George MacSpracken were both embroiled against their will in the conflict between the new and old religions; in the case of MacSpracken he was caught up in the clash between Roman Catholicism and Protestantism (Irishness and Britishness), whereas Mick is caught up in the conflict between the established Catholic Church in Ireland and the new religions fighting for influence and pushing at the boundaries of Catholic domination. Indeed, MacSpracken's confinement within the shrine of St Peter's in Drogheda may be symbolically interpreted as the way in which the ordinary people were metaphorically entrapped by the ideology of religion. Bolger satirises religious fundamentalism in all its guises, from the ridiculous and un-Christian beheading of MacSpracken for swindling a customer of a single apple, to the extreme self-denial of the Mormon missionaries, and fake Christianity of Mick's landlord who worries about saving Mick's soul yet still hounds him for his rent.

The carnivalesque style of this play is most likely aimed at destabilising the Catholic Church's ideological power that the author may have felt was still evident at the time of the play's production. Drawing upon Mikhail Bakhtin's theory of the carnivalesque, it seems reasonable to interpret this play as an attempt to use laughter as a weapon aimed at the undermining of

27. *Ibid.*, p 208.
28. *Ibid.*, p 209.

organised religion. The zeal of the Mormons in trying to convert Mick, and the equal zeal of the Legionaries of Mary in preventing his conversion is exaggerated to carnivalesque proportions in order to encourage the audience to contemplate how ridiculous it is to try and forcibly convince someone that one's own religion is the best for them. Yet it is important to note that Bakhtin did not see the carnival as a merely destructive social force; it was also the fertile origin for the instigation of a new order.[29] Bolger, therefore, concludes the play with Mick and MacSpracken barricaded into the bed-sit and with the possibility left in the mind of the audience that they will eventually decide on a way of life that suits them best, regardless of tradition or organised religion.

While the tone and content of *Blinded by the Light* and *The Holy Ground* are quite different, the conclusions appear very similar, since, at the end of both, the central characters lament the destruction caused to their lives by the intrusion of conservative religion on their private lives. The light-hearted tone of *Blinded by the Light* leaves the audience feeling that Mick will be able to survive his experience of religion, and as Mick is representative of youth in general, the suggestion offered to the audience may be that Ireland has the ability to evolve from its period of ideological domination. The relative solemnity of the conclusion of *The Holy Ground*, that sees Monica claim that the worst thing her husband ever did was to steal her Christ from her, may leave some audiences feeling that there is no positive hope for a post-Catholic Ireland, but Fintan O'Toole claims that Bolger's use of the spiritual in his work 'is no realist assault on mysticism: rather it is a search for new and better abstractions, new general ways of belonging which are more real and more generous than the old ones'.[30]

Several years after *The Holy Ground* and *Blinded by the Light*, Bolger's focus shifted somewhat with the publication of the novel *A Second Life*. Instead of presenting characters in the

---

29. For a succinct description of Bakhtin's concept of the carnival, see Pam Morris's introduction to *The Bakhtin Reader: Selected Writings of Bakhtin, Medvedev, Voloshinov*, (London: Arnold, 1998).
30. Fintan O'Toole, *Critical Moments: Fintan O'Toole on Modern Theatre*, Julia Furay and Redmond O'Hanlon (eds) (Dublin: Carysfort Press, 2003), p 108.

process of rejecting the dominant Catholic-nationalist ideology, he depicts a society engaging in a renegotiation of the past. In *A Second Life* Tom Sweeney betrays his unmarried sister's pregnancy to their parents. Thirty-six years later, now a priest, he is confronted by his estranged nephew, Sean Blake, in a confession box. Blake arrives intending to berate the priest for what he did to his mother, Elizabeth, yet Tom's version of the events leads him to in some way understand the cultural context in which it happened. In this novel, Bolger interweaves two conflicting strands of Irish identity that have caused a significant degree of division up to the present date: religion and sexuality. Tom recounts how, as a boy, he realised that he was homosexual, and that because of the taboo on homosexuality in Ireland in the 1950s, 'You think you'll wind up in the asylum. Then one day you find out and the asylum is not your worry any more. You realise that long before that you're likely to be found battered to death.'[31]

His quiet nature and lack of interest in girls caused people in the village to speculate about a possible vocation to the priesthood, and he discovered that 'it's hard to avoid rumours of sanctity, especially when you find out how they please your parents, especially when you want no other rumours started about you'.[32] Even though he knows he has no vocation, he chooses to enter the seminary where they are told that even if you have no vocation when you get to the altar on ordination-day, 'God would give you one'.[33] While Tom is home on a holiday from the seminary, Elizabeth confides in him that she is pregnant. He initially makes plans to run away with her to England where they can pretend to be husband and wife and raise the child. However, his fear of disappointing his parents and community by leaving the priesthood forces him to tell his parents, who brutally beat Elizabeth and send her to a Magdalene Laundry.

The Magdalene institutions operated in Ireland for over 100 years (the last one closing in the mid-1990s), and were usually overseen by religious sisters who supervised the work of young women who had often been committed to the institution by

---

31. *A Second Life*, p 279.
32. *Ibid.*, p 279.
33. *Ibid.*, p 281.

their families and against their will. James Smith claims that 'most Magdalene "penitents" were institutionalised for that peculiarly Irish sin, perceived sexual immorality.'[34] It is in this notion of perceived sinning that Bolger appears most interested in *A Second Life,* since the society he depicts seems overburdened with the concern to appear to be in conformance with established notions of moral behaviour. The problem for both Tom and Elizabeth is that, in a rural Irish environment of the 1950s, sexuality in any form, other than the matrimonial, is a taboo subject.

In bringing the Magdalene Laundries into *A Second Life,* which is essentially a discussion about an individual's search for identity, Bolger appears to have tapped into a pivotal debate about Irishness. He claims that the appearance of the laundries in this novel was somewhat accidental, and that he initially had no intention of writing about these institutions. However, he notes that on the day he posted the manuscript to his publishers 'there were two women outside, survivors of the Magdalene Laundries, who were getting people to sign a petition for a monument to the women who died in the Laundries'.[35] Far from the appearance of the laundries being a serendipitous occurrence, Bolger now feels that the tentative emergence of these women's stories somehow 'worked its way into the book because as a citizen that interested me at that time'.[36] It is this notion of the interested citizen that appears to characterise Bolger as a writer, and his writing seems intended to prod the reader into an awareness of aspects of identity that may be repressed.

One of the central themes of *A Second Life* is the social problems that stem from repression of identity, and in *Sexual Dissidence* Jonathan Dollimore claims that repression, particularly that of homosexuality, is an essential factor in the creation of a male-dominated society:

> There are those who believe it is possible in principle for gay culture to be integrated into the dominant culture, or at least

34. James M. Smith, 'The Magdalene Sisters: Evidence. Testimony … Action?', in *Signs*, 32 (2), 2007, p 431.
35. Damien Shortt, 'An Interview with Dermot Bolger', in *Irish Studies Review*, 14 (4), 2006, p 473.
36. Damien Shortt, 'An Interview with Dermot Bolger', *ibid.*, p 473.

find acceptance by it. But there are others who argue that, because the prevailing order in some sense requires the denigration of homosexuality, such integration is not possible. The work of those like Dennis Altman rather confirms the second view. Altman regards the repression of homosexuality as 'essential in the formation of male bonding, itself the psychological basis for authority, and male dominance, in virtually all existing societies'; he see its repression as especially formative in male institutions like the military – hence hostility to and anxiety about overt homosexuality in such institutions.[37]

This claim that the repression of homosexuality is pivotal to the creation of a patriarchal hierarchy has very interesting consequences not only for the analysis of *A Second Life*, but also for the analysis of the role of religion in Ireland throughout the twentieth century. Altman claims that male bonding is essential to the creation of male dominance, that if men are to maintain hegemonic control over society then they must act in one another's interests. The basis for Altman's and Dollimore's claim stems from the conflation of the ideas of identity, sameness and difference. They argue that the most basic definitions of masculinity and femininity, that appear to have helped define gender positions in the social hierarchy for many generations, are that a man is one who sexually desires women, while a woman is one who sexually desires men. Social groupings are usually formed through the claim that all members contain the same, or very similar, identities. The biological differences between men and women are the most obvious, and the difference between their positions in the social hierarchy, in Christian and Judaic societies, was determined in the Book of Genesis when God cursed Eve for having tempted Adam and punished her by decreeing that ever after man would dominate woman. In order to maintain this disparity of power between the genders, man, according to Toni O'Brien Johnson and David Cairns, must maintain

---

37. Jonathan Dollimore, *Sexual Dissidence: Augustine to Wilde, Freud to Foucault* (Oxford: Clarendon Press, 1991), pp 51-2. The Altman reference comes from: Denis Altman, *The Homosexualization of America* (Boston, Mass: Beacon Press, 1983), p 61.

the pretence that he is not dependent upon woman for his privileged position:

> Since the female is the object on which the masculine subject has been constructed, a hierarchical dynamic is inherent in this structure, and it is understandable that men should be fearful of having their dependence for 'masculinization' on the objectification of the female exposed, and of losing their privileged position.[38]

Thus, in order to preserve male privilege, masculinity must be presented as an essential quality, but this simplistic notion becomes problematic when homosexuals are introduced into the social equation. 'A lesbian and gay presence within any national literature', as noted by Eibhear Walshe, 'troubles privileged formations of what traditionally constituted "woman" and "man", therefore man and masculinity can no longer be termed essential where there is homosexuality.'[39]

John Hutchinson argues that 'during the struggle for independence, Gaelic authenticity, committed in blood to Pearse's vision of an Irish-speaking republic, based on the will of its native (Catholic) majority, became equated with political freedom'.[40] This equation of Irishness with Catholicism had important ramifications for the way in which Irish people would understand their identity in future years. In the aftermath of the achievement of a form of independence, Irish leaders set about framing the Constitution that would eventually become law in 1937, and which F. S. Lyons claims attempted 'to reconcile the notion of inalienable popular sovereignty with the older medieval conceptions of the theocratic state'.[41]

If Lyons and Hutchinson are correct, then as the State became somewhat theocratic it meant that official ideology would inevitably permeate popular consciousness and that Irish soci-

38. David Cairns and Toni O'Brien Johnson, *Gender in Irish Writing* (Milton Keynes: Open University Press, 1991), p 3.
39. Eibhear Walshe, *Sex, Nation and Dissent in Irish Writing* (Cork: Cork University Press, 1997), p 2.
40. John Hutchinson, *The Dynamics of Cultural Nationalism: The Gaelic Revival and the Creation of the Irish Nation State* (London: Allen and Unwin, 1987), p 307.
41. F. S. L Lyons, *Ireland since the Famine* (London: Fontana, 1973), p 538.

ety's mores would become synonymous with the mores of the Catholic Church. The relative newness of the Irish State, and the conflation within its laws of nationalism and Catholic morality, meant that in the popular, and perhaps simplistically syllogistic, mind anyone who was anti-nationalist was, *ipso facto*, anti-Catholic and vice versa. In the context of Irish society over the past seven or eight decades, it seems reasonable to claim that Lyons and Hutchinson are correct: Irishness seems to have been popularly imagined as being inherently defined by the synonymy of nationalism and Catholicism.

To bring the arguments of Walshe, Dollimore, Lyons and Hutchinson together, it may be seen that where patriarchy, nationalism and Catholicism are presented as interdependent fundamental identity formers, then homosexuality may create an identity problem. This problem is manifested by Bolger in *A Second Life* in the form of Fr Tom Sweeney. As a homosexual Catholic priest, Sweeney can be seen as an anomaly within the patriarchal and hierarchical structure of the Catholic Church, and as an anomaly he serves as an undermining tool in Bolger's attempt to reveal to his readers the fabricated edifice of traditional Irish nationalist identity. Sweeney's homosexuality means that he is at odds with both the teachings and patriarchal structure of the Church (since homosexual activities were not only banned by Church law, but also, as Dollimore points out, perceived as a threat to male dominated institutions) and, consequently due to the synonymy between the State and Church in Ireland at that time, Sweeney is also at odds with the moral ideology of the State. As an author who consistently challenges the notion of State and Church as a harmonious, symbiotic entity, Bolger perhaps uses Sweeney as a metaphor for the fabricated nature of this notion. Dollimore would claim that Sweeney, as a homosexual, undermines the idea of the patriarchy and hierarchy of the Catholic Church – since his sexuality is an anomaly in the gender-biased paradigm upon which the power of the clergy is based. If this is correct, then the rationale for the framing structures, morality and ideology of the 1937 Constitution may also be consequently challenged.

The nascent Irish State's overt and intentional marginalisation of women may be linked to *A Second Life*. Due to the complicity of Sweeney in the sending of his pregnant sister to the Magdalene Laundry, *A Second Life* may thus be read as an overt attack by Bolger on the role that the Catholic Church played in Ireland, and also as an implicit attack on the ideology of the State. Taking these two attacks in harness, *A Second Life* may therefore be read as a critique of Irish identity as it was popularly understood during the mid-to-late twentieth century. Many of the scandals that have beset the Church in recent years appear to have been exacerbated due to the difficulties the Church had in openly discussing sexuality and its role in the formation of both personal and communal identity. It appears that Bolger was quite prescient in his selection of subject matter for this novel in that it accurately reflected contemporary issues regarding the Magdalene Laundries. Bolger's particular social view appears to exist as a background to the actions performed by his characters in the texts, and this may explain why he appears to foreground the individual over the community – because he envisages the texts as primarily the depiction of a series of actions, performed by single autonomous individuals, that occur against the backdrop of a contingent *zeitgeist* that is of secondary importance.

In contrast to almost all of his other texts, Bolger's latest novel, *The Family on Paradise Pier*, marks a departure from the discussion of contemporary Ireland and explores the origins of the Irish State in the first quarter of the twentieth century. Interestingly, the rebellion of 1916 and the subsequent War of Independence form only a distant backdrop to the novel's action. Instead, Bolger focuses on a Protestant 'big-house' family (the Goold-Verschoyles) in Donegal, and discusses how their lives are affected more by international events such as World War I, the rise of communism, the Spanish Civil War and eventually World War II, rather than those solely happening in Ireland. In discussing the origins of the State in this manner, Bolger appears to attempt to diminish the importance of the British-Irish conflict as a font of twenty-first century Irish identity, and instead suggests a more eclectic international, or cosmopolitan, paradigm.

This novel portrays the Catholic clergy as somewhat oppressive in their endeavour to fill the power vacuum created by British withdrawal when they actively work to prevent the socialist organisation of the Irish working classes.[42] However, Bolger does not simply condemn the clergy for their perceived part in the creation of an isolationist and essentialist political and cultural milieu in Ireland during the twentieth century, the society in which he sets most of his other novels and plays. Instead, he offers a version of society that is more accepting of difference, is founded upon individuality first and society second, and which transfers spirituality from the public to the private domain.

The power of the clergy, and their control of many of the Irish working-class, is evidenced in this novel when three of the Goold-Verschoyles, Maud, Thomas and Art, unite in a bid to save the communist, Madame Despard, from an angry mob incited by priests to burn down her house. Even though Despard had supported the Irish Rebellion, Thomas remarks that she had been a suffragette before joining Sinn Féin, and a Protestant before she had become a communist, and that 'those are sins the priests won't forget.'[43] From this point of the novel onwards, Bolger presents a view of inter-war and Emergency Ireland in which the clergy steadily gain a stranglehold on power, albeit informally, but nevertheless real.

Bolger criticises the fickleness of the mob, especially 'slum shawlies' who, when not 'screeching for the old dame's blood', are 'queuing up to wheedle every penny out of her'.[44] Following the saying of the rosary out on the street, the mob burn Despard's house and the Verschoyles look down in dismay at 'the barefoot children staring up as if they were devils. At the ignorance and superstition and malnutrition and stunted growth and those protesters who were fervent and others swept up by the occasion who would just as easily join any other mob.'[45] Significantly, in this scene Bolger positions the Verschoyles on a balcony looking down on the angry mob, perhaps indicating an opinion that their double-liminality in the new Irish State afforded them a surplus of perspective not available to those more inculc-

---

42. In *The Family on Paradise Pier* (London: Fourth Estate, 2005) there are significant sections of the novel that present the clergy in this light, for example, pp 143-157, 167-176, 354-365
43. *The Family on Paradise Pier*, p 168.
44. *The Family on Paradise Pier*, p 170.
45. *The Family on Paradise Pier*, p 176.

ated into the new paradigm of Irish identity that was created at that time by the politicians and clergy.

Following the achievement of Irish independence, *The Family on Paradise Pier* charts the increasing marginalisation of the working-classes by the ruling elite. This is most clearly seen in their physical displacement from the heart of the capital:

> The city had cast its poor out to the edge of the mountains. It wasn't even a fodder farm for the capitalist factories because there was no work to be had. This was just a breeding ground for the emigrant boat.[46]

Due to the tone set by the author in the recurrent scenes of failed socialist rebellion, the reader cannot help but feel somewhat sympathetic towards the Goold-Verschoyles, and the manner of their depiction by Bolger suggests that the author also feels sympathy for their idealistic, but well-meaning intentions. This is not to suggest that Bolger is in any way an author with communist ideological leanings, but it seems that he is able to see in this family, and the historical figures upon whom they are based, a pioneering resistance to the alliance of nationalism and the Catholic Church in the new Irish State.

The heroine of *The Family on Paradise Pier*, Eva Fitzgerald, was a personal friend of Bolger and it is her life which seems to encapsulate much of Bolger's literary project to date. In the epilogue to *The Family on Paradise Pier*, Bolger describes Fitzgerald's funeral. He imagines her small coffin as a boat, a symbol of her individuality, which causes only the smallest ripple. However, that ripple spreads 'out across her lifetime to touch distant shores' and keeps 'moving on its own course long after many of the seemingly great waves of her time have died away'.[47] When researching the novel, Bolger attended some Quaker meetings (as Fitzgerald had done) and he was struck by the way in which the meetings were conducted on a basis of listening to what others had to say.[48] Perhaps, then, it is this durable impact of the individual life which characterises much of Bolger's work, and in

46. *The Family on Paradise Pier*, p 364.
47. *The Family on Paradise Pier*, p 550.
48. Damien Shortt, 'An Interview with Dermot Bolger', in *Irish Studies Review*, 14 (4), 2006, p 472.

Fitzgerald's singular existence of tolerance and understanding that the genesis of many of his characters can be found. Bolger's vision of twenty-first century Ireland may thus be a society in which the lone voices of individuals such as Mick in *Blinded by the Light*, Monica in *The Holy Ground*, Tom Sweeney in *A Second Life* and Eva Fitzgerald in *The Family on Paradise Pier* are heard. It is a society where politics and religion no longer converge in the public arena, but where the individual is free to privatise the sacred. Giving the last word to Bolger, it seems the most important thing to bear in mind when reading his work, is to avoid simplistically characterising him as an anti-religion author:

> I know a lot of priests, and I find that priests and poets have a lot in common. Francis Stuart once commented that we are not really valued as such, but we are called in the emergency occasions, when words of comfort are needed, at births, deaths and christenings. That's our role; we are asked to provide solace and then leave. That has always been the role of poets, and now it is the role of priests as well […] I think that in a very materialistic society religion is very interesting because it is irrational, and it says that there is more to life than simply working, so religion can be a very positive thing.[49]

---

49. Damien Shortt, 'An Interview with Dermot Bolger', p 472.

CHAPTER ELEVEN

Sifting the Remains of Irish Catholicism:
Relics and Nuns in Eiléan Ní Chuilleanáin's Poetry

Andrew J. Auge

In the spring and summer of 2001, the relics of St Thérèse of Lisieux came to Ireland and during their eleven-week tour of the country were venerated, according to the estimates of the event's organisers, by three million people, three quarters of the island's population. The *Sunday Business Post* went so far as to designate the crowds that greeted the relics as 'the greatest mass movement of the Irish people in the history of the country'.[1] This extraordinary outburst of traditional Catholic devotion was generally regarded as evidence that Catholicism in Ireland, despite the persistent rumours of its demise, was alive and well. It was as if an act of cultural homeopathy had been performed. The enthusiastic reception of these sacred relics seemingly inoculated the Catholic Church against the charge that it had itself been reduced to a relic, and re-established it as a legitimate counter-force to Celtic Tiger Ireland's increasing consumerism and secularisation. Such a view is belied though by the fact that the tour of St Thérèse's relics was marketed like the roll-out of some cutting edge consumer good or the appearance of a celebrity pop-star, with posters announcing that she 'would draw bigger crowds than rock legends U2' and that she 'was more popular than pop star Madonna.'[2] Moreover, the response to the relics that Bishop Brendan Comiskey of Ferns promulgated – a 'child-like' exercise of imagination that supersedes critical intelligence and submits to the presence of a mysterious power – is less a counter to than an extension of a consumerist ethos.[3] In this regard, we might

---

1. Audrey Healy and Eugene McCaffrey, *St Thérèse in Ireland: Official Diary of the Irish Visit, April-June 2001* (Dublin: The Columba Press, 2001), p 12.
2. Don Mullan, *A Gift of Roses: Memories of the Visit to Ireland of St Thérèse* (Dublin: Wolfhound Press, 2001), p 15.
3. Healy and McCaffrey, *St Thérèse in Ireland*, p 10.

recall that Marx fashioned his notion of 'commodity fetishism' from the analogous relationship between the enthrallment of the consumer with the commodity in capitalism and the worship of objects like relics in religions such as Catholicism. In each case the originating context of the object is obscured and the object itself is seen as imbued with animate and autonomous powers. When considered from this demystified perspective, the extraordinary popularity of St Thérèse's relics would appear to derive from their reification of a purer and seemingly more innocent Catholic faith, while their well-publicised introduction into twenty-first century Ireland looks suspiciously like an attempt to rebrand (à la Classic Coke) a superannuated and compromised product.[4]

In Eiléan Ní Chuilleanáin's poetry, the conjunction of relics and religious women takes on a much more destabilising valence. Instead of fostering traditional pieties, this motif in her poetry effects a winnowing of Irish Catholicism that brings forth both the seeds of a redeemed future and the chaff of past oppression. In her ground-breaking analysis of relics in their medieval climacteric, Caroline Bynum points out how they were predominantly associated with religious women and reflected an awareness and appreciation of the potency of female somatic experience.[5] A similar affiliation of relics with the corporeal reality of cloistered women characterises Ní Chuilleanáin's poetic rendering of these artifacts. This linkage does not, however, result in a conception of the relic that, like the popular view of St Thérèse's, casts it as a self-subsistent, palpable entity. In fact, Ní Chuilleanáin subverts precisely this vision of relics in the ironically titled poem 'The Real Thing,' from her volume *The Brazen Serpent* (1995), where the relic is envisioned as something more akin to what the philosopher Emmanuel Levinas refers to as a

---

4. An exception to this would be a group of women who hosted a conference on women's ordination in Ireland at the same time as the visit of the relics and who enlisted St Thérèse in their cause on the basis of the saint's expression in her personal writings of a desire to be a priest. See Mullan, *A Gift of Roses*, pp 191-196.

5. Caroline Walker Bynum, *Fragmentation and Redemption: Essays on Gender and the Human Body in Medieval Religion* (New York: Zone Books, 1992), pp 187-188.

'trace'. For Levinas, the trace is the wake left by something passing, a ripple in the fabric of things that lingers after that which produces it disappears. '[A]n absence radically withdrawn from disclosure ... [but] not reducible to concealment,' the trace hovers in the hinterland between present and past, being and nonbeing. It is a remainder that resists re-presentation and is manifested only as 'a disturbance imprinting itself ... with irrecusable gravity.'[6] In Ní Chuilleanáin's 'The Real Thing,' Sister Custos, whose name is Latin for 'guardian', adopts a posture similar to that of the conservators of the Thérèsian relics. She regards 'her major relic, the longest/Known fragment of the Brazen Serpent' – the Mosaic staff that was a type of the true cross – as 'the real thing'.[7] That is to say, she treats it as the hypostatisation of the essence of the faith, a treasure to be worshipped, sequestered, and safeguarded. Against this conventional understanding of the relic, the poem posits an alternative vision in which the heirloom of the faith is identified with '[t]rue stories/[that] wind and hang like this/ Shuddering loop wreathed on a lapis lazuli/ Frame' (BS, p 16). At the poem's conclusion, these stories are associated with the hidden vestiges of Sr Custos's own cloistered life. For Ní Chuilleanáin, this is the true relic: a remnant of a corporeal existence that is not memorialised, but that reveals itself instead in its disruption of the officially sanctioned and sanitised versions of the past:[8]

> The torn end of the serpent
> Tilts the lace edge of the veil.
> The real thing, the one free foot kicking
> Under the white sheet of history. (BS, p 16)

6. Emmanuel Levinas, 'Meaning and Sense', in Collected Philosophical Papers, trs Alphonso Lingis (Pittsburg, PA: Duquesne University Press, 1998), pp 102, 106.
7. Eiléan Ní Chuilleanáin, The Brazen Serpent (Winston-Salem, NC: Wake Forest University Press, 1995), p 16. Henceforth all quotations will be to this edition, denoted by BS, followed by the page number.
8. Guinn Batten's interpretation of this poem's conclusion touches upon this point by associating 'the secret authority of the sister's relics' with the 'missing narrative of women and desire'. See Guinn Batten's 'Boland, McGuckian, Ní Chuilleanáin and the body of the nation', The Cambridge Companion to Contemporary Irish Poetry, ed Matthew Campbell, (Cambridge: Cambridge University Press, 2003), p 174.

As the previous analysis suggests, from Ní Chuilleanáin's perspective the most significant traces that Irish Catholicism has left in the wake of its long triumphalist phase are those engendered by religious women. She has herself presented this 'preoccupation with nuns, and the reasons for their existence' as foundational to her effort to understand her cultural heritage, insisting that it 'explains or rather provides always the first syllable of an explanation of the world I grew up in and the many worlds I inherit.'[9] The definitive role that nuns play in Ní Chuilleanáin's poetry has been acknowledged by critics as well. In the article that first introduced Ní Chuilleanáin's work to an international critical audience, Peter Sirr designated her art as 'cloistered', not only because so many of her poems referred to 'nuns and convents', but because the form of the poetry itself – 'in its deliberate choice of marginal location, in its quiet rhetoric, in its discrete presentation of material' – had a 'cloistered' quality.[10] According to Ní Chuilleanáin, nuns entered her poetry not so much as invited guests but rather as unbidden emissaries from the recesses of her imagination. In the essay from which I quoted above, 'Nuns: A Subject for a Woman Writer', she describes how as a young writer in her late twenties she sought a 'vantage point' for her poetry that was based in experience, a theme 'really there, not made up, but intractably in the world I and others have lived in, hard and resistant to explanation.' But as her imagination groped for this experiential perspective, Ní Chuilleanáin was surprised to discover that her poetry was repeatedly invaded by 'the figure of a nun [who] would be standing quietly in the middle of a poem, as in a room in my house, before I had asked her in.'[11] While this fascination with nuns has a biographical basis – Ní Chuilleanáin was educated at convent schools and has three paternal aunts who were nuns – her interest in these religious women is ultimately driven by a deep-seated recognition of their cultural significance in Ireland.

9. Eiléan Ní Chuilleanáin, 'Nuns: A Subject for a Woman Writer', *My Self, My Muse: Irish Women Poets Reflect on Life and Art*, ed Patricia Boyle Haberstroh (Syracuse, NY: Syracuse University Press, 2001), p 22.
10. Peter Sirr, '"How things begin to happen': Notes on Eiléan Ní Chuilleanáin and Medbh McGuckian," *Southern Review* 31, 1995, p 459.
11. Ní Chuilleanáin, 'Nuns,' p 22.

Existing on 'a border, both inside and outside Irish society',[12] nuns occupied a crucially liminal position in relation to the dominant patriarchal social structure of late nineteenth and twentieth century Ireland. As such, they provide a kind of threshold experience that ostensibly upholds but more often interrogates the cultural codes in Ireland that have regulated the emplacement of women in society and in their own bodies.

Despite the primacy that Ní Chuilleanáin assigns to nuns in her imagination, they, like so many other entities in her poems, have a spectral rather than a substantive presence. They are never fully realised, but manifest themselves instead in brief glimpses and oblique gestures and allusions. Neither these nuns nor the poetic texts in which they appear can be reduced to commodities that are easily apprehended and readily consumed. Instead of being rendered as 'atomised, self-encapsulated things ... [whose] meanings and properties appear to lie within themselves alone' – the ontological perspective that according to Michael Taussig defines commodity fetishism – Ní Chuilleanáin's nuns are always presented in terms of a 'relational gestalt,'[13] always located in the context of her culture's formative assumptions about women's roles. One such assumption casts the social marginality of nuns as a form of diminution. It regards the lives of these women as attenuated because of their subjection to strict disciplinary regimes and their exclusion from the socially normative patriarchal family. Such an attitude is exemplified by the comment that one of Ní Chuilleanáin's uncles made in reference to the nuns who populate her poetry: 'When I see a nun I always think, "none".'[14] This 'depersonalisation' of nuns was widespread in Irish culture where, according to the historian J. J. Lee, 'nuns were de-humanised in public images to a far greater extent than priests.'[15] Against this prevailing view of the unattached female as defined by lack, Ní Chuilleanáin, paradoxically, em-

---

12. *Ibid*, p 23.
13. Michael Taussig, *The Devil and Commodity Fetishism in South America* (Chapel Hill, NC: University of North Carolina Press, 1980), p 35.
14. Ní Chuilleanáin, 'Nuns,' p 22.
15. J.J. Lee, 'Women and the Church since the Famine', in *Women in Irish Society: The Historical Dimension*, ed Margaret MacCurtain and Donncha Ó Corráin (Westwood, Ct: Greenwood Press, 1979), p 42.

phasises how the international nature of Catholic religious orders bestowed an expansiveness upon these cloistered women
that was generally lacking in their worldly counterparts con-
strained by the narrow provincialism of twentieth century Irish
middle-class life. Similarly, the nuns in Ní Chuilleanáin's poetry,
despite their spectral nature, are never seen as having been reduced to a kind of dismal ethereality by their ascetic practices.
Instead, Ní Chuilleanáin evokes in her poetry what she emphas-
ises in her prose: 'the way their lives, their attention were disci-
plined and directed to the physical world at all times', the manner
in which their habits far from inhibiting the body served as a kind
of habitat, an extension of the body that while containing it offered it room to move as freely and 'intently as a fish in water'.[16]

The touchstone for Ní Chuilleanáin's unorthodox assessment
of the nun's life is the poem 'J'ai mal à nos Dents' (from her 1989
book *The Magdalene Sermon*) which she chose as an epigram to
her essay on nuns and then reprinted, along with a brief commentary, as her contribution to a book of essays entitled *Religious
Women and Their History: Breaking the Silence*.[17] Dedicated to the
memory of Anna Cullinane or Sr Mary Anthony, who was one
of Ní Chuilleanáin's paternal aunts, this poem does not memorialise this woman's attributes but registers the implications of her
cloistered existence by contextualising the linguistic traces of
several disparate episodes of her religious life, most of which
was spent as a Franciscan of Calais. The fact that these verbal
remnants are in French and that the first of them is the strange
solecism that constitutes the poem's title highlights the alterity
and incongruity of the figure of the nun as epitomised by Sr
Mary Anthony. However, in the poem's opening and closing
lines, Ní Chuilleanáin invokes the more conventional view of
nuns as vitiated women, victims of a patriarchal Church that
stripped them of their freedom and alienated them from their
own bodies.

The Holy Father gave her leave
To return to her father's house

---

16. Ní Chuilleanáin 'Nuns, pp 23, 21.
17. Rosemary Raughter (ed.), *Religious Women and Their History:
Breaking the Silence*, (Dublin: Irish Academic Press, 2005), pp 116-118.

At seventy-eight years of age
....
They handed her back her body,
Its voices and its death. [18]

Focusing on these lines to the exclusion of the rest of the poem, readers might find themselves agreeing with one critic's assessment of the poem's tone as 'coldly angry', brimming with resentment at 'a patriarchal Church [that] has exploited this woman's strength until there was none of it left'.[19] But such a reading must be qualified by the fact that the poem itself holds this dismal view of Sr Mary Anthony's life up for criticism. For her brother back in Ireland listening to the war news on Radio Éireann, Sr Mary Anthony remains a distant and occluded object of concern – a 'name [that] lay under the surface' (*MS*, p 29) of the reports of German army advancing on Calais. Blinkered by his own assumptions about his sister's cloistered life, he cannot envision her active participation in the historical events to which he is merely a bystander.

> ... he could not see her
> Working all day with the sisters,
> Stripping the hospital, loading the sick on lorries,
> While the Reverend Mother walked the wards and
>   nourished them
> With jugs of wine to hold their strength.
> *J'étais à moitié saoûle*. It was done.
> They lifted the old sisters onto the pig-cart.
>
> And the young walked out on the road to Desvres,
> The wine still buzzing and the planes over their heads.
> (*MS*, p 29)

In lieu of the sterile asceticism stereotypically associated with religious women, these nuns, as the interposed French phrase

18. Eiléan Ní Chuilleanáin, *The Magdalene Sermon* (Loughcrew, Ireland: Gallery Press, 1989), p 29. Henceforth all quotations will be to this edition, denoted by *MS*, followed by the page number.
19. Paul Stanfield, 'How She Looks in That Company: Eiléan Ní Chuilleanáin as Feminist Poet', in *Contemporary Irish Women Poets: Some Male Perspectives*, ed Alexander Gonzalez (Westport, CT: Greenwood Press, 1999), p 109.

indicates, participate in a kind of bacchanal. Their drunken ecstasy contrasts, though, with that of the ancient Maenads in that it is conjoined with acts of succour rather than violent sacrifice. The physical engagement evoked in this passage – the communal sharing of the pleasures and burdens of the body – confirms the significance of the French phrase that appears as the poem's title and that is reiterated in the stanza prior to the one above. This bizarre locution – I have a pain in 'our' teeth – which the young Sr Mary Anthony utters during a visit to the dentist casts her body not as a reified and isolated substance owned by the self, the 'possessive individualism' that characterises modern self-identity,[20] but as an amorphous and shared corporeality that emanates, as the poem puts it, 'out of her first mother' (*MS*, p 29). As the last of the poem's French phrases (*Une malade à soigner une malade*/A sick woman to care for another sick woman) brilliantly illustrates, this blurring of the boundaries of self and other that characterises Sr Mary Anthony's experience as a religious woman continues when she returns to the family home, ill herself, to tend to her sick sister. Through its revelation of the hidden plentitude, both somatic and linguistic, of this nun's life, *'J'ai mal à nos Dents'* undermines the commonplace attitude that would equate the cloister with confinement, enclosure with erasure.

Ní Chuilleanáin's re-envisioning of the figure of the nun, although unconventional, is not unprecedented. In her comprehensive historical analysis of nuns in nineteenth century Ireland, Mary Peckham Magray offers substantial evidence to support her claim that convent life 'was far richer than ... constitutions and rule books would suggest ... [and] offered a style of living found highly desirable by many Irish women'.[21] Ní Chuilleanáin intensifies this point by presenting the life of the nun as a positive counter to the role of motherhood culturally and legally enshrined as the preferential option for Irish women. 'Chrissie', a poem from later in *The Magdalene Sermon*, employs this contra-

---

20. C. B. Macpherson, *The Political Theory of Possessive Individualism: Hobbes to Locke* (Oxford: Oxford University Press, 1962), p 3.
21. Mary Peckham Magray, *The Transforming Power of the Nuns: Women, Religion, and Cultural Change in Ireland, 1750-1900* (Oxford: Oxford University Press, 1998), p 47.

puntal theme to particularly powerful effect. Exhibiting the surreal mythic quality that makes so many of Ní Chuilleanáin's poems seem as though they emerge from the depths of the cultural imagination, this poem focuses on a young woman marooned with others on a bleak shore and hiding from them in a wrecked ship. The precise nature of the traumatic loss that she has suffered remains unknown, but the imagery associates it with sexual penetration and parturition. Utilising one of her favourite tropes, whereby the female body is recapitulated in an external structure, Ní Chuilleanáin casts the skeletal shipwreck as a kind of uterine form:

> Escaped beyond hope, she climbs now
> Back over the ribs of the wrecked ship,
> Kneels on the crushed afterdeck, between gross
> Maternal coils: the scaffolding
> Surviving after pillage.
> ....
> Four notches down the sky, the sun gores the planks;
> Light fills the growing cavity
> That swells her, that ripens to her ending. (*MS*, p 35)

Through its allusion to the placenta, umbilical cord, and womb ('crushed afterdeck,' 'gross/maternal coils,' 'growing cavity'), this passage envisions maternity as a kind of ship wreck whereby women are either left stranded in a socially sanctioned but desolate domesticity or else driven into desperate isolation, as may be the case here, to avoid the scandal of an illegitimate pregnancy. (The littoral setting and suggestion of a misbegotten birth make it hard not to see the contemporaneous Kerry babies case hovering in the background of this poem.[22]) That Ní Chuilleanáin is not so much indicting motherhood *per se* – she is

---

22. On 12 April 1984, Joanne Hayes, a 25 year old unmarried mother, gave birth in the fields of her family's farm near Tralee, County Kerry, after having hidden the fact of her pregnancy. When the baby died shortly after birth in confusing circumstances, she placed it in a plastic bag and deposited it in a pond on the farm. Two days later, another dead new-born baby with multiple stab wounds was found next to plastic fertiliser bags on the strand near Cahirciveen, County Kerry. Joanne Hayes was initially charged with the murder of this baby. The case against her began to fall apart with the discovery of the body of her

after all a mother herself – as the regressive *mythos* that coercively identifies femininity with maternity is evident from the poem's conclusion.

> And she goes on fingering
> In the shallow split in the wood
> The grandmother's charm, a stone once shaped like a walnut
> ....
> She clings, as once to a horned altar beside the well. (*MS*, p 35)

In these lines the young woman is associated with artifacts and sites – the walnut-shaped stone, the well, the horned altar recalling the Celtic fertility god Cernunnos[23] – that bind her over to something akin to an ancient fertility cult. Against this, the poem sets the image of another kind of mother, a Mother Superior, whose willingness to expose herself to the unfamiliar imbues her with the awful presence of an epic hero – '(Her tanned forehead more dreadful now / Than when helmeted and veiled)' – and who leads her charges, 'shoulder to the stern,' in 'pushing out boats' (*MS*, p 35) into the open sea. This action links the Mother Superior and her followers to the traditional Irish *imram* and casts the experience of these religious women as a courageous voyage away from the well-known terrain of domestic life and into an unfathomable realm suggestive of the infinite depths of both the feminine psyche and the divine.

In 'La Corona,' from Ní Chuilleanáin's next book, *The Brazen Serpent* (1995), the juxtaposition of nun and mother occurs in a mundane rather than mythic context. Here the poem's obliquity arises not so much from the setting as from the elliptical and disjunctive nature of the poem's narrative. The poem's central figure is a bed-ridden woman identified only as 'the mother' (*BS*, p 17). The status of this woman is ambiguous since she possesses the kind of religious paraphernalia – relics, a leather-bound prayer manual – that would seem appropriate for a Mother

own baby on the farm near Tralee and suggestions that the gardaí had coerced confessions from Hayes and her family. The charges against her were eventually dropped. For an extensive summary and analysis of this case, see Tom Inglis, *Truth, Power, and Lies: Irish Society and the Case of the Kerry Babies* (Dublin: UCD Press, 2003).
23. James Mackillop, *Oxford Dictionary of Celtic Mythology* (Oxford: Oxford University Press, 2004), p 86.

Superior, yet at the same time there is an allusion to her wedding day, and 'a daughter' (*BS*, p 17) is mentioned. This blurring of identities insinuates that the sterility typically associated with the nun's life is, perhaps, even more appropriately related to the traditional domestic role of wife and mother. The key to the riddle of this woman's identity lies, I believe, in the poem's allusion to St Rita, on whose feast day the poem is set and who provides one of the relics just referred to – a flower of the Holy Thorn that pierced the saint's forehead as she meditated upon the crucifixion. St Rita, as the story goes, wanted to be a nun but was coerced by her family into a loveless and abusive marriage from which she was released only by her husband's death. The character at the heart of this poem would seem to be in an analogous situation. She aspires to the religious life of a nun but has been immured within a domestic sphere that, as in Joyce's *Dubliners*, is characterised by a kind of moribund stasis. The fact that she has taken to her bed, perhaps in grief, and that black-bordered funeral cards appear at the poem's, conclusion suggests that, like St Rita as well, she may have been recently widowed.

The Joycean character of this poem extends to the way in which the paralysis of the poem's opening scene culminates in an epiphany, occasioned here by a solar eclipse which rends the quotidian routine of the mother's life just as it severs the poem itself:

> Through the high window light forces its wedge
> To blot the calendar; the mountainside
> Flooding, the water fanned in veins, backs
> Against a dark cloud with a bright snake at its edge. (*BS*, p 17)

Both the language here ('light forces its wedge') and the homonymic link between the aureole of light surrounding the eclipsed sun and the crown of thorns connect this event back to the Holy Thorn that is St Rita's relic. The implication is that the rupture in consciousness signalled by the eclipse should be equated with the liberating potential that emanates from this saint's tenebrous life. The possibility of redemptive transformation is highlighted by the figure that Ní Chuilleanáin uses to describe the corona since the image of the snake eating its tail, the *ouroboros*, is an archaic emblem of rebirth and resurrection.

For the mother in this poem then, this eclipse portends a change that would release her, like St Rita, from a desiccated and constrictive domesticity into a new and richer life as a nun. This hoped-for liberation is evoked once more at the poem's conclusion where the mother is described as dealing 'herself a new hand' (*BS*, p 17). Against the 'black borders' of the cards that she shuffles, emblems of her own death-in-life, are set the 'grey hatchet faces' (*BS*, p 17) of her cousins, an image that, however obliquely, calls to mind the sharp-edged profile of a nun wearing a wimple, a profile which Ní Chuilleanáin in another context describes as 'firm-faced' and 'formidable'.[24]

Ní Chuilleanáin's recognition of the nun's liminal status in Irish culture leads her not only to counterpoint this figure with the socially sanctioned role of mother, but also to align nuns and other religious women with women who were ostracised for violating the sexual norms of a rigidly patriarchal culture. This point is amplified in Ní Chuilleanáin's essay on nuns, where she suggests that in twentieth century Ireland the choice of the vocation of the nun involved 'a liberation from social constraints as wild as that of any girl who caused a scandal in her parish.'[25] In positing this alliance, Ní Chuilleanáin sets herself in stark opposition to prevailing public opinion in Ireland where the nun is more generally regarded as the oppressor rather than the ally of the sexually unruly woman. The revelations in the 1990s concerning the horrific conditions that pervaded the Magdalene Asylums and Mother and Baby homes that religious orders of women in Ireland ran throughout the twentieth century has led to a new stigmatising of nuns that presents them not as victims but as agents of patriarchal oppression. Nowhere is this more apparent than in Peter Mullan's harrowing *The Magdalene Sisters* (2002). Based on Steve Humphries documentary, *Sex in a Cold Climate* (1998), Mullan's film details the physical and psychological abuse inflicted upon three young Irish women consigned to a Magdalene laundry in 1964. Blame for this abuse is primarily directed at the nuns overseeing the laundary, who are cast in the film as the shock troops of a puritanical and patriarchal Church.[26]

24. Ní Chuilleanáin, 'Nuns,' pp 22, 28.
25. *Ibid*, p 26.
26. For an astute analysis of this film's reversion to gothic conventions

I will postpone until later the consideration of how Ní Chuilleanáin's addresses the collusion of religious sisters with the oppressive disciplinary regimes of the Irish state. For now, though, I want to focus on the way in which her poetry exhumes a hidden congruence between these divergent but similarly marginalised feminine figures and thereby elucidates the transgressive strand in the legacy of religious women in Ireland.

One of the most significant ways in which Ní Chuilleanáin effects this affiliation of women identified as spiritually superior and those labelled as sexually debased or deviant is by focusing upon a traditional figure – Mary Magdalene or St Margaret of Cortona – in whom these roles are conflated. In the poem treating the latter figure, the eponymous 'St Margaret of Cortona' from *The Brazen Serpent*, the relics of this medieval saint are presented as exerting an unsettling influence on the sexual politics of modern Ireland. Often referred to as the second Magdalene, St Margaret of Cortona was the mistress of a nobleman with whom she had a son. After his murder, she eventually entered a Franciscan monastery and spent much of the rest of her life redressing her earlier sins through harsh penitential practices. The poem focuses, however, less on St Margaret herself than on the appropriation of her legacy by institutional authorities, a point highlighted by the epitaph which follows the poem's title and identifies Margaret as 'Patroness of the Lock Hospital, Townsend Street, Dublin.' Established in England and Ireland in the latter half of the nineteenth century, Lock Hospitals were originally designated as places where prostitutes, ostensibly contaminated with venereal diseases, could be quarantined and subjected to religious and moral instruction.[27] This context is indirectly evoked at the poem's outset where a priest uses the occasion of her feast day to employ the saint as a homiletic tool. In the course of emphasising the illicit status of her early life – '*She had become*, the preacher hollows his voice, / A name not to be spoken' (*BS*, p 24) – the priest inadvertently reveals the extent to which

in its representation of nuns, see Elizabeth Cullingford's '"Our Nuns Are *Not* a Nation': Politicizing the Convent in Irish Literature and Film", in *Éire-Ireland*, 41 (1 and 2), 2006, pp 9-38.
27. Frances Finnegan, *Do Penance or Perish: Magdalen Asylums in Ireland*, (Oxford: Oxford University Press, 2004), pp 161-165.

St Margaret's life, and by implication the lives of women like her, resist the labels that society imposes upon them. It is, however, her relics that most fully manifest St Margaret's refractory nature:

Behind the silver commas of the shrine,
In the mine of the altar, her teeth listen and smile.

She is still here, she refuses
To be consumed. The weight of her bones
Burns down through the mountain. (*BS*, p 24)

The location of the relics parallels the syntactical placement of the epithets that would categorise and encapsulate this anomalous woman's life story. But what remains of St Margaret is an uncontainable trace, fragments of a body that, like the Cheshire cat's smile, mock those who would seek to reduce it to an apprehensible presence. The incendiary power of these relics links them to the fallen women in the Lock hospital, whose bodies burn alternatively with desire and disease. Reversing the trajectory of the traditional spiritual ascent through purgatorial flames that consume the vestiges of corporeality, the residue of St Margaret's bodily existence continues to exert a terrestrial influence. In Ní Chuilleanáin's rendering, St Margaret's relics are no longer tethered to the orthodox religious agenda of penitential reformation, but instead serve a more radical deconstructive purpose, proffering the possibility of a release from the social codes which would confine and regulate female sexuality.

All of this is recapitulated in the poem's typically evocative but enigmatic conclusion:

Her death did not make her like this:

Her eyes were hollowed
By the bloody scene: the wounds
In the body of her child's father
Tumbled in a ditch. The door was locked,
The names flew and multiplied; she turned
Her back but the names clustered and hung
Out of her shoulderbones
Like children swinging from a father's arm
Their tucked-up feet skimming over the ground. (*BS*, p 24)

What consecrates St Margaret, the poem suggests, is not her transcendence of the body through a process of mortification culminating in death. It is rather her illicit love and the suffering that she endures because of the loss of that love. The epithets thrust upon her are transmuted here from constrictive labels into markers of the fleeting movement of a life suspended between heaven and earth. But in stark contrast to the cruciform figure of the Son whose Father wills that he hang in agony, a testament to the irreconcilable opposition of worldly and celestial powers, the legacy of Ní Chuilleanáin's St Margaret is the vision of a different kind of patriarch, one who enables a playful straddling between the contravening demands of body and spirit.

A similar re-envisioning of the transcendental ideal underpinning patriarchy occurs in another poem from *The Brazen Serpent*, 'The Architectural Metaphor.' In this poem, however, the figures of the religious woman and the sexually transgressive woman are differentiated rather than conflated and the socio-cultural context in which the conjunction of these women actually occurred is fore-grounded. The title of this poem reminds us that in Ní Chuilleanáin's poetry, as Eamon Grennan has noted, 'one of the first things to strike a reader is the presence in it of some architecturally rendered space.'[28] Grennan casts Ní Chuilleanáin's use of architecture in exclusively spiritual terms, seeing it as 'sacramental, a solid outward sign of some inward truth: a monument, often literally, to an act of faith.'[29] But this poem registers her close attention to the way in which such spaces also manifest the agency of more secular powers, such as the nation-state. This realisation, in turn, precipitates a reconfiguration of a faith tainted by its complicity with state power. At its outset, 'The Architectural Metaphor' stresses how a shift in the border has moved the convent from its sheltered position on the periphery of society into the midst of the public sphere. The exact nature of the change brought about in this architectural space is hinted at in the poem's juxtaposed references to the cloister and the laundry. Ní Chuilleanáin acknowledges here the convent's incorporation in

---

28. Eamon Grennan, *Facing the Music: Irish Poetry in the Twentieth Century* (Omaha: Creighton University Press, 1999), p 284.
29. *Ibid*, p 285.

what James Smith refers to as Ireland's 'architecture of confine-ment': ·

> The archipelago of orphanages, mother and baby houses, Madgalene laundries, and reformatories that shored up the tenuous social structure of the newly independent Irish Free State.[30]

In her essay on nuns, however, Ní Chuilleanáin mitigates their responsibility, asserting that their role in this State-spon-sored disciplinary regime was ancillary and that blame would be more appropriately directed toward 'the real authority fig-ures: priests, doctors, and policemen ... politicians and bureau-crats who decide how little would be paid, and when nothing would be paid, for the up-keep of the powerless'.[31]

'The Architectural Metaphor' effects a similar rehabilitation of the legacy of nuns in Ireland from the stain of their appropri-ation by the patriarchal power structure. It does so by casting the dead foundress of the convent as the deliverer of a young girl on the verge of being assaulted by a man, precisely the type of girl who in the aftermath of such an assault could have found herself confined to a Magdalene laundry.

> Now light scatters, a door opens, laughter breaks in,
> A young girl barefoot, a man pushing her
> Backwards against a hatch –
>
> It flies up suddenly –
> There lies the foundress, pale
> In her funeral sheets, her face turned west
>
> Searching for the rose-window. (BS, p 14)

But the poem's power lies in the way in which it subverts our expectations by presenting this act of rescue as reciprocal. The young woman fending off her male oppressor could just as well be seen as reanimating the long deceased foundress, as re-call-ing the convent to its original sheltering mission. Because of

---

30. James M. Smith, 'Remembering Ireland's Architecture of Containment: "Telling" Stories In *The Butcher Boy* and *States of Fear*," in *Éire-Ireland* 36 (3 and 4), 2001, pp 111-130.
31. Ní Chuilleanáin, 'Nuns,' p 29.

pronominal ambiguity, the vision that concludes the poem cannot be consigned to either the foundress or the young girl, but must be seen as generated by the interfusion of their divergent yet coincident experiences. What most distinguishes this vision is its supplanting of the rose-window, the 'architectural metaphor' of the poem's title. This symbol embedded at the heart of countless Catholic Churches epitomises a conception of the divine as centripetal, harmoniously unified, and hierarchal – in short, as phallocentric. In lieu of this transcendent Rose (the prototype of the flower associated with the relics of St Thérèse of Lisieux), the poem offers a glimpse of a weed-choked graveyard with a foraging hen.

> It shows her
> what she never saw from any angle but this:
> Weeds nested in the Churchyard, catching the late sun,
>
> Herself at fourteen stumbling downhill
> And landing, and crouching to watch
> The sly limbering of the bantam hen
>
> Foraging between gravestones –
> Help is at hand
> Though out of reach:
> The world not dead after all. (*BS*, pp 14-15)

In this vision, the heterodoxy of which is marked by the concluding off-set lines, the pain and suffering of human existence are acknowledged as they are not in the artificial perfection of the rose-window. Hope is placed not in a distant panoptic deity but in a cunningly resistant and proximate femininity that offers the possibility of salvaging new life from out of the detritus of patriarchy.

As the poem's penultimate sentence 'Help is at hand/ Though out of reach,' reveals, there is a utopian quality to the vision that concludes 'The Architectural Metaphor'. That vision enacts a redemptive synthesis that elides the differences between the convent's dual roles as a protective enclosure that fostered a vibrant female-centred community and a place of near penal confinement that sequestered the most vulnerable of those women that patriarchy deemed recalcitrant. In Ní Chuilleanáin's most recent book, *The Girl Who Married the Reindeer* (2002), she backs away from any such synthesis and infers that the legacy of nuns and convent life in Ireland must ultimately remain an unresolved dialectic. This is most clearly revealed in the poems from this volume that evoke the motif of relics, 'Cloister of Bones' and 'Translation'.

'Cloister of Bones' culminates a set of loosely linked poems that can be seen as synopsising the provocative role that convents have played in Ní Chuilleanáin's imaginative life. The first of these poems, 'The Anchoress,' acknowledges, however obliquely, the recession of the figure of the nun from the contemporary social scene in Ireland and elsewhere. In the past, as the poem reveals in its final lines, there was a rich and enlivening exchange between cloistered religious women, such as the anchoress, and the surrounding community, an open sharing of their intimate and wondrous spiritual experiences with those on the outside.

> ... I remember
> When she would give me an hour of her visions,
> When she would levitate – she was always deaf –
> When thin pipe music resounded beyond the grilles.[32]

But as the anaphoric structure of these lines with their reiterated initial 'when' so insistently remind us, this condition belongs to an anterior time. In the poem's present, the engagement between the anchoress and the external world has become increasingly rare and attenuated, reduced to 'a few words, a command' and a promise of prayers exchanged at the 'mossgrown window beside the Church porch' (*GWMR*, p 4). The subsequent companion poems 'Sunday' and 'Chestnut Choir' expand upon this point by presenting us with a convent whose spatio-temporal location – the misty reaches of a mountain at winter's solstice – situates it in not so much in the realm of actuality as in an inner psychic landscape. It functions there more as a way-station than a destination, the locus of a spiritual impetus that pulls the per-

---

32. Eiléan Ní Chuilleanáin, *The Girl Who Married the Reindeer* (Winston-Salem, NC: Wake Forest University Press, 2002), p 4. Henceforth all quotations will be to this edition, denoted by *GWMR*, followed by the page number.

sona of these poems away from the familiar pleasures of ordinary life but that she cannot fully embrace. Having journeyed to
this site, the persona, instead of staying there and vigilantly
awaiting the arrival of the divine, decides to remain a wanderer
and ventures from this faith-full enclave into the freedom and
danger of the darkness outside.

If these preceding poems can be read as acknowledging the
declining viability of the convent as an external religious institution, 'Cloister of Bones' is Ní Chuilleanáin's most overt extrapol-
ation of its lingering emancipative potential. The cloister in this
poem is no longer the repository of relics but has become one
itself. This evocation of the convent as ruin all too accurately reflects the precipitous decline in late twentieth century Ireland of
women choosing the vocation of nun and the widespread closure
of convents that has accompanied it.[33] In the face of this loss, the
poem's speaker enacts an imaginative reconfiguration of the
cloister from its ruins. But instead of recreating this remembered
space as a spectacle, as her initial detached perspective might
suggest she will do, she finds herself subsumed within this ret-
rospective scene. This process of inter-animation reaches its climax
when in fulfillment of the promise of the poem's title the cloister
is transmogrified into the female body: 'arched and bouncing/
Naves, a corseted apse' (*GWMR*, p 9). By casting the female
body as a sheltered space invested with sacral power, this poem
brings to fruition what the experience of cloistered religious
women had long heralded – that is, a new conception of the relationship of women and the divine or what the poem in its last
line refers to 'the women's Christmas' (*GWMR*, p 9). In this gyno-
centric theophany, the female body is no longer merely a recept-
acle for a patriarchal deity but becomes a sacred site in itself.
And the eruptions of its somatic and psychic energy – the 'trem-
ble/Of women's laughter ... [and] mile-high panics' (*GWMR*, p 9)

---

33. Margaret MacCurtain points out that that during the 1980s over 30
convents closed and by the outset of the 1990s 57% of nuns were over 60
years old while only 2% were under 29. See 'Late in the Field: Catholic
Sisters in Twentieth-Century Ireland,' in *Chattel, Servant or Citizen:
Women's Status in Church, State, and Society*, ed Mary O'Dowd and
Sabine Wichert (Belfast: Queen's University Press, 1995), pp 39-40.

– are no longer regarded as manifestations of a disease, what patriarchy refers to as hysteria, but rather as a form of *jouissance* that the poem presents as a correlative to the act of worship.[34]

This eulogising of the cloister for its engendering of a distinctively feminine spirituality must, however, be juxtaposed with the lamentation for the victims of the Magdalene laundries in 'Translation'. The specific occasion for this poem, as its subtitle informs us, was the transfer of the remains of inmates from an unmarked mass grave at the Sister of Charity's convent in High Park, the site of Ireland's largest Magdalene asylum, to Glasnevin cemetery, where a memorial stone with the names of those whose remains could be identified was subsequently erected. If the preservation and veneration of relics such as St Thérèse of Lisieux 's represents an act of commemoration that fetishises an idealised past, the heedless dumping of the corpses of the Magdalene inmates fosters a collective amnesia that would erase the past sins of Church and state. There is a retributive logic at play here that, as Ní Chuilleanáin ironically puts it, 'evens the score' (*GWMR*, p 18). While alive, these women were regarded as impure or dirty and as punishment were charged with the task of expunging the dirt of others. Now as they are exhumed, the dirt they have become soils the nation's reputation. Their death exposes the dirty laundry, the humiliating trappings of a repressive past, that the nation has tried in vain to hide.

The amorphous remains of the Magdalene inmates contrast quite obviously with the carefully preserved and elegantly enshrined bodily fragments that constitute the traditional religious relic. And as this poem develops, they increasingly resemble the uncontainable and disruptive trace that characterises the notion of the relic articulated by Ní Chuilleanáin in 'The Real Thing' and repeatedly evoked throughout her poetry. This becomes especially apparent when we contrast 'Translation' with another work of art occasioned by the exhumation and reburial of the

34. For a more general analysis of *jouissance* in Ní Chuilleanáin that focuses upon her comments on Bernini's statue of St Teresa of Avila and her penchant for the baroque, see Dillon Johnston, " 'Our Bodies' Eyes and Writing Hands': Secrecy and Sensuality in Ní Chuilleanáin's Baroque Art", in *Gender and Sexuality in Modern Ireland*, ed Anthony Bradley and Maryann Gialanella Valiulis (Amherst, MA: University of Massachusetts Press, 1997), pp 207-208.

High Park Magdalenes – the author and performance artist Gerard Mannix Flynn's 'extallation' 'Call Me By My Name', erected in 2003. Prominently situated at the corner of Leeson Street and Stephen's Green, the very heart of Dublin and site of its first Magdalene Laundry, this 'extallation' consisted of a large mortuary wall with plaques, some of which contained the names and dates of deceased women buried in the mass grave at High Park, others of which simply indicated 'remains unknown'.[35] As Geraldine Meaney points out, Flynn's monument to these forgotten victims of the State directly challenged the 'official' heroic narrative of Irish history embodied in the myriad plaques and statues honouring Ireland's literary and political champions as well as its victims of colonial oppression.[36] Moreover, this work's naming of these previously anonymous women was in itself a powerful and profoundly moving act of reclamation. Ní Chuilleanáin's poem, on the other hand, resists any such attempt to memorialise the Magdalenes. She recognises that what remains after death is un-nameable, beyond words. Yet while the residue of these women's presence is literally untranslatable, it still somehow makes a claim upon us. Even in their silence, the victimised dead make themselves heard – theirs is, to quote Maurice Blanchot, 'the voiceless cry, which breaks with all utterances ... the cry [that] tends to exceed all language ... [to] remain outside of sense – a meaning infinitely suspended, decried, decipherable-indecipherable.'[37] Ní Chuilleanáin suggests something similar in a passage that brilliantly conjures this cry from out of the very forces, both natural and institutional, that would stifle it :

---

35. For a description of Mannix Flynn's 'extallation,' see Geraldine Meaney, 'The Gothic Republic: Dark Imaginings and White Anxieties,' in *Single Motherhood in Twentieth-Century Ireland: Cultural, Historical and Social Essays*, ed Maria Cinta Ramblado-Minero and Auxiliadora Pérez-Valdes (Lewiston, NY: Edwin Mellen Press, 2006), p 26, and Mary Raftery, 'Taking Mary Home', *The Irish Times*, 15 April 2004, http://ireland.com/newspaper/opinion.
36. Meaney, 'The Gothic Republic,' p 26.
37. Maurice Blanchot, *The Writing of the Disaster*, trs Ann Smock (Lincoln: University of Nebraska, 1995), p 51.

Assist them now, ridges under the veil, shifting,
Searching for their parents, their names,
The edges of words grinding against nature,

As if, when water sank between the rotten teeth
Of soap, and every grasp seemed melted, one voice
Had begun, rising above the shuffle and hum

Until every pocket in her skull blared with the note –
Allow us now to hear it, sharp as an infant's cry
While the grass takes root, while the steam rises: (*GWMR*, p 18)

In its conclusion, the poem intimates what effect the hearing of this cry would have. It does so, paradoxically, by adopting the persona of one of the deceased Magdalenes who asserts the untranslatability of her post-mortem condition, describing herself as 'washed clean of idiom,' even as she speaks:

I lie sifted to dust:
Let the bunched keys I bore slacken and fall:
I rise and forget: a cloud over my time. (*GWMR*, p 18)

It is as if the acknowledgement of the inexpressible suffering that the Magdalenes endured during life somehow releases them in death from the burden of that past. The hearing of their cry de-privatises and nationalises their pain, exorcising the shadow of oppression from them so that it may haunt the society as a whole. Detached from its particular context in this poem, this last line with its concurrence of liberation and miasma might serve as Ní Chuilleanáin's synecdoche for the legacy of nuns in Ireland. Her poetic sifting of the remains of religious women has disclosed that the hope for emancipation from patriarchal religious and social structures that their experience fosters must be tempered by a realisation of the institutional oppression that they facilitated. As Ní Chuilleanáin's poetry so powerfully demonstrates, the appropriate response to the tradition of Catholicism with which Irish culture is still imbricated is not a reification of the more venerable vestiges of its past, but rather an anatomising of the conflicting traces that it bequeaths to the present.

The Jesus Body, the Jesus Bones

John F. Deane

In the summer of 2000 I was lucky enough to have been offered a short residency on the island of Gotland in Sweden and flew from Dublin to Stockholm. We had to wait for a small plane to take us out to the island, about 40 minutes flight from Stockholm. As a group of us waited for that flight the weather got wilder; a storm was gathering, the winds grew in anger and the rain began to fall. It was announced that our flight would be the last one out of the airport that night. As we walked across the tarmac in failing light, I watched a young girl and her father ahead of me; she was nervous, she had a doll in her hand, and the father urged her on, almost pushing her up the small steps onto the aircraft. He settled her into her seat but she was crying; I could see she was brain damaged and in some anxiety.

During the flight our small plane was tossed like flotsam on the clouds and the girl cried out loud, adding to my own sense of fear and sympathy; her body rocked in unmanageable distress and her fingers bruised that half-forgotten doll. I remember thinking that, like the whole of creation, she shared in the suffering body of Jesus and in his bones. Later, as I eased myself into bed on the island, a bell chimed midnight from a dark tower nearby; for some reason, a memory of my serving Mass one morning on Achill Island came back to me, the memory associating itself with the child and with the body of Jesus. The congregation had been one old woman, in no great shape, physically or mentally, and the priest hesitated when he was laying the host on her cracked tongue; it fell, and he quickly picked out another one and gave it to her. Perhaps the priest himself was none too awake at that hour of the morning because it was left to me, in spite of all the warnings I had heard, to gather up the Deity from the floor; the perfect white of the bread was tinged where her tongue had tipped it; this, the necessary God, the beautiful, the patience. I swallowed it, taking within me Godhead and congregation, the long obedience of the earth's bones, and the hopeless urge to lay my hands in solace on the world.

This sense I have always had, that the world is one, and that it is graced through by the death and resurrection of Jesus, must have come to me from the wonder and beauty of the island on which I was born and reared. As I grew to relish that world, that earth, I also grew to an awareness of my Catholic heritage, but it was the words of Paul that stuck somewhere in my consciousness:

> Now there are varieties of gifts, but the same Spirit; and there are varieties of services, but the same Lord; and there are varieties of activities, but it is the same God who activates all of them in everyone. To each is given the manifestation of the Spirit for the common good. To one is given through the Spirit the utterance of wisdom, and to another the utterance of knowledge according to the same Spirit; to another faith by the same Spirit, to another gifts of healing by the one Spirit, to another the working of miracles, to another prophecy, to another the discernment of spirits, to another various kinds of tongues, to another the interpretation of tongues. For just as the body is one and has many members, and all the members of the body, though many, are one body, so it is with Christ. For in the one Spirit we were all baptised into one body – Jews or Greeks, slaves or free – and we were all made to drink of one Spirit. (1 Cor: 12)

Into one body, the Jesus body. This is, I suppose, that 'communion of saints' we spoke of in our creed; it is the prayer of Jesus himself, 'that they all may be one, as thou, Father, and I, are one'. One God. One creation. One people. And Paul also wrote:

> I consider that our present sufferings are not worth comparing with the glory that will be revealed in us. The creation waits in eager expectation for the sons of God to be revealed. For the creation was subjected to frustration, not by its own choice, but by the will of the one who subjected it, in hope that the creation itself will be liberated from its bondage to

decay and brought into the glorious freedom of the children of God. We know that the whole creation has been groaning as in the pains of childbirth right up to the present time. Not only so, but we ourselves, who have the first fruits of the Spirit, groan inwardly as we wait eagerly for our adoption as sons, the redemption of our bodies. (Rom: 18)

He is referring in these lines to the redemption of our bodies, and of the earth itself. Those bodies, that earth, that have been riddled through with the very flesh and blood of Jesus who died and was born again. If our hope rests on the resurrection of Jesus, and on the resurrection of our body, then it appears, too, that the whole earth will be resurrected in some way. The Catholic Church has always appeared to me to be in denial of so much that is physical in our being, it has been so alert with exclusions that gradually, down all the years that I have been seeking, I find myself now on the side of the world against that Church. I hesitate to call myself a Catholic. I hesitate, too, to call myself a Christian, a Christ-person, though this is what I want to be, because that name is so full of virtue, love, self-sacrifice, that I feel myself unworthy of the name. I believe, then, in the Jesus body, the Jesus bones.

With the admixture of a rural 1950s Catholicism and the physical beauty of Achill Island, perhaps it was inevitable that I turn to poetry. It is in a poetry that refuses to baulk at the reasonable and successful, and passes beyond into the unreasonable, the wonderful, that I find the deepest search into faith and how that faith may respond to the terrible demands of our time. To walk along a lazy, wet bog road on Achill Island, an island that has been riddled through with Christian faith and with time, beauty and the depredations of time, to idle on that track under an enormous sky, is to know something of the long reaching of God into one's life:

Towards a Conversion
There is a soft drowse on the bog today;
the slight bog-cotton scarcely stirs; for now
this could be what there is of universe, the far-off
murmuring of ocean, the rarest traffic passing, barely

audible beyond the hill. I am all attention, held
like a butterfly in sunlight, achieve, a while,
an orchid quiet, the tiny shivering of petals, the mere
energy of being. Along the cuttings

bubbles lift through black water and escape, softly,
into sunlight; this complex knotting of roots has been
an origin, and nothing new nor startling
will happen here, save the growth of sphagnum

into peat; if this is prayer, then
I have prayed. I walk over millennia, the Irish
wolf and bear, the elk and other
miracles; everywhere bog-oak roots

and ling, forever in their gentle
torsion, with all this floor a living thing, held
in the world's care, indifferent. Over everything
voraciously, the crow, a monkish body hooded

in grey, crawks its blacksod, cleansing music;
lay your flesh down here you will become
carrion-compost, sustenance for the ravening roots;
where God is, has been, and will ever be.

To mention God in poetry today, to bring God into any conversation, is to feel oneself placed at once to be viewed as hopelessly out-of-date. Faith, and particularly the Catholic faith, is seen as something once widely held but no longer to be taken seriously, like the penny farthing bicycle, like tansy as a cure for hysteria. Progress in economic terms has put faith into a box of strange curios; the world can and will do without faith. If so many of the wars of history can be ascribed to differences of faith, then the world will be better off without religion. Catholic teaching has never kept pace with scientific or economic or any other kind of progress, including developments in the equality of men and women, and therefore the Church has lagged away behind the world, behind a creation unified in the death and resurrection of Jesus. If the central sacraments are still insisted upon in the life of an individual, baptism, marriage, extreme unction, and if the Catholic rituals of bringing the dead to Church, of saying Mass for the dead, of Christian burial, are still carried out, it is often done so simply out of a sense of tradition, a kind of insurance, a method of channeling grief. Three or four nods to Catholic faith, but serious living looks elsewhere.

I think it has been the negative and divisive stance of the Catholic Church that has been alienating me over the years, together with the hierarchy's stress on glory-robes, status, authority and privilege. In my early years, priests were always a scary presence, dominant, judgemental and domineering, and everybody knows how that posture has been undermined by revelations of corruption. The sense of exclusivity, not only keeping women out of any real form of ministry, but insisting that any form of ecumenism be ruled by Catholic dogma, that liberation theology, particularly in Latin America, was somehow against the Church's authority, by standing, as it seems to me, always by the powerful and privileged and leaving the works of justice on behalf of the poor and oppressed to voluntary groups and non-governmental agencies. I never heard the Church speak out forcefully against the violence of our times; where are the voices now against the war crimes being perpetrated by Israel, by Bush and Rice and Rumsfeld, by Sharon and Olmert, the fanatics of another domineering faith currently in the ascendant ... In other words, how can I hold to a Church that denies in so many ways the possibilities of love, that love which moves towards the unification of all humankind in brotherhood and sisterhood.

John Donne expressed it well:

The bell doth toll for him that thinks it doth; and though it intermit again, yet from that minute that that occasion wrought upon him, he is united to God. Who casts not up his eye to the sun when it rises? but who takes off his eye from a comet when that breaks out? Who bends not his ear to any bell which upon any occasion rings? but who can remove it from that bell which is passing a piece of himself out of this world? No man is an island, entire of itself; every man is a piece of the continent, a part of the main. If a clod be washed away by the sea, Europe is the less, as well as if a promontory were, as well as if a manor of thy friend's or of thine own were: any man's death diminishes me, because I am involved in mankind, and therefore never send to know for whom the bell tolls; it tolls for thee ...

If the Christ has been crucified, entombed and returned to life, then in that faith must all our hope lie. And hence our universe is impregnated with the fact of the incarnation of God, the fact of the God's taking of flesh and bone, its partaking of our world and of our living, and hence the need for oneness and the hope that all of the earth, bone and fragment, hill and ocean depth, must partake of that wonder. I find the detailed implications of this belief difficult to frame in prose and so have tried to explore it in a series of poems, because poetry does not stop at the great blank wall before which reason comes to a dead end.

Mappa Mundi
Let this then be your diary and yearbook: make
    a frame of oak on which to fix
a sheet of finest vellum, stretched, like skin; draw

freehand, a not quite perfect circle; use black
    ink, some red, for the heart, let's say, for the Red
Sea; blue for rivers, veins, and brown-egg shapes

for mountain ranges, and for faith; focus it all
    towards the centre, Christ, his bones stretched wide
in crucifixion, colour him too insistent red

to confute the non-believers. Puce, for wars, but let it not
    predominate. Have angels flutterfly above
and devils snarl, scarlet, in the guts. Remember

that something within the frame of bones grows wiser
    as the bones grow heavier, the same that shifts
your being gratefully towards cessation. Now see

how down the long avenue the cherry trees once more
    have sifted all the juices of the earth
into extravagant blossoming, a canopy for wedding feasts, a
    Bach

cantata in the key of white, but in you, memory
    or the doleful rhythms of experience, hold the heart
from lifting in exultation, chill winds being possible

and unseasonable frosts. Remember, too, how the monks
    laboured years over their charts, finding in the corners
place for monsters, for the slithery ladder and the sulphur

lakes beneath. If there is time, etch in gold leaf your fabled
    places,
    Samarkand and Valparaiso, the pancreas, the afterlife.
Something within the frame of bones is in no rush

to clothe again the hard-won nakedness of spirit. Fig-leaf.
    Rue.
    When you are done, step back, and gaze awhile
into the mirror, note contour-lines about your face

and the curious light still shining in your eyes.

I point again to a belief in the harmony of all nature, and to
people's place in that harmony. We are in great danger, in our
time, of destroying that harmony. To damage our world is to
damage ourselves; not to cry foul when our ecology is threatened, when military powers are given free hand to undertake
any kind of warfare they feel they can get away with, when
over-the-steeple wealth is put on display for its own sake ...
then humanity is sliding down a loose-shale cliff towards the
abyss. When wealthy nations take unto themselves the right to
cheat and lie and torture, all in the name of a 'war on terror' and
the Church does nothing about it ... And I cannot help but remember how the Church in the Unites States stood behind
George W. Bush when he went for re-election, even though his
hands are bloodied and the Republican Party stands accused of
dealing in death, then I lose faith in that Church and its mission
to be 'one, holy, catholic and apostolic'. We have been, simply,
invited to love; in George Herbert's great poem 'Love', the God
invites the soul to come and sup at God's table but the soul
draws back, conscious of sin; then Love reminds the soul that
Jesus Christ supped with sinners, prostitutes and tax collectors
and it is not the worthiness of the soul that counts, but God's
own infinite giving, his mercy. When we grow aware of this invitation, it is not of our own merits we must think but of God's
overwhelming and unquestioning gifts of grace to us. We must
howl and scream and gesticulate against the inhumanity of our

times; it is of no earthly use to climb into an armour-plated popemobile and wave out of ermine glory to the common people, massed in their hope of hearing a new message of peace and love and sharing, a message wrung from the immediacy of our era. If there is a balance, then all of us must put on the scales even more and more of what is good and beautiful to counteract the evils that war and violence are placing on the other side.

The Poem of the Goldfinch
Write, came the persistent whisperings, a poem
on the mendacities of war. So I found shade
under the humming eucalyptus, and sat,
patienting. Thistle-seeds blew about on a soft breeze,
a brown-gold butterfly was shivering on a fallen
ripe-flesh plum. Write your dream, said Love, of the total
abolition of war. Vivaldi, I wrote, the four
seasons. Silence, a while, save for the goldfinch
swittering in the higher branches, sweet, they sounded,
sweet-wit, wit-wit, wit-sweet. I breathed
scarcely, listening. Love bade me write but my hand
held over the paper; tell them you, I said,
they will not hear me. A goldfinch swooped,
sifting for seeds; I revelled in its colouring, such
scarlets and yellows, such tawny, a patterning
the creator himself must have envisioned, doodling
that gold-flash and Hopkins-feathered loveliness. Please

write, Love said, though less insistently. Spirit, I answered,
that moved out once on chaos ... No, said Love,
and I said Michelangelo, Van Gogh, No, write
for them the poem of the goldfinch and the whole
earth singing, so I set myself down to the task.

If all of this comes across as a certainty in my life, then I am sorry; it is not so. I am conversant with poetry; I have been immersed in Catholicism; yet now I am lost and, like so many others, am seeking passionately for the truth. How desperately people are seeking, too, everywhere, all over the world. There are endless signs and symptoms of this searching and I have to say that the answers we are so often given are the negative, the

Thatcherite ones: 'Out! Out! Out!' The only certainty in my life, after my passion for poetry, after love and family, is that a man lived once, an anointed one, a Christ, and that his name was Jesus, meaning saviour. To him I cling, to his words, and his example. And to the hope that he offered to a (then, too) confused and violent world. I cling to the Jesus body, the Jesus bones. It is the urgency of the quest, and the imagery left on my soul by Achill Island, that spirits my writing, often against what I feel has been an original inspiration. The God intrudes! Often I am grateful, and often not. But then I realise, if the Bones and Body of Jesus are firm in the flesh of creation, then everything I write is stronger the closer it comes to those sacred bones.

> Take your pen, you urge, and write: God.
> But I resist and write
> sea-mew, fuchsia, city, moon.
> You insist, write: God. I say –
> I have no pen now, I use PCs.
> Then type out: God, you say, translate me
> into this your century.
> I type out: God; and then delete, type
> sea-mew, fuchsia, city, moon.
> And when I hear you laugh I know again
> you are the letters of every word I use, you
> the source and form of every poem. But,
> I plead, the people mock and say that God
> is not fit subject for our century. So I write again
> sea-mew, fuchsia, city, moon. And you say
> yes! you have written me down once more.

When I was growing up I suffered a severely repressive education in morality, emphasis almost always on sexual affronts. As the world today appears indifferent to such a morality, many disturbing questions rise in me. Questions to which I have no answers; I see a generation growing up in almost complete sexual freedom; I am aware of the potential diseases that this may bring, I am aware too of the values of family life and the fruits of stabilities in human relationships that may be lost in such an approach to loving. I hear around me only the same negative moral voices that I heard decades ago and the pointlessness of an undeveloped morality from the mouth of the Church hurts me still. Our technologically wizard younger generations have no time to consider questions of morality or faith; their duty is to themselves, to technology, to worldly possessions and 'success'. And what do I have to oppose to such attitudes should I, indeed, wish to oppose them? I believe, because of the Jesus body, the Jesus bones, that everything in the body of creation is good and that humankind has yet a great deal to discover in that body, that the search is good, and that a human balance will prevail. That is, however, a view depending on one's faith in the inherent goodness of a humanity that moves without the guidance of a progressive Church. And so, once again, I propose … Christ.

In the hidden sutures of my own mind I grow aware, too, of death. How can we not be aware of it, we who have been grieving witnesses to the terrible power of modern technology to destroy human life and the infrastructures of an ancient nation. How suddenly did Israel, backed up by Britain and the criminal regime of George W. Bush, rain death down on the innocent lives of children, in Southern Lebanon, in Palestine, in Quana? And how imperfect the most highly-boasted techniques of mass destruction in their pinpoint accuracy fail so abysmally; death, overlord and ever-present cackling ghost, death indiscriminate and carefree, hovering over their precision-guided bombs? What is there to offer the generations in opposition to such inhuman terror? Christ, again Christ, Christ only.

I want to push further down this uncertain, yet sustaining lane. I assert, in all humility and with all the stays of vagueness, insubstantiality and wilfulness, that I try to call myself a Christian, a Christ-follower, and eschew Catholicism as it is currently conceived. And if, as Joseph Mary Plunkett touched on, 'I see His blood upon the rose, and in the stars the glory of His eyes', then I must partake more closely, and perhaps more foolishly, in the great sacrament of Communion with that Jesus body. Hence the great moment of the Mass still means a lot for me, that moment of transubstantiation, and then of taking that sacred body within my own. If there is even a scintilla of truth in that, then the substance of the being of Jesus enters my substance: 'Body of Christ', the priest says, and I answer fervently, 'Amen!' 'Blood of Christ', he offers, and I agree again, 'Amen!' And then, when I walk down a beautiful country lane, the world around me is transubstantiated, too, the great sacrament extending into the landscape with which I am in league.

Kane's Lane
The substance of the being of Jesus
sifts through the substance of mine; I
am God, and son of God, and man. Times I feel

my very bones become so light I may
lift unnoticed above Woods's Wood and soar
in an ecstasy of being over Acres' Lake; times again

I am so dugged, so dragged, my flesh
falls granite while a fluid near congealed
settles on my heart. The Christ – frozen in flight

on the high-flung frame of his cross
leaves me raddled in the grossest of mercies
and I walk the length of Kane's Lane, on that ridge

of grass and cress and plantain
battening down the centre, I sex my tongue
on the flesh juices of blackberries, cinch my jaws on the chalk

bitterness of sloes, certain and unsettled,
lost and found in my body, sifted through a strait
and serpentine love-lane stretched between dawn and night.

To make the statement that sets one quite apart from so many of one's contemporaries, especially when that statement is made with a modicum of doubt and a deal of uncertainty, must appear a very foolish thing. The lane I have travelled is not in itself a scientific one, quite the opposite, it partakes of the craziness of the imagination and of the foolishness of a trust in the movements of the heart and the track of poetry. That statement is a belief in the truthfulness of the gospels, made in my mind even more truthful because of the inconsistencies and contradictions between the four evangelists. I trust in the actual existence of Jesus, and in the value of his words and example. I trust that, if the God was crazy enough to stir out of eternal restfulness to create a world filled with the doubtful wonder that is humanity, then that God is a poet, and a hugely masterful one. Because, along-side reason and its offshoots, there is the invisible door that one must open and go through for a full faith in Jesus as incarnate God; here I can do no more than hope. But poetry can go beyond that hope; poetry can take the invisible key, open the door that is not there in the great blank wall of reason and step out into the wonder and beauty of what is beyond. This is the ultimate power of the Jesus presence in the whole of the created world; this is the finest power of poetry. Down the centuries, the great poets have taken this key and opened that door: Donne, Herbert and Marvel, Milton, Blake and Hopkins, Eliot, Dickinson and Thomas, and many, many more. The trust is in the Word; and the word is, ultimately, love. Whether or not this love is radiated by the Catholic Church is a matter of personal decision; for me, the Church does not mediate that love. I go back to what I already mentioned, the morality and greatness of a life devoted to family, to the love of one person, to the treasure that is marriage.

Your Name
A warm rain falls outside, sowing its dust-motes
softly onto soft ground; I will sit here
beside you while you sleep. All my thoughts again, will be
concerning you. Your body lies
easeful, your breathing gentle as the fall of dusk.
You have gifted life and death to me
and given both your name, and with that name
I will go down proudly to my grave, my lips
holding to these exceptional words: I have lived.
The dark blue of the walls around us, here
where we have loved, will be the colour
waiting for me when I close my eyes. You
to me are truce in the long war, a tent
fixed firmly against the waging desert storm.

I will have laid the jewel of my death
in your kindly palm, or you
will have laid yours in mine, the hand
closing over it will wait, in warmth, in quietness.
They will speak of me, when they speak,

in terms of you, the way they say a stream
meanders through its chosen country. Remember
how we found each other, hurt, migrating birds
resting on a green island; remember
how we kissed, under the unblinking eye
of Mars. Here now I write your name in sand-dust
and it will blow about this favoured earth forever.

I sometimes wonder how deep was the faith of the people of my generation, and of the generations before them, when they followed without demur every rule and regulation of the Catholic Church. I have spent a week in Drumshambo, Co Leitrim, and during three days of that week the local people were offered their annual 'mission'. This triduum was known as the days of the Portiuncula, after the little Church in Assisi founded by the great St Francis. In the earlier decades, crowds overran Drumshambo and assisted at every Mass, penitential service, confession, prayers, blessings ... It was a festival atmosphere, something like the crowds that now throng the Galway races, with obvious differences. There were stalls erected and people bought their religious objects, the rosaries, medals, scapulars, holy water, holy pictures ... and took them to be blessed on the final evening. And the priest thundered at them, sinners that they were, outlined the fires of hell, the sufferings of purgatory, the narrow and strait way that would lead to heaven. They worked for plenary indulgences, for themselves and for the souls in purgatory. And they went home purified, full of resolutions and hope, and went back to their difficult lives.

But was all of that really faith? Was not a great deal of it a matter or custom, of tradition, of fear? There were half-held convictions, upheld by the authority of Rome and their local priesthood, convictions that we have seen fall away so fast and so easily. How we trusted in those men who dressed in gorgeous robes and processed about our Churches, chanting in a foreign tongue, performing rituals of which we had only a general understanding. There was security there; there was an absence of personal responsibility; there was a path to follow. Ireland is, I believe, currently in a phase of adolescence, being a young country in its freedom, and for the first time in its history finding itself with a great deal of money to spend. We are still far from maturity. It is easy to blame the Church now for taking that responsibility from us, for holding us in the palm of her hand, for threatening and cajoling us down the path she insisted we must take. But that will not do; nor will it do for the Church to fall back, as she appears to be doing, on those same old simplistic rules and sanctions and threats, withdrawing into a fortress and refusing to admit the modern world and its advances and its sorrows. Who will guide the country through its adolescent and foolish phase? Or what country should we take as example to follow? The Church itself must constantly work with the world towards a common maturity; it, too, appears to be in an adolescent phase, in denial of its need to grow up, in its constant iteration of objections and refusals. To be vocal and authoritative in this world the Church, too, must accept the oneness of all people in God, the oneness of all the creation in God, and strive, with the original Jesus, to convince the world of love, of the Jesus body, the Jesus bones.

We are witness, in our time, to an evil that grows in tandem with technological advances and economic wellbeing; that evil is selfishness, the opposite to what I am speaking about. It is clear and is shouted about often enough, God knows, that technological advances and economic wellbeing are showing the way to bring ease and health to regions that are yet in dreadful straits. The fact that the 'developed' world is turning those assets to its own egotistical ends, again proves the point that I am hoping to make. I am offering a picture of our world: I am offering words that go too far, yet that is where poetry must go, and that is where I find my hope:

> Lank yellow cranes, like migratory birds, stilted, are feeding in the shallows of our suburbs and our village outposts and this building frenzy seems a part of our adolescent rush yet this, too, is part of God's creative urging; the finely-speckled breast of a mistle thrush, proud yet startled in the shadow of an old ash-tree, this, too, is listed with our hurrying in the one, ongoing annals of the world; yet soon branch and bole of the ash-tree will lift naked out of mud, like lopped limbs in a war zone; men in daffodil-yellow hard hats move like

robots carrying wooden planks; earth shakers, world movers. Beyond this frenzy it is easy to lose heart, and I have been figuring, in a place apart, if this is stitching or unstitching of the world. Times now I feel like hosting requiem before our ocean juggernauts, road juggernauts, sky juggernauts and before mosquito jets masterful in their economies, their deconstructions; in our economic victories such spiritual defeat!

I stand before him and he says: 'Body of Christ' and I chew on flesh, he says 'Blood of Christ' and I taste a bitter, small intoxication; I take the substance deep into my substance and can say I, too, am Jesus; and I pray – that after all, through the Jesus body, the Jesus bones, the deaf will hear the breezes siffling through the eucalyptus trees, will hear the breaking of waves along Atlantic's shingle shores; that the blind, after darkness and the shadows that darkness throws, will see the moonlight play like fireflies along the undersides of leaves, that those of us botched in brain and limb will be gazelles across an intimate terrain and that the tears of the too-old woman, inward-dwelling, wheelchair-locked who lost her lover-man to death some twenty years ago will step out giddily again into blue erotic light.

The Jesus Bones
It was full summer and the skylarks soared
over the wild meadow;
across ditch and hedgerow the dogrose
was draping its pink-rose shawl while the flowering
 brambles reached

dangerous fingers
towards the flowerbeds. A bat lay dead on the garage
window-ledge, amongst webs
and husks; it was curled up tight, perfect as a babyfist

though flies already
had laid their eggs in the sacred caverns of the ears;
I touched the fur and brushed the unresisting skin of night.
The holly leaves hymned in the sun

and small birds flitted through it;
it was shaping in torsion – all of us subject to corruption – a
   green
promise of clusters of the most scarlet of all berries; tree, I
   imagined,
of the knowledge of good and evil, its bitter roots

driving into the humus of our sleep. I would be, at times,
animal, thread of the skein
of earth, free of the need of redemption. Once I crept along a
   ditchtop,
in a tunnel of rhododendron, on earth mould,

leaf mould, on blossom-droppings, the tiny hardnesses
stippling palms, and knees;
this was everyday adventure,
the eyes of blackbirds following and their alarm calls,

with the strange and beetly
insects frightening me, their throbbing, their pebble-eyes.
I could fall silent there, hidden on the pulsebeat of the earth,
   mind
vacant, body stilled. Part of it. To receive.

And watched the fox slip by the drain outside,
there, uncareful, in daylight,
each russet hair sun-burnished, the breathfilled brush
like an old guardianship, a queen's train, that sorrowing eye

rounded where a moon-sliver shape of white
startled me; her long tongue lolling, the teeth were visible
in a grim fox-smile. My breathing stopped and a tiny shiver
   of fellowship
touched my spine. A moment, merely. Then

she was gone. A magpie
smattered noisily in the trees: *one for gloria, for hosanna.* If, in
   our waking,
we could mould it all into a shape, beautiful and at peace
the way the electrically burnt heart of Jesus

found rest in the rock tomb
though we are many, seam and femur, root-system,
belly, spleen. Night, and the moon dressed the storm-black
   clouds
in scarves of buttermilk-white while a solitary star, as if
   hastening, sat

over the eucalyptus tree. We –
not animal enough and cruel beyond thought –
go scattering blood over the earth
as we might scatter water off our fingers,

big-headed man, articulate, stitching and unstitching
mindlessly as we pass. The Jesus bones
have been nailed into the timber of the tree, the blood
in its revolutions

pouring through the puncture-holes, this man,
of localised importance, this Jesus-fox, who broiled fine fish
on a nest of stones by the lakeshore; this
rag-and-bone man, this stranger, this lover, giver, priest.

Catholicism at a Crossroads:
Jean Sulivan's Message for post-Catholic Ireland

Eamon Maher

Jean Sulivan (1913-1980) is not a name that triggers automatic recognition among literary cognoscenti in France or in Ireland. 'Sulivan' is the nom de plume adopted by the Breton priest, Joseph Lemarchand, who published his first book in 1958, when he was 45 years old. Between that and his death in 1980, he produced about one publication a year, mostly fiction (novels and short stories), but also a significant spiritual journal, *Morning Light,* and a memoir recounting his youth on a Breton farm and his close relationship with his mother, *Anticipate Every Goodbye,* which I translated into English and to which I will return later. In this chapter, I will illustrate the way in which Sulivan's prophetic voice transcends boundaries, geographical and temporal, and resonates in a special way in what many commentators refer to as post-Catholic Ireland.

In order to situate Sulivan's writings a little better, it is necessary to travel back to the France of the middle of the last century. The Second World War had been a major source of embarrassment to a nation that prided itself on its military prowess and long colonial history. The total capitulation to the invading German army, the collaboration of many French people with the occupying forces' relentless pursuit and extermination of the Jewish population, left France feeling vulnerable and uncertain in the wake of its liberation in 1945. In such a climate, it is not surprising that existentialism became the dominant philosophical and literary trend at this time. Issues of social responsibility came to the fore as people began to ask questions like: How does one find meaning in existence when one no longer believes in God? What is the best way to live a life that will both improve society and fulfil one's moral obligation towards the common good? The human psyche appeared absurd, incomprehensible to a number of intellectuals. Camus, in *The Myth of Sisyphus*, put forward the theory that the only serious moral issue that people had to face was the decision whether to commit suicide or prolong a life bereft of meaning.

In literature, there was the emergence of the New Novel, with its fragmented style and absence of organic development of character, and the waning of the Catholic Novel, which had enjoyed such a glorious period at the end of the nineteenth and the beginning of the twentieth centuries with talented practitioners such as Bloy, Barbey d'Aurevilly, Mauriac and Bernanos. When Sulivan began writing, he was hailed as a successor to Bernanos, with whom he shares a prophetic vision. However, in a move that was to characterise his future literary development, he chose a different path. He knew that the spiritual climate of the nineteen fifties in France demanded a fresh approach from a writer like him:

> But whether it is that genius cannot be imitated, because former cultural and religious signs have become outdated, they can only communicate with a public living in the past. Spiritual heirs are either out of touch or else forced to renew themselves and follow a new direction, or else return to silence.[1]

He was clearly seeking something different, to devise a new way of presenting aspects of religious experience. After winning the *Grand Prix catholique de littérature* for his novel *The Sea Remains*, in 1964, he deliberately distanced himself from both the Catholic Novel and traditional literature in general. The Catholic Novel still had a considerable audience in France at this time. However, in Sulivan's estimation it made no sense to attempt to prolong this genre of writing when its era had passed. He wrote, once more in *Petite littérature individuelle*: 'It is in invention that the future of Christian writers lies if they want to be something more than specialists, scribes or efficient instruments in the market of religion.'[2] What he conceived or invented was a strange type of conversational style in which the author intervened regularly to address challenges to his readers like the fol-

---

1. Jean Sulivan, *Petite littérature individuelle* (Paris: Gallimard, 1971), p 142. My translation.
2. *Ibid.*, p 131. My translation.

lowing from what is perhaps his most disjointed book, *Joie errante* (*Wandering Joy*):

> Your anxiety moves me. All these comings-and-goings in space and time [...] You would like an accomplished book that would grab you by the throat! I don't want to lie to this extent. Why should I allow myself to be carried along by the mechanics of a plot? [...] Why should I extend for you this trap, while I'd hide behind the smooth rampart of literature, totally unblemished, watching you look at yourselves, delighted with my posturing.[3]

In lines like these, Sulivan questions all the usual features associated with the novel genre: plot, classical style and linear character development. But he is also debunking the tools of his trade by telling his readers that he refuses to 'hide behind the smooth rampart of literature', or to maintain a pretence in relation to a literary process that he considers outdated and ineffectual. In his later novels, in particular, Sulivan writes more and more of social marginalisation through the experience of his characters, many of whom live in liminal spaces, often as tramps. He never experienced marginalisation first hand, but his characters frequently dispense with the veneer of social respectability, and this affords them a keener vision of what is really important in the development of a strong inner life. He reveals the transformation that can take hold of people who are suddenly deprived of material and physical comforts and experience all that is synonymous with living as a down-and-out in any large city. They remain for the most part unseen and ignored by those who go about their daily routine without a thought for how people on the margins are faring. Sulivan believed that material impoverishment could be a gateway to happiness, a liberation. Hence his declaration in *Morning Light*:

> From the start I feel close to all those whom society has marginalised – tramps, addicts, freaks, even 'establishment' types, empty of spiritual substance and beginning to realise it. They live in the midst of steel, glass high-rises, highways

---

3. Jean, Sulivan, *Joie errante* (Paris: Gallimard, 1974), p 147. My translation.

that have become cemeteries, sex shops, and the rubble of human failure. But at the same time I notice with amazement that a song of freedom flows through everything, a paradoxical joy more powerful than my pain and mediocrity, the hope which those who bear it within them say they recognise.[4]

At the time he was writing these lines (the 1970s), the old Catholic order in France was giving way to a new, underground religion. Young people in particular were disenchanted and dissatisfied with the Church's teachings and were choosing to live in marginal communities where they believed a more fulfilling spiritual life could be realised. Sulivan is thus very much a writer of his time, a time of questioning of, and revolt against, traditional values. It is significant that many of his agnostic and atheistic characters are more sympathetic and possess more genuinely Christian qualities than those who claim membership of the Church. In fact, there is a sense in which Sulivan was dismissive of many aspects of organised religion:

> In itself religion is conservative; it emphasises the fear of death, protection against evil, and a taste for the miraculous as an escape from reality. The gospel, in contrast, implies constant revolution, rousing those who hear it from the sleep of fable and magic, as well as from any political absolute. (*Morning Light*, p 65).

His commitment to the Gospel, with its calls for uprooting and rebirth, and the accompanying distrust of certain aspects of the institutional Church – particularly all the remnants of dogmatic, repressive religious teaching – may well have been at the root of Sulivan's literary vocation. He saw himself as prolonging the *Logos*, or the Word, whose mysterious breath can transform lives, whose enigmatic quality forces readers to come up with their own answers, to question their belief system and to take risks in their personal lives. Sulivan believed that inner conversion was the path to self-fulfilment and that this conversion was often only possible when one detached oneself from the centre of society, with its emphasis on the accumulation of material

3. Jean Sulivan, *Morning Light: The Spiritual Journal of Jean Sulivan*, trs Joseph Cunneen and Patrick Gormally (New York: Paulist Press, 1988), p 100.

goods and instant gratification, things that were often achieved at the expense of spiritual contentment. As a writer, he decided to steer clear of the path that would lead to celebrity and high book sales and to concentrate on reaching the small band of readers who were open to his particular brand of writing, those who were not put off by the chaotic nature of the style or by the provocation contained therein. We read in *Miroir brisé*: 'It is possible that the music of my books is not made for you. One comes across numerous and diverse melodies in books that are only suited to the small number capable of responding to their call.'[5] Sulivan wanted at all costs to avoid falling into the trap of edification and self-congratulation. He mused about the future of Christian writing in *Anticipate Every Goodbye*:

> Where are the prophets, I ask myself? In truth, literature has become a career for many writers. There is an obvious contradiction between pursuing a career and living out the paradoxes of the gospel. I keep on waiting to hear a breath, a voice of rebellion. Instead all we're treated to is writers playing around with political or moral ideas and telling us about their pious aspirations. All I hear are well-rounded, balanced truths that will not upset the apple cart.[6]

When reading pronouncements like this, one must ask oneself why there have been so few of the prophetic figures of whom Sulivan speaks in Ireland. After all, it is not as if we live any more on an island cocooned from the inroads of modernity. We have had our period of disenchantment with organised religion, to the extent that the Church of Ireland bishop, Richard Clarke, in a book of essays on what he refers to as 'post-Catholic Ireland', feels justified in suggesting that 'the Irish Church is now discredited and moribund in the eyes of many detached onlookers'. Clarke senses that the revelations of child sexual abuse involving Catholic clergy, while causing a massive loss of confidence in the institution, were not in themselves anything like the full reason for the current crisis within Irish Catholicism. They provided ammunition to those who had harboured a

---

5. Jean Sulivan, *Miroir brisé* (Paris: Gallimard, 1969), p 51. My translation.
6. *Anticipate Every Goodbye*, trs Eamon Maher (Dublin: Veritas, 2000), p 82.

grievance against the powerful institution and an opportunity to gain some long-awaited revenge. The major issue for many people in relation to child sexual abuse, in my view, was the reluctance within the leadership of the Church to risk the reputation of the institution by dealing in an adequate manner with those few who had disgraced their calling. Clarke notes: 'Yet, had all been well in every other aspect of the life of all the Christian traditions, this loss of reputation might have been overcome. But much else was going awry.'[7]

Ever since Vatican II, increased access to education, the appearance of televisions in most Irish homes, foreign travel and, finally, the phenomenal prosperity heralded by the Celtic Tiger, led to people questioning in a much more stringent manner the basis of their faith. They were no longer prepared to be dictated to as they had been in the past. Slowly, but inexorably, the once unstinting dedication and commitment to the Church began to falter. To such an extent that the favourite Sunday activity among Irish people is more likely to be a visit to a shopping centre than a Church. Tom Inglis, in his book *Global Ireland*, captures the transformation very well:

> What was crucial during the second half of the twentieth century was how, for some people, that sense of difference moved from a predominantly Catholic culture to one of commodity capitalism. Instead of realising ourselves through the language of the Church and its teachings and practices, we gradually switched to realising ourselves through the language of the market and its teachings and practices.[8]

The result of this, in Inglis's view, is the shift among Irish people from 'Catholic to consumer capitalism', from 'a culture of self-denial and self-surrender to one of self-realisation and self-indulgence.' (*Global Ireland*, p 33) In previous times, many of our writers, who suffered at the hands of a repressive Censorship Board that was viewed as being dominated by the Church even though its members were lay people, felt estranged

---

7. Richard Clarke, *A Whisper of God: Essays on post-Catholic Ireland and the Christian Future* (Dublin: The Columba Press, 2006), p 27.
8. Tom Inglis, *Global Ireland: Same Difference* (London: Routledge, 2007), p 30.

from the dominant religion. As Colum Kenny notes:

'Throughout the decades following independence, the new state certainly had among its citizens vibrant artists and interesting writers. However, a stifling blend of nationalism and conservative Catholicism made it increasingly difficult for many to express themselves freely or to work in ways that they believed to be moral and necessary.'[9]

John McGahern, someone who was extremely attached to the rhythms and rituals of the Catholicism of his youth, came to resent the intrusions made by priests and religious into the sexual lives of people. Many couples got married without any sexual knowledge, or indeed without any knowledge of the person they were marrying. Contraceptives were not available, and it was sinful to use them in any case. As a result, a large number of children came into the world, often more than could be adequately catered for in terms of food and clothing. The hold of the Church over the people was draconian: 'The ideal of society was the celibate priest. The single state was thus elevated. The love of God was greater than the love of man or woman; the sexual was seen as sin-infected and unclean.'[10]

Given this stifling and repressive attitude to sexuality, it is in some ways logical that Irish people, many of whom jettisoned their religion when it was no longer of social or political advantage to them, were very happy to welcome the dawning of a new, liberal, economically prosperous, secular society in the 1990s. However, the recently appointed Cardinal Seán Brady, in a speech delivered at Knock, a place where the most significant Irish Marian shrine is located, on 17 August 2007, warned of the dangers of the new 'Ireland of stocks and shares'. He remarked: 'The truth is that many of those who claim to have set Ireland free from the shackles of religious faith in recent years are now silent in the face of the real captivities of the 'new' Ireland.'[11] The Cardinal went on to declare that there were signs that the secular

---

9. Colum Kenny, *Moments That Changed Us* (Dublin: Gill and Macmillan, 2005), p 229.
10. John McGahern, *Memoir* (London: Faber&Faber, 2005), pp 51-2.
11. Cited in Patsy McGarry, 'Back with a Belt of the Crozier', in *The Irish Times* (Weekend Review), 25 August, 2007.

project in Ireland did not bring happiness, mainly because of its failure to address the really important questions of people's lives. It is actually difficult to ascertain whether or not our newly found prosperity has had an overall positive or negative effect. For those arguing the latter case, there is the evidence of increased addiction to alcohol and drugs like cocaine and heroin, unacceptably high rates of suicide among young people, carnage on our roads, criminality, sexual deviance, a loss of reference points in the wake of the decline in religious practice. The positive effects would be perhaps greater disposable income, cheap foreign travel, more enlightened attitudes towards sexuality, heightened levels of freedom, better access to education, more tolerance of difference. It is probably fair to say that on balance most people are better off than they were a few decades ago.

John McGahern was certainly of that view. Living as a young person in Leitrim and Roscommon, he would have seen a huge number of his contemporaries being forced to emigrate to find work. Many never returned. He was also the victim of clerical interference when he lost his job as a primary school in Clontarf after the banning of his second novel, *The Dark*, in 1965. The then Archbishop of Dublin, John Charles McQuaid, used his influence with the INTO to ensure that McGahern be removed from his position. The fact that he had got married in a registry office in London to a Finnish woman, Annikki Laaksi, the previous summer, did nothing to improve his standing with the Church. As someone whose life was negatively influenced by the Catholic Establishment, one might expect McGahern to have harboured hostility towards the Church. But remarkably that was not the case. Thus we read at the end of *Memoir*:

> I have affection still and gratitude for my upbringing in the Church: it was the sacred weather of my early life, and I could no more turn against it than I could turn on any deep part of myself. (*Memoir*, p 222)

McGahern is not alone in retaining affection for the Church's role in introducing him to mystery and a sense of the sacred. While he remained staunchly an unbeliever, he nevertheless appreciated the sincere faith of his mother and recognised that for people like her – and they were numerous – the Church was the most important influence in their sometimes harsh existence. McGahern is representative of a generation of Irish people who, while they were no longer formally members of the Catholic Church, still retained a respect, even nostalgia, for the symbolism of the religious ceremonies of their youth. But there is a lot in McGahern that reminds me of Sulivan and it is to this parallel that I now turn in comparing two very different, yet similar, autobiographical accounts, *Anticipate Every Goodbye* and *Memoir*. These books provide evidence of much common ground in terms of religious practice in Brittany and rural Ireland. Sulivan, while he was describing his youth and early adulthood from the First World War until the death of his mother in the 1960s, comes up with comments like the following, which are so appropriate to the Ireland described by John McGahern:

> The priests at this time tended to preach about laws and obligations. In this way, they had succeeded in transforming Christianity into something approaching a natural religion. In their eyes the rural order in which the Church still played a dominant role was an expression of the divine will. They had forgotten about freedom, without which there is no real faith. (*Anticipate*, p 52)

McGahern resented the authoritarian nature of religion as it was enforced during the Ireland of his youth. He believed that Church and State worked hand in hand to ensure the preservation of a conservative, traditional way of life, free from what they considered the corrupt influences of continental Europe. Women were given a particularly raw deal in this society: they were usually forced to give up work when they got married and were denied access to artificial contraception, which would have allowed them control over the number of children they conceived. But there were even more sinister practices: 'The breaking of pelvic bones took place in hospitals because it was thought to be more in conformity with Catholic teaching than Caesarean section, presumably because it was considered more "natural".' (*Memoir*, p 210) What is striking about both writers' accounts is the extent to which their devout mothers completely accepted the authority of priests. In the case of Margaret McGahern, this blind acceptance could be said to have cost her

her life. After undergoing a mastectomy, the consultant strongly advised her and her husband that another pregnancy could prove fatal. McGahern was amazed to discover through letters exchanged between the couple that they were still risking intercourse in spite of the dire and well-founded warnings of the consultant. But when one considers the deep religious belief of this woman, and how closely linked this was to her role as dutiful wife, such an attitude is more understandable. Hence these sentiments in a letter she wrote to her husband: 'God has given me near-perfect health for forty years and now that he has taken that health away, it must be for some inscrutable reason of His own to test my faith. In Him and by Him and for Him I live and place my trust, and to Him alone I pray.' (*Memoir*, p 47) Such a strong faith allowed her to face up to her imminent death with equanimity, but it also left a large family without a mother and in the care of an extremely tough and authoritarian father:

> He was religious too, but his religion was of outward show, of pomp and power, edicts and strictures, enforcements and all the exactions they demanded. In his shining uniform he always walked with slow steps to the head of the Church to kneel in the front seat. She [McGahern's mother] would slip quietly into one of the seats at the back. (*Memoir*, p 47)

Because of his stern exterior and noble bearing, Frank McGahern reminded his son at times of God the Father. Sulivan lost his father at the front in Argonne during the Great War when he was only a baby. His mother, in order to hold on to the farm she leased from a local doctor, was forced to remarry. This event had a traumatic effect on her son. He deliberately ran off prior to the wedding ceremony and was found in the woods by a neighbour, who dragged him back to the reception. As he approached the table, he noticed his mother looking at him with eyes filled with tears. He spoke of the impact of this event in an interview with Bernard Feuillet:

> There is always one image that comes back to me. Crying, I run on a pathway through the fields. Why am I late? I have no idea. I arrive at the house – it's my mother's wedding. She isn't dressed in white as it's her second time to get married.

> She is also crying as she comes over to me [...] My writing
> has been a constant attempt to cure myself of this scene. The
> death of my father, the remarriage of my mother have
> marked my whole life.[12]

Writing became a form of therapy for Sulivan – it operated in much the same way for McGahern. As an adult, he would realise that his mother was forced by economic necessity to remarry, but for the little boy dressed in the sailor suit that was reserved for special occasions, the sight of his mother giving herself to a man who was not his father was a cruel psychological blow. *Anticipate Every Goodbye* concentrates almost exclusively on the relationship between the mother and the only son of her first marriage. The children of the second union are barely mentioned, in the same way as the stepfather is only alluded to briefly, as Sulivan attempts to come to terms with the most important relationship in his life. In the same way, McGahern seems to have jealously cherished the time he spent alone with his mother. Sulivan had the advantage of resolving some of the pain he endured during his weekly Sunday visits to his mother, living alone now in Montauban-de-Bretagne – McGahern would not have the same opportunity, as his mother died when he was ten years old.

Anticipate Every Goodbye begins as the priest is driving down from Rennes to see his mother, now in her seventies. He turns the corner and the village of Montauban comes into view, with its familiar Breton landscape. His mind then jumps forward to the mother's funeral, when he, as the eldest child, will walk at the front of the cortège. Some day he knows she will not be there to greet him, a thought that fills him with anguish. As he arrives at the house, he can make out with relief his mother's shadow moving about in the house. They are not demonstrative in their affections towards each other:

> I kiss my mother at the root of her hair. I will kiss her like this
> on her deathbed. She won't return my kiss, no more than she
> does now; that is the custom we have adopted. Everything
> takes place on the inside. (*Anticipate*, p 10)

12. *L'instant, l'éternité : Bernard Feuillet interroge Jean Sulivan* (Paris: Le Centurion, 1978), p 36. My translation.

The restraint in the writing does not disguise the depth of the feelings these two people have for one another. It was she who read the Bible aloud to him on a daily basis, she who inculcated him with her own strong faith. It was thus in the natural order of things that he should be the best in his class at catechism, his mother obliging him to reel off both the answers and the explanations! His decision to go to Junior Seminary was equally greeted with great joy – it was the fulfilment of a long-held maternal desire. John McGahern's mother made him promise regularly that he would become a priest:

> After the Ordination Mass, I would place my freshly anointed hands in blessing on my mother's head. We'd live together in the priest's house and she'd attend each morning Mass and take communion from my hands. When she died, I'd include her in all the Masses that I'd say until we were united in the joy of heaven, when time would cease as we were gathered into the mind of God. (*Memoir*, p 63)

As can so often be the case, the vocation was more the mother's than the son's and soon literature replaced the priesthood as McGahern's vocation in life: 'Instead of being a priest of God, I would be the god of a small, vivid world.' (*Memoir*, p 205) Art fulfilled the role of religion in the writer's life as soon as he discovered that he no longer had the faith that his mother had attempted to pass on to him. He began to see how writing was his way of working out the complex tissue that constitutes human existence. Through 'naming' his world, through bringing it to life in words, he was, in a way, performing a divine function. Sulivan's mother often asked him why he wrote and he would have loved to explain to her that he did so in order to find himself, to find God who is already found, but never really found, in order to discover a hidden path: 'Writing, it seemed to me, limited my chances of telling lies.' Later, in the same page, he states: 'I'd express myself, and by extension the faith that was peculiar to me while hoping not to betray anything: such was my manifest ambition.' (*Anticipate*, p 79)

The death of their mothers impacted harshly on both writers. The rupture of the loss of someone so dear is related with a rawness that conveys the full anguish of the writers. McGahern, although urged by his mother to pray for his father and sisters, always made the same wish, 'that she would never go away again and be with me forever.' (*Memoir*, p 75) On receiving the dreaded news that his mother had taken ill, Sulivan had a similar reaction: 'Forms and sounds became dim, the countryside was shifting uncontrollably. Love was like death; I had never known up until then what it was like to fall into nothingness.' (*Anticipate*, p 93) Although he was in a position, unlike McGahern, to say Mass for his mother, when she finally passed away he was so bereft he could not even concelebrate the funeral Mass. Once more, we come across the cathartic power of literature for Sulivan, as the writer assumes the function of the priest in his hour of need: 'You are not present at your own death. But it is impossible to escape from the death of someone you love. When you write, you love once more, suffer the pain all over again.' (*Anticipate*, p 104)

McGahern was not allowed by his father to attend his mother's funeral and he was forced to conjure up in his mind's eye the various stages of the ceremony: 'The priests come through the altar gate to bless the coffin. An altar boy holds the vessel of holy water; another carries the smoking thurible, and yet another the small boat that holds the incense.' (*Memoir*, p 133) He then imagines the dull thud of the clay on her coffin and reproaches himself for not having spent all the time he could with her before they left in the lorry their father had sent to collect them and the furniture from the house in which their mother was dying and transport them to the barracks in Cootehall: 'If I could have that hour or hours out on the cinders by the lorry back, I could portion out the time so that I could lay eyes on her face from time to time and she would not be gone forever.' (*Memoir*, p 135)

In the hospital in Rennes, before she was moved to Nantes, Sulivan first noticed the fault lines beginning to appear in his mother's faith and it hit home to him how difficult it is to die: 'Only at that precise moment did I know that she was going to die, that she was replacing Christ on the naked cross, experiencing all the feelings of abandonment. I could see her eyes – I couldn't, I wouldn't read what they were saying. I would only know later.' (*Anticipate*, p 111) To her son's amazement, she refused to pick up the rosary beads that never left her side throughout her life; when he mentioned that she might like to invoke Our Lady of Lourdes, to whom she had great devotion, she shook her head. But he was also aware that 'in the unseen part of her soul she was still attached to the living and true God.' (*Anticipate*, pp 110-111) As the initial hopes of her recovery disappeared, the consultant told Sulivan that there was nothing further they could do for her, other than to allow her to die in her own house. Shortly after they got her into the ambulance, she died. Hospital regulations would normally decree in such circumstances that the patient be brought back inside but the driver agreed to continue, provided they left her eyes open. As they drove along the country roads, the trees and the landscape were reflected in these eyes and gave the impression of a great peace that had been hard won. The son was far from such a state, however. For him, there was only the terrible knowledge that there would be no more Sunday visits, no more glimpses of her silhouette behind the curtains, no more discussions about his dead father, about religion and writing. The following lines have a particular relevance for contemporary Ireland:

We are all blind thinking that life consists of possessing material goods, holding on to this, then that, getting to know one thing, then another, trying desperately to ignore the fact that the whole process inevitably amounts to absolutely nothing. Life isn't just a game where you have to possess and know as many things as possible. Rather, it is about reducing yourself to zero, living in a new and more authentic way. (*Anticipate*, p 114)

In today's globalised world, economic concerns dominate our awareness and tend to occlude our spiritual growth. What McGahern and Sulivan manage to capture in their autobiographical accounts is that faith is much more than a collection of ideas, that it has really got to do with rebirth, with 'reducing yourself to zero', recognising the transience of the things of this world. After McGahern died in 2006, he had arranged for a traditional funeral Mass, concluding with a decade of the rosary at his graveside (he was laid to rest alongside his mother in the cemetery of Aughawillan). There was no death-bed reversion to the Catholic faith. No, the funeral was more a mark of respect for his mother's deep faith, as well as for the customs of the local community. *Memoir* concludes with the following lines:

> I would want no shadow to fall on her joy and deep trust in God. She would face no false reproaches. As we retraced our steps, I would pick for her the wild orchid and the wind-flower. (*Memoir*, p 272)

I trust that the relevance of Sulivan's writings to the Ireland in which we live is evident from this brief discussion. He shares with John McGahern a keen awareness of nature as well as an appreciation of the importance of local rituals and religious practices. Their mothers imparted something more important to them than social standing and material wealth: the two women demonstrated by their life and death that a belief system is vital in combating the vicissitudes of life. Both writers discovered also that literature was their method of dealing with the pain of loss. As Sulivan stated: 'Writing these anecdotes, expressing ordinary feelings, which quite possibly millions of people secretly feel after seeing their own mother dying, reassures me and comforts me a bit. It sometimes seems to me that my mother is the humble mother of a great number of people.' (*Anticipate*, p 124) The same can be said of Margaret McGahern, who in *Memoir* assumes many of the qualities of mothers all over the world. Strongly imbedded in the local, these women attain a universal significance through the moving portraits provided by their writer-sons.

I asked the question earlier if there were any prophets in present-day Ireland who could compare favourably with Jean Sulivan. McGahern, because he was an unbeliever, is undoubtedly quite different from the French priest-writer, although they share a number of similar interests. When looking within the confines of the Church in this country, the name of the Benedictine monk, Mark Patrick Hederman, is someone who has the philosophical knowledge, keen intelligence and independence of mind to be considered on a par with Sulivan. Having studied in Paris during the 1960s under Emmanuel Levinas, he was undoubtedly exposed to a very different world view to what would have existed in Ireland at that time. He wrote in his thought-provoking *Kissing The Dark*:

There are those who no longer believe in any God or any religion because of disappointment with the Churches or because of disillusionment caused by the scandalous and criminal behaviour being daily reported among so-called professional representatives of the clergy and the religious orders. Nothing of the sort should allow us to be deflected from our own particular journey, our own connection with the living God.[13]

Quotes like this one show Hederman to have the same ability to criticise the abuses of the institution while still remaining within its fold. Sulivan wrote, for example, in *Morning Light*: 'I see the Church detaching its members from structures of profit, conventional security, and mythologies of happiness in order to make them spiritual nomads, capable of commitment without illusion, always ready to absent themselves in order to go somewhere else, straining for the impossible and necessary.'[14] It is not always easy for priests or religious to distance themselves from the party-line or clerical mindset. Sometimes they can lose sight of the enthusiasm and sincerity of their early vocation and content themselves with performing their priestly function in a desultory fashion. Similarly, many sincere Catholics can go about their lives without a thought for how far removed they are from the Gospel message of unconditional love. Sulivan was convinced that there was hope in the midst of despair and that the 'dechristianised' France in which he lived had the potential for rebirth and regeneration, albeit among the 'few' who were able to see beyond the faults and failings of the institution and devote time to modelling their lives on the example of Christ. In this way, his testimony is invaluable in the Ireland of the third millennium.

---

13. Mark Patrick Hederman, *Kissing the Dark: Connecting with the Unconscious* (Dublin: Veritas, 1999), p 160.
14. *Morning Light*, p 158.

The Contributors

ANDREW AUGE is a Professor of English at Loras College, Dubuque, Iowa, USA. He has published articles on Seamus Heaney, Eavan Boland, and Paul Muldoon and is currently working on a book examining the interconnections between Catholicism and modern Irish poetry.

JOHN F. DEANE was born on Achill Island. He founded Poetry Ireland, the national Poetry Society and its journal, *The Poetry Ireland Review*. Founder and editor for many years of The Dedalus Press, he has won several awards for poetry, notably the Marten Toonder Award and the O'Shaughnessy Award. His work is translated into several languages. His latest poetry collection is *The Instruments of Art* (Carcanet, 2005) and his latest fiction is *The Heather Fields* (Blackstaff, 2007). Columba published a collection of essays of poetry and religion, *In Dogged Loyalty*, and in late 2008 Carcanet will publish his next poetry collection, *A Little Book of Hours*.

EOIN FLANNERY is Lecturer in English Literature at Oxford Brookes University. He has published widely in the area of Irish Studies, on contemporary Irish literature, visual culture, and postcolonial studies. His books include: *Versions of Ireland: Empire, Modernity and Resistance in Irish Culture* (2006) and *Enemies of Empire* (2007). He is currently completing a book on Ireland and postcolonial theory entitled *Fanon's One Big Idea: Ireland and Postcolonial Studies*, and editing two books: *Seeing Things: Irish Studies and Visual Culture*, and *Modern Irish Gothic: From Bram Stoker to Patrick McCabe*. He recently edited a special issue of *Postcolonial Text* on Irish culture.

COLUM KENNY teaches journalism and media policy at Dublin

City University. His books include *Moments that Changed Us* (Gill & Macmillan: 2005), a review of developments in Ireland since 1975. An honorary life member of Glencree Centre for Reconciliation, he is a columnist in the *Sunday Independent*. He designed and co-ordinates 'Belief and Communication', an innovative module taught jointly at DCU by staff from DCU, St Patrick's College and Mater Dei Institute.

PATRICIA KIERAN is a British Foreign and Commonwealth Chevening Scholar. She currently teaches Religious Education at Mary Immaculate College, University of Limerick. She is co-author of *Children, Catholicism and Religious Education* (Veritas, 2005) and co-editor of *Exploring Theology: Making Sense of the Catholic Tradition* (Veritas, 2006). She has published numerous chapters and articles on the subject of Roman Catholic Modernism, inter-religious education and Catholic education.

PEADAR KIRBY is Professor of International Politics and Public Policy at the University of Limerick. Until September 2007 he was co-director of the Centre for International Studies and associate professor in the School of Law and Government, both at Dublin City University. He has published extensively on globalisation and development, both in theoretical terms and in relation to Ireland and to Latin America. A book entitled *Contesting the State: Lessons from the Irish Case* (co-edited with Maura Adshead and Michelle Millar) is currently in press with Manchester University Press. His latest published book is *Taming the Tiger: Social Exclusion in a Globalised Ireland*, co-edited with David Jacobson and Deiric Ó Broin (Tasc with New Island Books, 2006) and earlier in 2006 he published *Vulnerability and Violence: The Impact of Globalisation* (Pluto Press, 2006). Recent books include *Introduction to Latin America: Twenty-First Century Challenges* (Sage, 2003) *The Celtic Tiger in Distress: Growth with Inequality in Ireland* (Palgrave, 2002), *Reinventing Ireland: Culture, Society and the Global Economy*, co-edited with Luke Gibbons and Michael Cronin (Pluto Press, 2002), *Poverty Amid Plenty: World and Irish Development Reconsidered* (Trócaire and Gill & Macmillan, 1997), and *Rich and Poor: Perspectives on Tackling Inequality in Ireland*, co-edited with Sara Cantillon, Carmel Corrigan and Joan

O'Flynn (Oak Tree Press in association with the Combat Poverty Agency, 2001). In 2003, the UN Economic Commission for Latin America and the Caribbean (CEPAL) published his paper on the lessons of the Celtic Tiger for Latin America and he has recently written a study on the relationship between growth and poverty in the Irish growth model for the United Nations Research Institute for Social Development (UNRISD) which will be published as part of a larger international study on policy regimes and poverty reduction. He has published journal articles in *New Political Economy, Review of International Political Economy, The European Journal of Development Research, Globalizations, Development Review, Irish Studies in International Affairs, The Irish Review* and *Administration*. He holds a PhD from the London School of Economics.

JOHN LITTLETON, a priest of the Diocese of Cashel and Emly, is Head of Distance Education at The Priory Institute, Tallaght, Dublin. He has taught theology, religious studies and religious education in several colleges and institutions in Ireland and the UK, and is a well-known preacher and retreat director. He served for six years (2001-2007) as President of the National Conference of Priests of Ireland. He is a regular contributor to theological and pastoral journals, and writes weekly columns for *The Catholic Times* and the *Tipperary Star*. With Louise Fuller and Eamon Maher, he co-edited *Irish and Catholic? Towards an Understanding of Identity* (2006).

EAMON MAHER is Director of the National Centre for Franco-Irish Studies in ITT Dublin (Tallaght) where he also lectures in Humanities. He completed his PhD in NUI Galway on the theme of marginality in the life and works of the French priest-writer Jean Sulivan and a book based on this research was published by L'Harmattan in 2008. Other monographs include *John McGahern: From the Local to the Universal* (2003) and *Crosscurrents and Confluences: Echoes of Religion is 20th-century Fiction* (2000). He is the series editor of *Reimagining Ireland* and a General Editor with Grace Neville and Eugene O'Brien of *Studies in Franco-Irish Relations*, both with Peter Lang. He is currently preparing another monograph titled *'The Church and its Spire': John McGahern and the Religious Question* for The Columba Press.

CATHERINE MAIGNANT is Professor of Irish Studies at the University of Lille and President of the French Association for Irish Studies. After completing a PhD on early medieval Irish Christianity she has specialised in contemporary Irish religious history. Her research interests include the new religious movements, the response of the Catholic Church to secularisation, interreligious dialogue, Celtic Christianity and the religious aspects of the globalisation process.

LAWRENCE J. MCCAFFREY is Professor Emeritus of History at Loyola University of Chicago. In 1954, he received his PhD from the University of Iowa. He has written and edited a number of books on Irish and Irish-American history, published articles on the same subjects as well as on Irish and Irish-American literature. In 1960, he co-founded the American Conference for Irish Studies (ACIS). He served as President of ACIS and of the American Catholic Historical Association. He was a consultant to, and appeared in, the 1997 documentary *The Irish in America: Long Journey Home* and technical advisor to the 2002 film *The Road to Perdition*. In 1982, St Ambrose University, his undergraduate alma mater, awarded McCaffrey an Honorary Doctor of Humanities; five years later the National University of Ireland designated him Honorary Doctor of Letters.

PATSY MCGARRY has been Religious Affairs Correspondent at *The Irish Times* in Dublin since March 1997. From Ballaghaderreen, Co Roscommon, he was educated at St Nathy's College, Ballaghaderreen, and at University College, Galway. He began in journalism in 1983 with Sunshine Radio in Dublin. He later worked for the *Sunday World, Magill*, the *Irish Press*, Capital Radio, the *Sunday Independent* and the *Irish Independent*. In 1992 he won a national media award for analysis and comment following articles in the *Sunday Independent* on the fall of Charles Haughey as Taoiseach. In 1994 he began working with *The Irish Times*. He was awarded the John Templeton European Religion Writer of the Year Award in 1998 for coverage of Pope John Paul II's visit to Cuba in January of that year; the Irish Churches' failure to practise rather than just preach reconciliation; and for a profile of Rev John Pickering, then rector of Drumcree parish in

Co Armagh. In 2001 his *The Book of Jesus Reports* was published by *The Irish Times* and *Christianity*, a collection of essays which he edited, was published by Veritas. In 2006 his book *While Justice Slept* was published by The Liffey Press.

JEAN-CHRISTOPHE PENET is a Research Fellow at the National Centre for Franco-Irish Studies (NCFIS), ITT Dublin. He is currently completing a PhD thesis on the impact of secularism on Catholic practices in France and in Ireland under the joint supervision of Eamon Maher and Eugene O'Brien.

DAMIEN SHORTT is a lecturer of English at Edge Hill University. Following three years teaching in a Swiss boarding school, he completed his PhD on the Dublin author, Dermot Bolger, at the University of Limerick in June 2006. At Edge Hill he is a research fellow, with particular focus on exploring the utilisation of computer aided assessment in literature degrees and also the analysis of postgraduate education from a post-structuralist theoretical perspective.